Blindsided

Why the Left Tackle Is Overrated and Other Contrarian Football Thoughts

KC Joyner

WILEY

John Wiley & Sons, Inc.

Published by John Wiley & Sons, Inc., Hoboken, New Jersey
Published simultaneously in Canada

Design and composition by Navta Associates, Inc.

For general information about our other products and services, please contact our Customer Care Department within the United States at (800) 762-2974, outside the United States at (317) 572-3993 or fax (317) 572-4002.

Wiley also publishes its books in a variety of electronic formats. Some content that appears in print may not be available in electronic books. For more information about Wiley products, visit our web site at www.wiley.com.

Library of Congress Cataloging-in-Publication Data:
Joyner, KC
  Blindsided : why the left tackle is overrated and other contrarian football thoughts / KC Joyner.
    p. cm.
  Includes index.
  ISBN 978-0-470-12409-3 (cloth)
  1. National Football League. 2. Football—United States. I. Title.
  GV955.5.N35J65 2008
  796.332'640973—dc22

                                                              2007046859

Printed in the United States of America

10 9 8 7 6 5 4 3 2 1

For my wife, Heather. I couldn't have done any of this without you.

CONTENTS

Introduction

Hello! For those of you who are already familiar with either my articles on ESPN.com or my *Scientific Football* books, it's great to talk to you again! For those of you who are new to the discussion, let me take a moment to tell you a little something about what I do and how it is that I started doing it.

The best way to describe my work is to call it analytical football studies. I started doing this type of analysis in 1984 after I read that season's edition of *The Bill James Baseball Abstract*. James's unique way of viewing baseball caused me to want to try to view football through a similar prism. Over the years I did a number of research projects as a hobby, but that didn't satiate my intense curiosity. I knew that if I ever wanted to dig really deep and answer all of the questions I had about football, I was going to have to find a way to do this type of analysis for a living.

In 2003, I did just that. I cashed in my retirement savings accounts (with the blessing of Mrs. Scientist) and quit my job. A year and a half later I wrote a book called *Scientific Football 2005*. I sent copies of that book to sportswriters and newspaper editors across the country, hoping that one of them would like it and help me find my audience.

Dr. Z from *Sports Illustrated* read the book, liked it, and ended up doing an article on it for SI.com. His article was the big break I needed. It helped me land a job with ESPN.com and *ESPN The Magazine* and it also served as my introduction to many people throughout the NFL, including scouts, coaches, and executives of multiple NFL teams.

The ESPN gigs kept me in business and allowed me to expand the scope of my research to the kinds of areas that James reached later in his career. The eclectic nature of James's work is actually one of the great, and seemingly most misunderstood, facets of his writing career. There are those who aren't familiar with his work who sometimes portray him as being merely a rogue statistician, but his writing range was incredibly varied. He was just as likely to muse on baseball history or managerial philosophy as he was to talk about some new statistic.

James himself said that the key to his writing wasn't in the statistics, but rather in the questions he asked. His most effective method for coming up with questions was to listen to some of the conventional wisdom of the day and run the numbers to see if it was true. If some sportswriter or talking head on a television broadcast said that Fenway Park favored right-handed hitters, James would run the numbers and see if the evidence backed this up.

What was most refreshing about this approach was that James was not willing to take the conventional wisdom at face value, even though it was often baseball professionals who were spouting these nuggets of information. James had such an independent mind-set that he wanted to find the truth on his own, even if that required hundreds of hours of research. Once this research started showing that the accepted truths were often somewhat inaccurate or, in some cases, completely false, it reinforced James's notion that any and all conventional wisdom should have to go through a debunking process.

When I started writing the *Scientific Football* series, I decided to take that same approach to player personnel analysis. For example, I wasn't satisfied to hear NFL insiders say that Champ Bailey was the best cornerback in the NFL. I wanted to do the legwork and see if it was true. When I found that the research proved that a significant portion of the big-name players weren't nearly as good as they were touted as being by many members of the media and NFL coaches, I knew that I was on to something.

Blindsided is much like *Scientific Football* in that it strives to question pro football's conventional wisdom. Whereas *Scientific Football* does this in an annual player personnel analysis format, *Blindsided* will take a more macro view and analyze some of the larger questions of the game.

The first part of the book will tackle three of pro football's conventional wisdoms:

1. The true value of the left tackle position

2. Whether free agency and the salary cap have killed the dynasty

3. Whether the 2007 Patriots will be the last undefeated team we will see this generation

The second part is a collection of statistical reviews covering various topics such as:

1. Which makes for a more successful playoff team: a tough schedule or a schedule filled with creampuff matchups?

2. Does it take a great running back to win a Super Bowl?

The third part will look at another area of the NFL that is overrun by myth and legend: the coaching profession. Much, if not most, of the analysis of head coaches today revolves around trying to understand the cult of personality that these men use to lead and motivate their teams and organizations. While I would never try to say that leadership and motivation are unimportant parts of the coaching process, there are many other areas of the profession that deserve as much attention as the personality side. The four areas covered in this part are:

1. The coaching profession is divided into four distinct strategic/philosophical alignments, and Bill Belichick is succeeding in part by using the most difficult of these philosophies

2. Whether there is a ten-year window of success for head coaches

3. The Hall of Fame standards for coaches, with the underlying question of whether Marty Schottenheimer has done enough in his career to qualify for the Hall of Fame

4. The background demographics of coaching and whether they indicate that there should be more black coaches in the NFL because of the high percentage of black players in the league

The fourth part of the book is titled Historical Iconoclasm. The reason I decided to do this section is that I am somewhat appalled by the way pro football looks at its past. Pro football doesn't do quite as good a job of embracing its history as baseball does, but it does a much better job of embracing its mythology. I have no issue with good mythology, but I don't like it when the facts get in the way of the real story.

That has been the case in the storytelling of two of the most respected elder statesmen from the NFL's glory days, Art Rooney and Bert Bell. This section will help shed light on their real stories. I will also review the multiple reasons that show why I believe that the Steel Curtain defense and Jerry Rice are the best ever in their respective fields, hands down.

The fifth section of the book will review some of the NFL's business practices and the damage they could possibly cause the league.

The last section of the book is titled "A Call for a Historical Statistical Revolution." It is my effort to help jump-start the statistical revolution that the world of football is on the precipice of but still hasn't completely embraced.

PART ONE

DEBUNKING MYTHS

1

What Is the True Value of the Left Tackle?

Most of you are probably familiar with Michael Lewis's book *The Blind Side*. It recounts a young player's struggles to adapt to his new environment, but from a football sense Lewis paints a very compelling picture of how valuable the left tackle position is for NFL teams.

As excellent as Lewis's research was, after reading the book I was still left with some doubt as to the real value of the left tackle. I understood how much it meant to Bill Walsh to have someone capable of blocking Lawrence Taylor. I also had a better understanding of why left tackles are paid so much. But I still didn't get a good sense as to how much more valuable a left tackle was than, say, a right guard.

So what is the real value of the left tackle? We are told that the position is crucial in pass blocking, but where does run blocking fit into the equation? And when it comes to pass blocking, is the left tackle just an airbag (saves you from catastrophe in an accident) or is it antilock brakes (prevents the catastrophe and then some).

I believe the best way to find this out is to gauge both the run- and the pass-blocking value of left tackles by asking questions such as:

- How many sacks does the typical left tackle give up versus sacks given up by other linemen?

- How often do most teams run behind their left tackle versus running behind other linemen?

- How many yards per attempt are gained on running plays behind the typical left tackle versus runs behind other linemen?

Let's start with the running game. In researching *Scientific Football 2006*, I broke down every running play in the NFL with a system that centered around which offensive linemen were being run behind on a particular play. It took four months of breaking down tape to get the database built, but at the end I had a very clear picture.

Here are the numbers by positional type:

POSITION	ATTEMPTS	% OF TOTAL ATTEMPTS
Tackles	4,888	32.6%
Guards	6,602	44.1%
Centers	3,494	23.3%
Total	14,984	100.0%

(These attempts don't include certain types of plays such as kneeldowns or fumbled handoffs, as those plays would not have any run blocks to account for. There can be multiple blockers on each play as well, so the total number of carries is higher than the total number of runs during the NFL season.)

Tackles as a whole accounted for just under one-third of all run blocks. Here is how the numbers divided up between left and right tackles:

POSITION	ATTEMPTS	% OF TOTAL ATTEMPTS
Left Tackles	2,458	16.4%
Right Tackles	2,321	15.5%

(Tackles who alternated between playing the left and right side were not included in either total.)

So from a running standpoint, left tackles accounted for only 16.4 percent of all run blocks in the 2005 season. This number shows that they really don't occupy an extra-special part of the running attack. That isn't entirely surprising, but it does give evidence as to their value in the running game.

In addition to tracking which lineman plays were being run behind, I also tracked the number of yards that were gained on those runs. Here are the numbers:

POSITION	ATTEMPTS	YARDS GAINED	YPA
Tackles	4,888	23,079	4.7
Guards	6,602	31,288	4.7
Centers	3,494	16,064	4.6
Total	14,984	70,431	4.6

And here are the totals for left and right tackles:

POSITION	ATTEMPTS	YARDS GAINED	YPA
Left Tackles	2,458	11,644	4.7
Right Tackles	2,321	11,000	4.7

When I first saw these numbers, I was a bit perplexed by the similarity of the yards per attempt (YPA). Each position had a wide range of yards per attempt from the best to the worst. For example, the best left tackle had a YPA of 7.8 yards, while the worst came in at 2.6 yards. There were similar variances at the other positions.

What I realized after thinking about it for a short while was that these metrics show what coaches have been saying for years: it takes an effort by the entire offense to make the running game work. Even though there are wide variances from lineman to lineman in yards per attempt, the overall YPA indicates that positional success in this category typically occurs when a group of linemen is successful. That indicates that even the best run blockers are dependent on the success of their offensive line mates.

The run studies confirm what we really already knew: left tackles aren't paid the big money to be anchors in the running game. Their perceived value is in the passing game, so let's take a look at that area.

The starting point in this discussion will be how many sacks the left tackles in the league gave up in 2005 (the season that was studied in *Scientific Football 2006*). Here are those numbers:

RANK	TEAM	STARTING OR PRIMARY LEFT TACKLES	LEFT TACKLE SACKS ALLOWED
T1	Denver	Matt Lepsis	1
T1	Philadelphia	Tra Thomas	1
3	Pittsburgh	Marvel Smith	2
4	Atlanta	Kevin Shaffer	2.5
T5	Cincinnati	Levi Jones	3
T5	Seattle	Walter Jones	3
T5	Detroit	Jeff Backus	3
T5	Jacksonville	Khalif Barnes	3
T5	Arizona	Leonard Davis	3
T5	San Francisco	Adam Snyder	3
T11	Indianapolis	Tarik Glenn	3.5
T11	Minnesota	Bryant McKinnie	3.5
T13	Miami	Damion McIntosh	4
T13	Washington	Chris Samuels	4
15	New York Giants	Luke Petitgout	5
T16	Green Bay	Chad Clifton	5.5
T16	Tennessee	Brad Hopkins	5.5
T16	Tampa Bay	Anthony Davis	5.5
T16	Baltimore	Jonathan Ogden	5.5
T16	Cleveland	L.J. Shelton	5.5
T16	St. Louis	Orlando Pace	5.5
22	New Orleans	Wayne Gandy	6
23	Buffalo	Mike Gandy	6.5
T24	New England	Nick Kaczur/Matt Light	8
T24	Chicago	John Tait	8
26	Carolina	Travelle Wharton	9
27	San Diego	Leander Jordan/Roman Oben	9.5
28	Kansas City	Willie Roaf/Jordan Black	11
29	Houston	Victor Riley/Chester Pitts	11.5
30	Oakland	Barry Sims	12.5
31	Dallas	Torrin Tucker/Flozell Adams	15
32	New York Jets	Adrian Jones/Jason Fabini	15.5

These totals look remarkably similar to the individual defensive sack totals from the 2005 season in that the worst linemen gave up 15.5

sacks, while the best pass rusher, Derrick Burgess, totaled 16 sacks. This means that a bad left tackle can lose a team as many games as a great pass rusher can win.

That poor tackle play can hurt a team really isn't a compelling argument for the position's value, because bad players at any position can cause a team to lose games. For example, the center position is often manned by an offensive line's weakest blocker, but if a team has to put in a backup center who isn't used to making the line calls, it will equal a loss just as quickly as a mediocre left tackle.

The next set of numbers I reviewed was the percentage of overall team sacks that each left tackle allowed. Putting the total in a percentage format will help put each left tackle's individual performance into perspective with the rest of the pass blockers on his team. I have included these totals below as sorted by the number of total sacks allowed by the team (for reasons that I will explain in a moment):

RANK	TEAM	TOTAL SACKS ALLOWED	STARTING OR PRIMARY LEFT TACKLES	LEFT TACKLE SACKS ALLOWED	LT % OF TOTAL SACKS
1	Indianapolis	20	Tarik Glenn	3.5	17.5%
2	Cincinnati	21	Levi Jones	3	14.3%
3	Denver	23	Matt Lepsis	1	4.3%
4	Miami	26	Damion McIntosh	4	15.4%
T5	Green Bay	27	Chad Clifton	5.5	20.4%
T5	Seattle	27	Walter Jones	3	11.1%
T7	Carolina	28	Travelle Wharton	9	32.1%
T7	New England	28	Nick Kaczur/Matt Light	8	28.6%
T7	New York Giants	28	Luke Petitgout	5	17.9%
T10	Chicago	31	John Tait	8	25.8%
T10	Detroit	31	Jeff Backus	3	9.7%
T10	San Diego	31	Leander Jordan/Roman Oben	9.5	30.6%
T10	Tennessee	31	Brad Hopkins	5.5	17.7%
T10	Washington	31	Chris Samuels	4	12.9%
T15	Jacksonville	32	Khalif Barnes	3	9.4%
T15	Kansas City	32	Willie Roaf/Jordan Black	11	34.4%
T15	Pittsburgh	32	Marvel Smith	2	6.3%
18	Atlanta	39	Kevin Shaffer	2.5	6.4%
T19	New Orleans	41	Wayne Gandy	6	14.6%

(continued)

(continued)

RANK	TEAM	TOTAL SACKS ALLOWED	STARTING OR PRIMARY LEFT TACKLES	LEFT TACKLE SACKS ALLOWED	LT % OF TOTAL SACKS
T19	Tampa Bay	41	Anthony Davis	5.5	13.4%
T21	Baltimore	42	Jonathan Ogden	5.5	13.1%
T21	Philadelphia	42	Tra Thomas	1	2.4%
23	Buffalo	43	Mike Gandy	6.5	15.1%
T24	Arizona	45	Leonard Davis	3	6.7%
T24	Oakland	45	Barry Sims	12.5	27.8%
T26	Cleveland	46	L.J. Shelton	5.5	12.0%
T26	St. Louis	46	Orlando Pace	5.5	12.0%
28	San Francisco	48	Adam Snyder	3	6.3%
29	Dallas	50	Torrin Tucker/Flozell Adams	15	30.0%
30	New York Jets	53	Adrian Jones/Jason Fabini	15.5	29.2%
31	Minnesota	54	Bryant McKinnie	3.5	6.5%
32	Houston	68	Victor Riley/Chester Pitts	11.5	16.9%
		1,182		190	16.1%

When I ran these figures, I noticed a trend, but the trend really only shows up when the previous list is sorted by the left tackle sack percentage, which I have done below:

RANK	TEAM	TOTAL SACKS ALLOWED	STARTING OR PRIMARY LEFT TACKLES	LEFT TACKLE SACKS ALLOWED	LT % OF TOTAL SACKS
T21	Philadelphia	42	Tra Thomas	1	2.4%
3	Denver	23	Matt Lepsis	1	4.3%
T15	Pittsburgh	32	Marvel Smith	2	6.3%
28	San Francisco	48	Adam Snyder	3	6.3%
18	Atlanta	39	Kevin Shaffer	2.5	6.4%
31	Minnesota	54	Bryant McKinnie	3.5	6.5%
T24	Arizona	45	Leonard Davis	3	6.7%
T15	Jacksonville	32	Khalif Barnes	3	9.4%
T10	Detroit	31	Jeff Backus	3	9.7%
T5	Seattle	27	Walter Jones	3	11.1%
T26	Cleveland	46	L.J. Shelton	5.5	12.0%
T26	St. Louis	46	Orlando Pace	5.5	12.0%
T10	Washington	31	Chris Samuels	4	12.9%
T21	Baltimore	42	Jonathan Ogden	5.5	13.1%
T19	Tampa Bay	41	Anthony Davis	5.5	13.4%

(continued)

(continued)

RANK	TEAM	TOTAL SACKS ALLOWED	STARTING OR PRIMARY LEFT TACKLES	LEFT TACKLE SACKS ALLOWED	LT % OF TOTAL SACKS
2	Cincinnati	21	Levi Jones	3	14.3%
T19	New Orleans	41	Wayne Gandy	6	14.6%
23	Buffalo	43	Mike Gandy	6.5	15.1%
4	Miami	26	Damion McIntosh	4	15.4%
32	Houston	68	Victor Riley/Chester Pitts	11.5	16.9%
1	Indianapolis	20	Tarik Glenn	3.5	17.5%
T10	Tennessee	31	Brad Hopkins	5.5	17.7%
T7	New York Giants	28	Luke Petitgout	5	17.9%
T5	Green Bay	27	Chad Clifton	5.5	20.4%
T10	Chicago	31	John Tait	8	25.8%
T24	Oakland	45	Barry Sims	12.5	27.8%
T7	New England	28	Nick Kaczur/Matt Light	8	28.6%
30	New York Jets	53	Adrian Jones/Jason Fabini	15.5	29.2%
29	Dallas	50	Torrin Tucker/Flozell Adams	15	30.0%
T10	San Diego	31	Leander Jordan/Roman Oben	9.5	30.6%
T7	Carolina	28	Travelle Wharton	9	32.1%
T15	Kansas City	32	Willie Roaf/Jordan Black	11	34.4%

The rankings in this chart are carried over from the total sacks allowed chart because I believe they make a great point: The left tackles with the fewest sacks allowed oftentimes play for the teams that allow the highest number of sacks.

For proof, consider that of the bottom fourteen left tackles on this list (starting with Miami's Damion McIntosh), nine played for teams that finished in the top ten in overall sacks allowed. If the six multiple left tackle pairings are removed from the bottom fourteen, seven of the remaining eight tackles still come from teams that ranked in the top ten in overall sacks allowed.

So what does this mean? In a nutshell, I think it means that defensive coordinators know the old adage that the shortest distance between two points is a straight line. If a team has a weak offensive line, a defense will not bother attacking the left tackle.

To further illustrate this point, let's take two teams with identical sack numbers, the Cleveland Browns and the St. Louis Rams.

The Browns and the Rams tied for twenty-sixth in overall sacks allowed. Despite that lousy overall showing, both of their left tackles, Orlando Pace and L. J. Shelton, allowed only 5.5 sacks.

Pace and Shelton started all sixteen games, so their playing time was equal. There was a difference in the number of passes thrown by the Browns and the Rams. St. Louis passers threw 599 times versus Cleveland's total of 497. That equates to Shelton allowing a sack on 1.1 percent of total passes versus Pace's 0.9 percent, or one more sack on every 500 pass plays.

There was also a significant difference in the number of vertical passes for each team, as the Rams threw around 100 more vertical passes (11-plus yards or more downfield) than Cleveland did. That certainly raises Pace's performance over Shelton's significantly, but from a pure numbers standpoint it still wouldn't seem to justify the perceived performance difference between these two. Pace made both the Pro Bowl and one of the All-Pro teams in 2005. Shelton's overall play was so bad that the Browns let him go in free agency without much, if any, of a fight.

I believe the reason that Shelton and Pace had such similar numbers is that in both cases, the rest of the offensive linemen were mediocre. The blocking metrics from *Scientific Football 2006* showed that Claude Terrell and Alex Barron were both struggling to hold their own for the Rams that year. St. Louis also had numerous offensive line injuries to deal with as well.

Cleveland had a similar, if not worse, situation. The metrics showed that Mike Pucillo was one of the worst offensive linemen in the NFL in 2005, yet he was in the lineup for ten games. Jeff Faine was an undersized center who had his share of troubles and was traded away after the year. The metrics also indicated that the rest of the Browns blockers were middle-of-the-road linemen.

Beating a left tackle to the corner to get to the quarterback requires a defensive player to go a long way. Beating an offensive line up the middle is a much faster way to get pressure, so defenses will choose that option whenever it is available. Since the middle of both Cleveland's and St. Louis's lines contained many potential pass-rush targets for a defense, there was no reason to target the left tackles very often. That is why Shelton's and Pace's sack totals were so close to each other.

When an offensive line is strong up the gut, however, the defense knows that coming up the gut is a low-percentage play. They will then put most of their pass-rushing eggs in the basket of beating the left tackle to the corner, especially if that left tackle isn't an elite pass blocker. What this would seem to indicate is that a team should not aim to pick up a top-of-the-line left tackle unless it has the rest of its offensive line already in place.

The other part of the 2005 numbers that stood out is that there didn't seem to be much of a correlation between having a great left tackle and winning. Of the ten teams with the lowest percentage of sacks allowed by the left tackle, only four made the playoffs. Contrast that to three playoff teams that had left tackle sack percentages in the bottom ten of that same category and it provides some evidence that it doesn't take a great left tackle to win.

In addition, look at the left tackles of the past few Super Bowl winners. The past six Super Bowl left tackles have been David Diehl, Tarik Glenn, Marvel Smith, Matt Light twice, and Roman Oben. Glenn was certainly one of the premier blindside protectors in the NFL, but Diehl, Smith, Light, and Oben have tallied only two Pro Bowl appearances and zero All-Pro nominations between them in their entire combined careers.

I believe the reason for this is that teams have known for a long time that dominant left tackles are very hard to come by. Because of this, offensive coordinators and personnel directors have tailored their play-calling and personnel acquisition efforts accordingly.

That would seem to go against what Lewis said in *The Blind Side*, but let's put his comments into perspective. In the pro football historical section of his book, Lewis was mostly giving us a review of the evolution of pass rushing and blocking in the 1980s. As important as it was for the 49ers to block Lawrence Taylor, and as much of an impact as Walsh's moves had on the NFL as a whole, let's not forget that a player of the talent level of the original LT comes around maybe once in a generation at most. There hasn't been another edge pass-rushing linebacker with the impact of Taylor since he left, so Walsh was responding to a rare personnel issue.

Edge pass-rushing linebackers are still around today, but contemporary 3–4 schemes use more deception than the 3–4 schemes from the early 1980s. Today's defenses don't rely as much on getting the edge linebacker in a one-on-one matchup against a left tackle, but instead try to get a mismatch anywhere they can on the line. That makes building a solid offensive line across the board much more important than just having one great pass-blocking left tackle.

Another way to put this is that a team can scheme to get by without a great left tackle until they play a team with a dominant pass-rushing linebacker. At that point, they have to either have an incredibly talented pass blocker or a good pass blocker combined with a very adaptable blocking system that can adjust for that level of pass rusher.

In the end, I hope that this study is only the first of many on this subject to be performed by future researchers. As it stands, the research seems to indicate that while the left tackle is important, the position doesn't seem to justify the huge salaries being thrown at it. And it likely won't be that valuable until another Lawrence Taylor appears on the horizon.

2

How Can I Miss You If You Won't Go Away? Why the End of the NFL Dynasty Period Is Not Here

There doesn't seem to be a week that goes by without some television announcer or writer commenting about how free agency and the salary cap have made it much more difficult to build dynasty teams. This idea is so prevalent that the 2000s Patriots are often given extra credit for having established a dynasty during this period.

Rather than just accepting this premise at face value, let's instead ask this question: What effect should we expect free agency and the salary cap to have on the establishment of dynasty teams?

I think the best way to start this type of review is to remember that free agency and the salary cap are but two ways of controlling player movement. Since the history of the NFL has seen varying levels of player movement, it might be enlightening to take a look at what the

NFL record books have to say about how player movement has affected the building of dynasties over the years.

A Way to Measure a Team's Dynastic Impact

Before we can measure any of those effects, however, we first must define some parameters for measuring dynastic teams. I believe the most objective way to do this is by establishing a set of team accomplishments and assigning values to each of them (a method that Bill James pioneered for measuring team greatness in baseball).

There are any number of things a team can do to be considered successful, some of which are more valuable than others. The list of team accomplishments I decided to use for this analysis includes the following:

- Have a winning season
- Post .600 record, .700 record, .800 record, and so on
- Make the playoffs
- Win secondary-level playoff games
- Win conference championship
- Win league championship

Each of these has a set point value. A winning season nets a team one point. A team is also awarded half a point for each step up the incremental winning percentage success ladder. For example, if a team posts a 12–4 record (.750 winning percentage), they receive one point for a winning season, half a point for posting a .600-plus record, and another half point for posting a .700-plus record.

A team is awarded one point for making the playoffs, regardless of what level of playoff the team achieved. For a win in the wild-card round, a team is awarded one point. A win in a divisional or second-round playoff game (or in a conference/divisional championship tiebreaker game during the 1930s–1960s) nets a team two points. For winning a conference championship game, a team is given three points. These three points are also awarded to teams that appeared in an AFL or NFL championship game prior to the advent of conference championship games. Winning a league championship (NFL, AFL, or AAFC) gives a team four points.

The idea behind the system is to award teams an ever-increasing number of points for the largest accomplishments. Teams are not considered dynasty-level unless they win championship games, so the scale is heavily weighted for that achievement.

The biggest flaw I see in this system is that it will award a modern team that wins two or three playoff games before winning a championship a much higher number of points than a pre–expanded playoff tournament team had available to it. That reduces or precludes the use of the system as a balanced historical gauge of dynastic success, but since the system is being used to gauge teams from very specific eras, it fits the needs of this particular analysis.

A New Chronology for Dynasties

In reviewing the history of dynasties, most historians use a decade-by-decade approach. Since our discussion revolves around what effect a specific set of personnel acquisition rules had on dynastic teams, I think the best way to look at this would be to review it by the distinct player personnel distribution eras in NFL history. These eras are the following:

1920–1932: The Barnstorming Era. This period was marked by the beginnings of the standard player contract that limited player movement, but it also had barnstorming teams, some short-term player contracts (often on a game-by-game basis), varying levels of free agency for players from defunct teams, and open bidding for college players.

1933–1945: The Divisional Era. This era saw the end of barnstorming, the beginning of the set schedule, and the start of the NFL draft, all of which combined to virtually eliminate any level of player free agency.

1946–1959: The AAFC/CFL Era. The AAFC war made open player competition a reality for the NFL for the first time in over a decade. After winning the AAFC war, the NFL had a border skirmish with the CFL, which also resulted in some level of competition for player contractual rights.

1960–1969: The AFL/NFL Era. The AFL-NFL war saw competition for players increase every year until the merger was implemented. The rivalry was mostly limited to the draft, but there was also competition for undrafted players and players not wanted by the other league (a phenomenon that occurred mostly from the NFL to the AFL, especially in the early years of the war).

1970–1988: The Rozelle Rule Era. The merger killed off all meaningful competition for players, but in this era the league went even further to stop player movement by implementing the Rozelle Rule, which effectively punished teams for trying to sign players from other teams. The new rule gave the commissioner the ability to award compensation (either existing players and/or draft picks) to any team that lost a player to another team. It had been in place prior to 1970, but the war with the AFL had limited its efficacy.

1989–1993: The Plan B Era. This was an era with a limited form of free agency where each team could protect a large core group of players. Since the typical unprotected player was one who was on the fringe of making an NFL roster, this style of free agency was only useful in opening up competition for those types of players.

1994–today: The Salary Cap/Free Agency with Player Movement Tags Era. This system allows for open competition for players under a hard salary cap, and with the top players' movement limited by franchise/transition tags.

For those of you wondering why I didn't include the World Football League war as a separate era, I point to two reasons. The first is that the WFL lasted for only a season and a half, so many of its signings that would have impacted the NFL didn't occur.

The second reason is that the player defections that did happen only adversely affected one team from a dynastic standpoint, that being the

TEAM	.500+	.600	.700	.800	.900	1.0	PO	WC WIN	DIV P/O WIN	CONF WIN	CHAMP WIN	POINT TOTAL
1920–1932: THE BARNSTORMING ERA												
Green Bay Packers	12	11	7	2	1	1	0	0	0	1	3	38.00
Decatur/Chicago Staleys/Bears	12	11	8	6	3	0	0	0	0	1	2	37.00
Canton Bulldogs	4	4	3	2	2	2	0	0	0	0	2	18.50
New York Giants	6	5	3	2	2	0	0	0	0	0	1	16.00
Frankford Yellow Jackets	5	5	4	2	1	0	0	0	0	0	1	15.00
Chicago Cardinals	6	4	3	1	0	0	0	0	0	0	1	14.00
Providence Steam Roller	4	3	1	1	0	0	0	0	0	0	1	10.50
Akron Pros	2	2	2	1	1	1	0	0	0	0	1	9.50
Rock Island Independents	5	5	2	0	0	0	0	0	0	0	0	8.50
Cleveland Bulldogs	1	1	1	1	0	0	0	0	0	0	1	6.50
1933–1945: THE DIVISIONAL ERA												
Chicago Bears	12	11	9	6	2	2	7	0	1	7	4	73.00
New York Giants	10	10	6	3	1	0	8	0	0	7	2	57.00
Green Bay Packers	12	11	7	5	2	0	5	0	0	4	3	53.50
Boston/Washington Redskins	10	8	5	4	1	0	6	0	1	6	2	53.00
Detroit Lions	8	7	3	0	0	0	1	0	0	1	1	21.00
Cleveland Rams	1	1	1	1	1	0	1	0	0	1	1	11.00
1946–1959: THE AAFC/CFL ERA												
Cleveland Browns	13	12	11	9	5	1	12	0	2	11	7	109.00
Detroit Lions	6	6	4	2	0	0	4	0	2	4	3	44.00
New York Giants	10	6	6	3	0	0	5	0	1	4	1	40.50
Los Angeles Rams	10	8	5	1	0	0	5	0	1	4	1	40.00
Philadelphia Eagles	8	5	2	2	1	0	3	0	1	3	2	35.00
Chicago Bears	11	10	5	3	0	0	3	0	0	2	1	33.00
San Francisco 49ers	9	8	3	1	0	0	2	0	1	1	0	22.00
Baltimore Colts (rev 2)	3	2	2	0	0	0	2	0	0	2	2	21.00
Chicago Cardinals	5	2	2	1	1	0	2	0	0	2	1	20.00
1960–1969: THE AFL/NFL ERA												
AFL RESULTS												
Los Angeles/San Diego Chargers	9	7	4	2	0	0	5	0	0	5	1	39.50
Dallas Texans/Kansas City Chiefs	7	5	4	2	0	0	4	0	1	3	2	35.50
Houston Oilers	4	4	3	0	0	0	5	0	0	4	2	32.50

(continued)

TOP TEAMS AND ERAS *(continued)*

TEAM	.500+	.600	.700	.800	.900	1.0	PO	WC WIN	DIV P/O WIN	CONF WIN	CHAMP WIN	POINT TOTAL
1960–1969: THE AFL/NFL ERA *(continued)*												
AFL RESULTS												
Buffalo Bills	5	3	2	1	0	0	4	0	0	2	2	26.00
Oakland Raiders	6	6	4	3	2	0	3	0	2	1	0	23.50
New York Titans/Jets	3	3	2	0	0	0	2	0	0	1	1	14.50
Boston Patriots	5	4	1	0	0	0	1	0	1	1	0	13.50
NFL RESULTS												
Green Bay Packers	9	8	5	3	1	0	6	0	2	6	5	65.50
Cleveland Browns	10	9	6	0	0	0	5	0	2	2	1	36.50
Baltimore Colts	8	6	4	3	2	0	3	0	1	2	0	26.50
New York Giants	4	4	3	1	0	0	3	0	0	3	0	20.00
Chicago Bears	5	3	1	1	1	0	1	0	0	1	1	16.00
Dallas Cowboys	4	4	3	2	0	0	4	0	1	0	0	14.50
Philadelphia Eagles	3	3	2	1	0	0	1	0	0	1	1	14.00
Los Angeles Rams	4	3	3	1	1	0	2	0	0	0	0	10.00
Minnesota Vikings	3	2	1	1	0	0	2	0	0	1	0	10.00
1970–1988: THE ROZELLE RULE ERA												
Dallas Cowboys	16	14	11	1	0	0	14	2	10	5	2	88.00
Miami Dolphins	14	14	12	3	1	1	12	1	6	5	2	77.50
Oakland/Los Angeles Raiders	15	13	8	3	1	0	11	2	8	3	3	77.50
Pittsburgh Steelers	13	10	7	2	0	0	11	0	7	4	4	75.50
Washington Redskins	14	13	8	2	0	0	10	2	5	4	2	67.50
San Francisco 49ers	10	9	4	3	1	0	8	0	6	3	3	59.50
Minnesota Vikings	13	8	6	4	0	0	11	3	5	3	0	55.00
Los Angeles Rams	15	13	6	2	0	0	13	1	6	1	0	54.50
Denver Broncos	12	9	3	2	0	0	7	0	3	3	0	41.00
Chicago Bears	7	7	4	2	1	0	7	0	3	1	1	34.00
Cincinnati Bengals	10	7	6	0	0	0	6	0	2	2	0	32.50
Baltimore/Indianapolis Colts	7	6	5	1	0	0	6	0	2	1	1	30.00
Cleveland Browns	10	7	2	0	0	0	8	0	2	0	0	26.50
New York Giants	7	4	1	1	0	0	4	3	1	1	1	26.00
Boston/New England Patriots	11	6	1	0	0	0	5	1	1	1	0	25.50
Houston Oilers	7	6	1	0	0	0	5	4	2	0	0	23.50
1989–1993: THE PLAN B ERA												
Buffalo Bills	5	4	3	2	0	0	5	1	4	4	0	35.50
San Francisco 49ers	5	5	3	3	0	0	4	0	4	1	1	29.50

(continued)

TOP TEAMS AND ERAS *(continued)*

TEAM	.500+	.600	.700	.800	.900	1.0	PO	WC WIN	DIV P/O WIN	CONF WIN	CHAMP WIN	POINT TOTAL
1989–1993: THE PLAN B ERA *(continued)*												
Dallas Cowboys	3	3	2	1	0	0	3	1	2	2	2	28.00
Washington Redskins	4	3	1	1	0	0	3	2	1	1	1	20.50
New York Giants	3	3	2	1	0	0	3	1	1	1	1	19.00
Kansas City Chiefs	5	4	0	0	0	0	4	2	1	0	0	15.00
Denver Broncos	3	2	1	0	0	0	3	0	2	1	0	14.50
Houston Oilers	5	3	1	0	0	0	5	1	0	0	0	13.00
Philadelphia Eagles	4	4	0	0	0	0	3	0	1	0	0	11.00
Los Angeles Raiders	3	2	1	0	0	0	3	1	1	0	0	10.50
1994–2006: FREE AGENCY/SALARY CAP ERA												
New England Patriots	11	9	4	3	1	1	10	3	6	5	3	72.00
Pittsburgh Steelers	10	9	3	2	1	0	9	3	6	2	1	51.50
Green Bay Packers	11	9	5	3	0	0	10	4	4	2	1	51.50
Indianapolis Colts	10	8	6	3	0	0	10	4	3	1	1	45.50
Denver Broncos	9	7	4	3	0	0	7	1	3	2	2	44.00
Philadelphia Eagles	8	8	3	1	0	0	8	4	4	1	0	37.00
San Francisco 49ers	7	7	5	2	0	0	7	3	2	1	1	35.00
Dallas Cowboys	8	6	3	1	0	0	8	1	2	1	1	33.00
New York Giants	6	5	1	0	0	0	6	1	2	2	1	30.00
Tampa Bay Buccaneers	7	5	1	0	0	0	7	1	2	1	1	29.00
Los Angeles/St. Louis Rams	4	4	3	2	0	0	5	0	2	2	1	27.50
Minnesota Vikings	8	4	1	1	1	0	7	3	2	0	0	25.50
Houston Oilers/ Tennessee Oilers/ Tennessee Titans	5	5	3	2	0	0	5	2	2	1	0	24.00
Jacksonville Jaguars	7	5	2	1	0	0	6	3	2	0	0	24.00
Miami Dolphins	10	5	0	0	0	0	7	4	0	0	0	23.50
Baltimore Ravens	5	4	2	1	0	0	4	2	1	1	1	23.50
Seattle Seahawks	7	3	1	1	0	0	5	2	1	1	0	21.50
San Diego Chargers	6	4	2	1	0	0	5	0	2	1	0	21.50
Carolina Panthers	3	3	1	0	0	0	3	2	3	1	0	19.00
New York Jets	7	4	1	0	0	0	5	2	1	0	0	18.50
Chicago Bears	5	3	2	2	0	0	4	1	1	1	0	18.50
Kansas City Chiefs	8	4	3	3	0	0	5	0	0	0	0	18.00
Atlanta Falcons	4	2	1	1	0	0	4	1	2	1	0	18.00
Los Angeles/Oakland Raiders	4	3	1	0	0	0	3	1	2	1	0	17.00
Buffalo Bills	5	4	0	0	0	0	4	1	0	0	0	12.00

Dolphins. The Steelers, Cowboys, and Raiders were not affected in any significant way by the WFL. The failure of Miami to regain any semblance of its dynasty after losing a backup running back (Jim Kiick), an aging wide receiver near the end of his career (Paul Warfield), and a dominant running back (Larry Csonka) is a partial indicator that Miami wasn't quite as strong as the other dynasty candidates of that era. Add those reasons up and I simply couldn't find a way to justify assigning a separate era to the WFL. The USFL also doesn't warrant a separate era for similar reasons.

Using the dynastic point system described above, let's take a look at the point totals for the top teams in each of these eras.

One of the first things that stood out to me when I completed these lists is that there are not only major dynasties in each of the eras, but also a large number of mini-dynasties.

ERA	MAJOR DYNASTIES	MINI-DYNASTIES
1920–1932: Barnstorming	Green Bay, Chicago	Canton, New York Giants
1933–1945: Divisional	Chicago	New York Giants, Green Bay, Boston/Washington Redskins
1946–1959: AAFC-CFL	Cleveland	Detroit, New York Giants, Los Angeles Rams, Philadelphia, Chicago
1960–1969: AFL/NFL	Green Bay	Los Angeles/San Diego Chargers, Dallas Texans/Kansas City Chiefs, Houston, Cleveland
1970–1988: Rozelle Rule	Dallas, Miami, Oakland/Los Angeles Raiders, Pittsburgh	Washington, San Francisco, Minnesota, Los Angeles Rams
1989–1993: Plan B	Dallas	Buffalo, San Francisco
1994–2007: Free Agency/Salary Cap	New England	Pittsburgh, Green Bay, Denver, Indianapolis

One of the precepts of the death-of-the-dynasty idea seems to be that if a particular dynastic team did not exist for some reason, a different dynastic team would not have risen up in its place. The above analysis shows that even if any of the dynastic teams had not been able to claim their spot, there were always multiple teams primed to take their place.

For example, had the Belichick Patriots not been so dominant, I think it is quite likely that the Indianapolis Colts would have become the dynastic team of the early free agency/salary cap era. Buffalo certainly would have done so in Dallas's place in the plan B era. The Cowboys of the 1970s were actually quite close to laying claim to being the team of that decade and would have had a legitimate claim had they beaten Pittsburgh in either of their Super Bowl meetings.

The second item that stood out is that, regardless of the type of player distribution system used, there have been dynastic teams in all of the distinct player personnel distribution eras in NFL history. Dynastic teams and near-dynastic teams have never stopped occurring regardless of how much or how little player movement there was. There simply isn't any historical evidence to back up a claim that says otherwise.

Having said that, there is one trend I saw that seems quite significant. The two eras that had the closest competition between the top teams were the barnstorming era and the AFL side of the AFL-NFL era. Both of these eras happen to be the ones with the greatest amount of player movement, so that is a feather in the cap of the idea that it is somewhat harder to build a dynastic team during a free agency era. Even with that greater difficulty, however, I should point out that both of those leagues were still dominated by two or three teams and the Packers won three straight championships during the barnstorming era.

All It Takes to Be an Expert Is to Be One Page Ahead in the Book

So why is it that free agency and the salary cap haven't killed off the dynasty? I think it comes down to a simple matter of the player acquisition rules being a sinking or rising tide that affects all boats. A good example of this is that the salary cap rules are record-neutral and can negatively impact both good and bad teams. The only reason those rules tend to adversely affect the best teams is that winning breeds greed, but that can be managed if a team plans for it just like they would for aging and/or injured players.

Free agency is a bit different in that players on championship teams are often able to cash in on their inflated value, but don't forget that the free agency road also flows both ways (e.g., the Patriots and Corey Dillon). Free agency gives the dynasty hopefuls more options to address player personnel deficiencies, but it also gives dynastic teams more options to fill their gaps. In addition, free agency and the salary cap can adversely affect the dynastic candidate's competition if they don't manage greed and inflated player value well.

Having said that, I do have a theory as to why the NFL always has dynastic teams. I believe that a team doesn't need to try to become the best team of all time to be a dynasty. All they have to do is find an edge over their competition. If you take a detailed look at how every dynasty was built, it becomes clear how and why every one of them found this edge.

Let me show you what I mean by taking a look at each dynasty.

Era: Barnstorming (1920–1932)

Dynasty Team: Green Bay Packers

Dynastic Edge: Able to acquire three Hall of Famers between 1928 and 1929 seasons

From 1920 to 1928, the NFL had only one team that could have possibly been considered a dynasty, that being the Canton Bulldogs, but by 1928 the Bulldogs were defunct. The Packers certainly weren't anything close to a dynasty by then, as their best finishes up to that point were a second- and third-place ranking in 1927 and 1923 respectively.

That all changed in 1929 when Curly Lambeau took full advantage of three personnel opportunities that passed his way that year. The first of these was due in large part to the financial strain of the New York Yankees franchise. Dan Topping, the Yankees owner, was in debt and doing all he could to cut his costs. One of these costs was a $400 contract owed to Mike Michalske, one of the best linemen in the league who was coming off two consecutive first team All-Pro seasons. In exchange for waiving the $400 owed to him, Topping allowed Michalske to become a free agent and Lambeau quickly signed him.

The second opportunity was Cal Hubbard's dissatisfaction with life in the big city. Hubbard played two seasons with the New York Giants and made either first- or second-team All-Pro in both years. He wasn't a fan of living in New York, however, and longed to get back to small-town life. He enjoyed his visits to Green Bay so much that he told the Giants they could either trade him to the Packers or he would retire. The Giants acquiesced with his request and Lambeau, in two strokes, had built one of the best lines in the entire league.

As if that weren't enough, Lambeau pulled off one more coup that offseason. Johnny "Blood" McNally was an extremely talented runner and receiver who had bounced around among three different teams during his first five years in the NFL. When Blood's latest team, the Pottsville Maroons, disbanded after the 1928 season, he became available and Lambeau signed him to a $100 per game contract.

Gaining three players of this caliber would be a huge benefit in any generation, but its impact in an era with twenty-man roster limits and sixty-minute players cannot be overemphasized. These three helped the Packers run off a 12-0-1 record in 1929 to win the NFL title for the first of three consecutive years. All totaled, Green Bay's record during that three-year run was 34-5-2. Lambeau certainly displayed a very good eye for talent, but it was a set of extremely favorable circumstances that allowed him to get a significant talent edge over the rest of the league.

Era: Divisional (1933–1945)

Dynasty Team: Chicago Bears

Dynastic Edge: George Halas as owner/coach

Four teams dominated the NFL during this era: Chicago, Green Bay, Washington, and the New York Giants. To give you an idea of just how dominant these four teams were, consider that there were twenty-six possible slots in the thirteen championship games played during this time frame, and these teams filled twenty-four of those slots.

Three of these four teams were also run by dominant coaching figures: Lambeau in Green Bay, Steve Owen in New York, and Halas in Chicago. The bulk of the Redskins' success came under Ray Flaherty, but he was only able to stand George Preston Marshall's overbearing personality for seven seasons, thus preventing Washington from becoming the dynastic team of this era. Lambeau and Owen were certainly giants of the coaching profession at a similar level to Halas, so the question here is, why was Halas able to clinch this dynastic title for the Bears?

I think it was a simple matter of Halas being able to leave coaching every ten years to recharge his batteries. The ten-year rule is a subject I cover in much greater depth in the coaching section of this book, but I can sum the theory up thus. History shows us very clearly that a coach has his greatest successes during his first ten years with a team and his record drops fairly dramatically from there, no matter how great the coach is.

In this case, the ten-year rule certainly reared its ugly head. For proof, consider the following comparisons. Curly Lambeau was only one season removed from his third straight championship campaign when this era started but he was in his thirteenth season as coach. Halas coached from 1920 to 1929 but then took a three-season hiatus as head coach, during which time he maneuvered his partner Ed Sternaman out of the Bears organization. He restarted his coaching career right as this era began.

Over the next ten seasons, the Packers posted a 78-34-4 record and appeared in three championship games, winning two. During that same time frame, Halas guided his team to an 85-22-4 record and led the team to five championship games, winning three. The Bears also beat the Packers in their only playoff meeting during this time, a divisional playoff game after the 1941 season when both teams were tied with a 10–1 mark.

As favorable as that comparison is for Halas, it looks even better when you consider that his coaching record doesn't include the entire 1942 season. He was commissioned in the navy and had to leave the team in midseason after posting a 6–0 record. Hunk Anderson and Luke Johnsos took over the coaching reins and guided the Bears to five more wins and a berth in the championship game, thus giving the Bears a sixth title appearance during this time. The Bears and Packers both won one more title during the rest of this period, so the Bears' fill-in coaches were able to keep the lead over the Packers that Halas had built up during his second ten-year run as coach.

A similar ten-year point can be made with Owen, or more accurately an eleven-year point. During Owen's first eleven seasons (1931–1941), the Giants had an 81-42-9 record and they appeared in six championship games, winning two. For the last four seasons of this era, the Giants had a 22-15-4 record and appeared in only one championship game. Halas's backups led the Bears to two championships and helped the team finish off one undefeated season during that time frame, both of which helped them extend their dynastic lead over the Giants.

Halas never had to face the ten-year demon full-bore during his career because he left the coaching profession four different times after coaching exactly ten seasons. Lambeau and Owen, great though they were, were never able to get away from things for even one season, and as time wore on, they wore out. Recharging his coaching batteries was the advantage Halas had over his competition.

Era: AAFC/CFL (1946–1959)

Dynasty Team: Cleveland Browns

Dynastic Edge: Paul Brown's inside info on amateur personnel/ the unique personnel setup of the early AAFC

When discussing the success of the Cleveland Browns during this era, it is often said that Paul Brown's pioneering of certain techniques (i.e., a classroom style teaching of players, messenger guards, the face-mask, and intelligence testing) were the biggest difference-makers in Cleveland's success. While each of those techniques certainly gave them some kind of an edge, I contend that their biggest edge came from Brown's inside knowledge of the amateur players of that era.

Prior to his tenure with the Browns, Brown coached at Massillon High School from 1932 to 1940, Ohio State from 1941 to 1943, and the Great Lakes Naval Training Center from 1944 to 1945. All of these teams were chock-full of good players. Massillon was the premier high school team in the country, Ohio State won the national championship in 1942, and the Great Lakes team was one of the best in the military ranks. Brown's coaching history gave him a much wider body of amateur personnel knowledge than anyone else in professional football.

For proof of the impact of this knowledge, take a look at some of the players Brown picked up from either Massillon, Ohio State, Great Lakes, or opposing Big Ten teams: Otto Graham, Lou Groza, Dante Lavelli, Marion Motley, Bill Willis, Mac Speedie, Lin Houston, Horace Gillom, and Tommy James. The first five on that list are Hall of Famers. Speedie probably would have been a Hall of Famer had he stayed in the NFL instead of transferring to the CFL. Brown rated Houston as one of the fifteen best players he had while coaching the Browns. Gillom was one of the best punters of his generation and James was a onetime Pro Bowler and ballhawk who notched thirty-four interceptions in his eight years with the Browns. One of Brown's assistant coaches with significant college and high school contacts, Johnny Brickles, was also instrumental in getting Frank Gatski, another Hall of Famer, a tryout with the Browns in 1946.

In most eras, Brown would have picked up some of these players, but he was able to stock up and cherry-pick the best of the bunch due to the unique circumstances that ruled the pro football world during and after World War II. The AAFC-NFL war afforded players the first true free agency the professional football ranks had seen since before the advent of the draft in the mid-1930s. In addition, the AAFC did not hold a draft until after its first season, so Brown had an unfair advantage not only over the NFL, but also over his own league.

Brown took advantage of this free agency by signing many of his best players while they were still in the service. He offered them contracts that began after the war and also paid some of the players retainers while they were still serving on active duty.

In the case of other players such as Lou Rymkus, Brown had to wait until after their war service was over. Rymkus had been an All-America and team MVP in his senior season at Notre Dame and then was drafted by the Redskins in 1943. He played for Washington for a year and went to serve in the war for two years. After the war he chose to sign with Cleveland and went on to be named first- or second-team All-Pro six times during his career.

Under normal circumstances, Brown would never have had the chance to sign most of these players, but he took full advantage of the personnel opportunities afforded to him. Every team had the opportunity to sign these players, mind you, but Brown was the best prepared for it given his background. The combination of the unlikely sets of player acquisition circumstances, Brown's inside knowledge of the best available players, and the Browns ownership's willingness to finance the early payments to players gave Brown an unprecedented opportunity to hoard talent. It was that hoarding of talent that gave Cleveland a dynasty.

Era: AFL/NFL (1960–1969)

Dynasty Team: Green Bay Packers

Dynastic Edge: Jack Vainisi

When most teams have a lot of success, they are usually either blessed with a great coach or a great personnel man. Rarely does a team end up having great men at both positions at the same time, but that's exactly what the Packers had in the late 1950s. Everyone knows that Vince Lombardi was the best motivator of his era, but much of the Packers' success during Lombardi's coaching run was due to the efforts of a relatively unknown personnel man named Jack Vainisi.

Vainisi was the Gil Brandt or Bill Polian of his day in that he lived to find talented football players. His track record of finding those players is second to none. He was the hardest-working scout in the business, often putting in eighteen-hour days at a time when many teams had part-time scouting departments. Vainisi was driven to be successful as quickly as he could because he had a heart condition that doctors said was going to curse him with an early death.

Vainisi's hard work paid off with a collection of great football players that reads like a Who's Who of the Packers Hall of Fame: Bart Starr, Paul Hornung, Jim Taylor, Forrest Gregg, Henry Jordan, Jim Ringo, Ray Nitschke, Willie Wood, Boyd Dowler, Jerry Kramer, Hawg Hanner, and Max McGee. And that list isn't even all-inclusive. Vainisi died a mere five weeks prior to the 1961 NFL draft, so he probably also deserves a good amount of credit for the Packers' selections that year, picks that included Herb Adderley (another Hall of Famer), Ron Kostelnik, and Elijah Pitts.

I don't mean this to take away anything from Lombardi's coaching prowess, as he certainly got the most out of the players given to him. Lombardi's post-Vainisi draft record, however, proved he was nowhere near being in Vainisi's league as a talent evaluator. Thankfully for the Packers, no one else in the league was in Vainisi's league, either.

Having the combination of both the best coach and the best talent evaluator of their era gave the Packers one of the biggest edges of any team in any era. That is the primary reason their dynasty numbers are among the greatest of all time.

Era: Rozelle Rule (1970–1988), Part 1

Dynasty Team of the 1970s: Pittsburgh Steelers

Dynastic Edge: Inside information on players from predominantly black colleges

The 1970s were similar to the 1940s in that there were a lot of teams that could have ended up being the dynastic team of the generation. The Steelers, Cowboys, and Raiders all had legitimate chances of being the best of this era, and the Dolphins and Vikings weren't far behind. Since each of these teams had excellent personnel departments and top-notch coaching staffs, how could any of them gain an edge over the other?

The answer lay in the fact that there were still some college football programs that were not scouted very thoroughly, most notably the predominately black southern colleges. The Steelers were able to effectively tap into the talent pool in these schools because of the information provided by one man: Bill Nunn Jr.

Nunn worked for one of the local Pittsburgh newspapers, and at the end of each season he compiled a Black College All-America team. His picks were noticed by Art Rooney Sr., who hired him to help the Steelers in grading players from these relatively unknown schools.

Nunn's input was a tremendous help, as evidenced by Pittsburgh's draft picks from those schools: L. C. Greenwood (Arkansas AM&N), John Stallworth (Alabama A&M), Mel Blount (Southern), and Donnie Shell (South Carolina State). Blount and Stallworth are both Hall of Famers, while Greenwood and Shell have both been finalists for the Hall of Fame. The Cowboys and Raiders certainly racked up their share of top talent, but the Steelers matched them player for player even before taking the Nunn-influenced picks into account. Add the Nunn picks in and it was just the edge that Pittsburgh needed to beat Oakland and Dallas in the quest for dynasty team status.

Era: Rozelle Rule (1970–1988), Part 2

Dynasty Team of the 1980s: San Francisco 49ers

Dynastic Edge: Bill Walsh's realization of the value of quantity versus quality of draft picks

By the time Bill Walsh took over the 49ers in 1979, the edge that could be gained by mining unknown talent pools was diminishing rapidly. He realized that hustle and hard work by scouting staffs would no longer be enough to win the talent acquisition battle. If Walsh wanted an edge, he was going to have to apply strategy to the issue.

Luckily for Walsh, he had a role model for this: Don Klosterman. Klosterman was the Rams personnel chief in the 1970s and a master of two draft strategies. The first of these was trading veterans for draft picks. This strategy paid off quite well for the Rams, as evidenced by some of his best players-for-picks trades, which are detailed below.

1973–The Rams sent eleven-year veteran quarterback Roman Gabriel to the Eagles in exchange for Harold Jackson, Tony Baker, the Eagles' number 1 pick in 1974, and their number 1 and number 3 picks in 1975. Klosterman then drafted John Cappelletti, Dennis Harrah, and Dan Nugent with the Eagles' picks.

Since Los Angeles had already traded for quarterback John Hadl, the Rams were set at that position and could afford to let Gabriel go. Hadl won the NFC MVP award that year, Jackson was one of the better vertical threats for the five seasons he played with the Rams, and Harrah started 168 games in thirteen seasons. Gabriel earned a Pro Bowl berth in his first year with the Eagles but only started twenty-four games in the three following seasons so Klosterman definitely got the better of this deal.

1974–Los Angeles traded Hadl to Green Bay for the Packers' number 1 and number 3 picks in 1975, their number 1 and number 2 picks in 1976, and Baltimore's number 2 pick in 1975 that the Packers had acquired in a previous deal. The Rams turned those picks into Mike Fanning, Monte Jackson, Ron Jessie, and Pat Thomas. This trade wasn't quite as good as the Gabriel trade, but considering that Hadl was in his thirteenth season and the Rams had Ron Jaworski on their roster, it was certainly another winning deal for Klosterman.

1978–Los Angeles traded Monte Jackson to Oakland for their number 1 pick in 1979, number 3 pick in 1980, and number 2 pick in 1981. The Rams turned two of those picks into George Andrews and LeRoy Irvin and used the other to garner a later multiple-picks trade in their favor.

Klosterman also combined these trades with other trades that would allow the Rams to move down in the draft in exchange for extra draft picks. To illustrate the real value of these trades, take a look at the number of picks the Rams were able to stockpile in the first four rounds of the 1972–1980 drafts:

1972: four picks in rounds 1–4

1973: six picks in rounds 1–4

1974: five picks in rounds 1–4

1975: eight picks in rounds 1–4

1976: five picks in rounds 1–4

1977: seven picks in rounds 1–4

1978: six picks in rounds 1–4

1979: seven picks in rounds 1–4

1980: five picks in rounds 1–4

That is a total of fifty-three picks in the first four rounds over nine seasons, or seventeen more picks than what the Rams would normally have. That is nearly two extra picks in the first four rounds of every draft for almost an entire decade.

The extra picks helped make the Rams consistent winners during this decade. They were not able to turn this mother lode of talent into a Super Bowl because their owner, Carroll Rosenbloom, was too impatient for a winner and was constantly changing coaches and quarterbacks, but that doesn't invalidate Klosterman's draft strategies.

Putting together a Super Bowl winner wasn't an issue for long with the Walsh 49ers, but Walsh didn't utilize Klosterman's volume draft-pick lessons at the beginning of his head-coaching career. San Francisco had a habit of trading away their high draft picks during the early portions of Walsh's tenure and they didn't typically get draft picks back in return. The 49ers lacked either a first- or second-round pick in four of Walsh's first seven seasons. In 1985, the Niners had only four picks in the first six rounds and six picks overall, although it must be pointed out that their first-round pick was Jerry Rice.

By 1986, the 49ers were one of the best teams in the NFL, but they were by no means a cinch for dynasty status. Truth be told, the Niners at that point looked to be a team on something of a decline. They had won the Super Bowl in the 1984 season but were thrashed in the playoffs the next two seasons to the tune of 66–6. If San Francisco wanted to turn the dynasty corner, it was clear they were going to have to embrace changes in their team-building strategies. That's when Walsh decided to use Klosterman's idea of success through volume of picks.

Part of the reason Walsh did this was that he believed the 1986 draft had a lot of depth and he was determined to take full advantage of that depth. He engineered multiple trades that allowed San Francisco to repeatedly trade down and stockpile picks until they were able to draft nine players in the first six rounds of that draft. Those picks included Larry Roberts, Tom Rathman, Tim McKyer, John Taylor, Charles Haley, Steve Wallace, Kevin Fagan, and Don Griffin. All of those players turned out to be starters and many were Pro Bowl–caliber players. That one draft was the catalyst that allowed the Niners to run off two more Super Bowl wins in the late 1980s and grab the dynasty title for themselves. Because it led to Super Bowl success, it also illustrated to the rest of the league the value of quantity versus quality in the draft in a way that Klosterman's Rams never could.

Era: Plan B (1989–1993)

Dynasty Team: Dallas Cowboys

Dynastic Edge: Mike Lynn's gaffe, Jimmy Johnson's knowledge of college players and revising the draft value chart

After Walsh's 1986 draft coup, it was inevitable in the copycat world of the NFL that other teams would adopt his strategy. When multiple teams are trying to trade down, however, the draft stockpiling strategy becomes much more difficult to implement effectively.

Widespread use of this strategy also made teams very value-conscious of their picks. Even with this value-consciousness, however, most NFL teams still lacked an effective way to accurately determine their picks' value. What was needed was an actuarial method for gauging the value of each draft pick, and that's where Jimmy Johnson comes into the picture.

Johnson and his staff had recently moved up from the collegiate coaching level. Since his entire staff had been involved in the college scouting and recruiting process, Johnson had access to a collegiate personnel knowledge base not unlike Paul Brown's in the 1940s. But he wasn't satisfied with merely having a knowledge edge; he also wanted to find the best methods possible for maximizing its usefulness.

Johnson's first method was to find creative ways to use the Walsh method of stockpiling picks. He was able to accomplish this in part because Mike Lynn gave away the Vikings' draft farm in exchange for Herschel Walker in the NFL's most infamous trade. The Walker picks gave Dallas a good supply of personnel ammunition, but it was just the beginning for the Cowboys. Johnson traded many of those picks to build up even more draft-day value.

The reason he was so effective in doing this is the revisions he ordered made to the Cowboys draft value chart. Dallas had been using a chart showing the relative value of draft picks for a few years, but it was in need of updating. Johnson had a member of the Cowboys staff review the success/failure rates of each draft slot and used that information to revise the point values on the value chart.

The benefit of this for Dallas was twofold. First, they were able to make rational, analytical trade decisions in a hurry, while their competitors were scrambling around trying to determine the proper trade value without having completed any prior research. Second, because Dallas had the best information on college players, they were able to properly value which picks they were willing to reach for.

Personnel expertise was an edge the Cowboys staff had over the rest of the league, but they also found ways to utilize this knowledge to the fullest. As much as the Walker picks helped the Cowboys, it was the creation of an intelligent structure with which to value those picks that really gave Dallas the dynasty edge.

Era: Salary Cap/Free Agency (1994–Today)

Dynasty Team: New England Patriots

Dynastic Edge: Modular use of defensive players, pioneered game plan agnosticism

By the time the Patriots started their dynasty run every team had their own draft value charts, so the jockeying and fleecing of teams that occurred in the draft rooms of the 1970s–1990s was diminished. If any team was going to dominate the salary cap/free agency era, it was going to have to find a way to get increased value out of any draft pick, as it was much more unlikely that a team was going to corner the market on talent.

The Patriots found two ways to accomplish this. The first was by expanding the role of the linebacker in their 3–4 defensive scheme. Most teams employing the 3–4 used two-gap defensive linemen to occupy the offensive linemen in order to free up the linebackers to make plays. The linebackers were also divided into two types: pluggers (run stuffers) and edge pass rushers.

The Patriots got around the limitations of that version of the 3–4 by changing the nature of the 3–4 linebacker. Instead of dividing the front seven into specialists, New England made the linebacker position modular in nature.

The modular change had three benefits. First, it gave New England a strategic edge by better disguising their linebackers' intentions. In the Patriots' system, each linebacker could now line up anywhere in the front seven and his role could change from play to play. On one play, a linebacker might line up as a defensive end and two-gap. On the next play, he might end up rushing the passer or playing back and defending the run at the linebacker level.

The second benefit is that it allowed the Patriots to better absorb injuries. Most teams have only two or three players for each position on their depth chart. Since each linebacker was taught how to play any of the front seven positions on defense, it effectively gave New England as many as four and five players on the depth charts of every one of their front seven positions.

The third benefit was that New England's coaches were able to do what they do best. Bill Belichick built his defensive reputation by coaching linebackers, and many members of his staff also had line-backer-coaching backgrounds. The increased role of the linebacker in their defensive scheme allowed the Patriots to maximize their coaching acumen. The combination of these three benefits gave New England the best defense in the NFL.

The other innovation the Patriots used to gain an advantage was game plan agnosticism. Most teams have a specific game plan ideology that they want to use every Sunday. These ideologies typically revolve around either attacking the opponent's matchup weaknesses or trying to attack the weakness in an offensive/defensive scheme. For example, the Colts' passing offense under Peyton Manning is designed to find the weakest player in the secondary and attack him as often as possible. This is very different from the many West Coast offenses that are designed to attack the soft spot in a defensive coverage scheme and often pay little attention to which defender the ball ends up being thrown at.

The Patriots under Belichick had no such set game plan ideology. One instance of this occurred when New England faced the Steelers in the 2002 season opener. The Patriots coaching staff realized that they were not going to run the ball with very much success against Pittsburgh. They also knew that the Steelers secondary was quite suspect. When faced with this type of a matchup, many if not most coaching staffs would throw more often than run, but they would still try to maintain a balance between the two.

The Patriots suffered from no such offensive balance pangs. On their first seven drives, New England had Tom Brady drop back to pass thirty-three times and had him hand off only four times. The run/pass balance eventually started to come once New England established a 17–7 lead early in the third quarter, but up until then the Patriots were perfectly content with attacking the Steelers' weakness to the exclusion of doing anything else.

This wasn't the only time the Patriots utilized this type of play-calling imbalance, and it wasn't exclusive to their offensive play calling. New England had their share of dominant players on defense and did all they could to isolate these great players in the right matchups, but during their dynasty run they also displayed their ability to play schemes well by being the best zone coverage team in the NFL. In addition, the Patriots were one of the best teams at identifying and exploiting an opponent's personnel weaknesses while masking their own. They also knew when to avoid attacking an overwhelming strength.

Phil Simms may have put it best when he said the Patriots were hard to prepare for because they were capable of doing anything and therefore made their opponents prepare for everything. One of the reasons that most teams of this era didn't approach game planning in the same manner as the Patriots is that it takes a lot of coordination and effort to build a play-calling structure with this level of flexibility. It takes creativity, intelligence, and an extremely adaptable mind-set. That is a combination of traits that most coaching staffs simply don't have, at least to the level that Belichick's staffs possessed. It was this unique utilization of coaching acumen that gave the Patriots their dynastic edge.

When to Expect the Next Dynasty

Even with the overwhelming historical record and the fact that the NFL is still in the midst of a dynasty (the Patriots' loss to the Giants in Super Bowl XLII notwithstanding), some people will still claim that the football world of today is extra-special. These pundits will say that the Patriots were an exception to the new rule of no dynasties and that no other team will be able to duplicate their success.

The same thing has been said numerous times in the past. I was reminded of this when I watched the 1972 NFL Films season review recently. John Facenda spoke about how Dallas, the winner in Super Bowl VI, was expected to become a dynasty but didn't. Facenda even said at one point that the Dallas dynasty had died.

I can understand why that would have been the feeling at the time. After the 1972 season, there had been a new champion crowned in four straight Super Bowls. It would be understandable at that moment to believe the league was seeing the start of a new world order where repeat champions were a thing of the past.

The trouble is that the long arc of football history seems to be lost to most pundits who claim that the dynasty is dead. Once two or three years have passed without a new dynasty establishing itself, these dynastic nonbelievers will come out of the woodwork and claim to be dancing on the dynasty's grave.

My response to this is to point out something about pattern recognition. If you look through United States presidential history, it seems that a dynamic executive appears on the scene every forty years. In 1780, it was George Washington, followed by Andrew Jackson in 1820,

Abraham Lincoln in 1860, Teddy Roosevelt in 1900, FDR and Harry Truman in the 1940s, and Ronald Reagan in 1980. This isn't to say that any of the other presidents weren't dynamic, but this group of presidents is among the most accomplished in U.S. history. I would say that the United States hasn't had a dynamic chief executive since Reagan, but if history is any indicator, we shouldn't expect one until around 2020.

That same rule applies to the beginnings of each NFL dynasty. These beginnings typically become evident every ten to fourteen years or so, or at least that has been the case since the Browns dynasty established itself around 1948. The Packers dynasty started to become evident around 1961 or 1962. The Steelers dynasty had its first inklings in 1972, but they weren't seen as a dynastic candidate until around 1975. The 49ers had fits and starts to their dynasty, but it wasn't until 1987 or 1988 that they were recognized as a dynastic team. The Cowboys of the 1990s were an exception to this delay, as their dynasty started to be touted as early as 1993, but there was then another ten-year delay before the Patriots started to be thought of as a dynastic team in 2003.

By these historical measurements, we should not expect to see another dynastic candidate until sometime between 2013 and 2017. In other words, if you hear a funeral announcement for the dynasty before then, do yourself a favor and skip renting a tuxedo for the occasion.

The bottom line of this chapter is simply that none of the structural changes in the NFL should prevent dynasties from happening. Free agency and the salary cap are meant to balance out the field, but if NFL history is any indication, some sharp operator will find a way to use those very rules to get an edge of his own. If that doesn't happen, some scout might use some of the new statistical tracking methods for college players and become the Bill Nunn of his generation. Another possibility is that in ten to twenty years the NFL might have a very strong Mexican or European presence and some scout or team might find a way to gain a personnel edge there. It could be any of a number of things, but all it will take is one of these to give a team the edge it needs to become a dynasty.

3

Is It Like Winning the Lottery, or Is It More Like Winning at the Bingo Hall?

Prior to New England's undefeated run during the 2007 regular season, most media members and fans said that the combination of parity, free agency, and the salary cap would ensure that the 1972 Miami Dolphins would be the last undefeated team we will ever see. Since the 2007 Patriots were the only team since then to even have a postseason chance at going unbeaten, it might seem that we will have to wait at least another thirty-five years to see another team have a similar Super Bowl chance at immortality.

One of the primary goals of my work is double-checking the validity of conventional wisdom, so I decided to investigate that assumption. Will we have to wait until Super Bowl LXXVII to see another team finish the regular season unbeaten? Just how often should we expect a team to enter the postseason with zero losses?

There are two main factors that go into how often we should expect to see an undefeated team. The first factor is the talent level of the team (i.e., what is their expected winning percentage?). To illustrate what I mean, let's start by taking a good but not great team, say one whose talent level suggests that we would expect them to have an 11–5 record (or .688 winning percentage). How often would a team of that caliber be expected to go undefeated?

It depends on how many games they play, which is the second factor. If they played only one game, they would finish undefeated 68.8 percent of the time. If they played two games, they would be expected to win both games 47.3 percent of the time (.688 × .688 = .473). Extrapolate that equation out to sixteen games and the expected undefeated percentage for an 11–5 team is .0025 percent, or only one time in four hundred seasons. Luck may have something to do with going undefeated, but it is obvious that a team will need to have more than an 11–5 talent level if they want to seriously entertain this achievement.

Since an 11–5 team won't go undefeated, just how good does a team have to be to be expected to go undefeated? Let's run the numbers.

- A 12–4 team (.750 winning percentage) should be expected to go undefeated in a sixteen-game regular season about 1 percent of the time, or once every hundred years.

- A 13–3 team (.813 winning percentage) should be expected to go undefeated in a sixteen-game regular season about 3.6 percent of the time, or about once every twenty-eight years.

- A 14–2 team (.875 winning percentage) should be expected to go undefeated in a sixteen-game regular season about 11.8 percent of the time, or about once every eight or nine years.

- A 15–1 team (.938 winning percentage) should be expected to go undefeated in a sixteen-game regular season about 35.9 percent of the time, or about once every three years.

What these numbers show is that there are very few teams that should be expected to go 14–2 or better in a season. The reason I say this is that if there were at least one team that could be expected to go 14–2 in every season, the percentages say that undefeated teams would be much more common than they are.

Another interesting aspect of these numbers is how well the 13–3 win percentage fits into the NFL's historical patterns. Let me show you what I mean.

Between 1933 and 1960, the NFL played twelve-game seasons for the most part. A 13–3 caliber team should be expected to win twelve straight games about 8.3 percent of the time. During that time frame, there were thirty-seven teams that finished with a .813 or higher winning percentage, or an average of 1.3 per season. If those teams' winning percentages were considered true indicators of their talent level, then it would be expected that three of them would have finished the season undefeated.

That is exactly what happened. The Bears went 13–0 in 1934 and 11–0 in 1942, and the 1948 Browns finished their AAFC season undefeated.

The NFL expanded to a fourteen game-schedule in 1961 to match the AFL's fourteen-game schedule. The two leagues ran this schedule length from 1961 through 1977. During that time, there were thirty-four teams that finished with a .813 win percentage or higher. An .813 team would be expected to win all of its games in a fourteen-game schedule about 5.5 percent of the time. That pace would mean there should have been nearly two undefeated teams during this time, which is one more than actually occurred.

The NFL adopted a sixteen-game schedule in 1978. An .813 team would be expected to go undefeated in a sixteen-game schedule about 3.6 percent of the time. There were fifty-four teams with .813 or better win percentages between 1978 and 2007. The expected number of undefeated teams in that case would be two. Again, the expected number is higher than the actual number of unbeaten teams, but it is still the closest prediction of any of the win percentages detailed earlier.

The one major variable that I haven't accounted for yet is that all of those numbers assume the .813 teams are legitimate thirteen-win contenders. It is quite likely that a significant percentage of those teams are not quite that good talent-wise but were able to put up thirteen wins due to other factors (luck, lack of injuries, easy schedule, etc.). That can flow both ways and it is rather impossible to state with certainty how many of those teams have thirteen-win talent levels, but for the sake of argument let's assume that 25 percent of the .813 teams are actually teams with 12–4 talent levels. If that is the case, the percentages for each group end up as follows:

- 1933–1960: 37 teams × .75 = 27.75 teams × expected undefeated percentage of 8.3% = 2.3 expected undefeated teams (three actual undefeated teams)

- 1961–1977: 34 teams × .75 = 25.5 teams × expected undefeated percentage of 5.5% = 1.4 expected undefeated teams (one actual undefeated team)

- 1978–2007: 54 teams × .75 = 40.5 teams × expected undefeated percentage of 3.6% = 1.5 expected undefeated teams (one actual undefeated team)

Add the eras up and they say the NFL should have seen 5.2 undefeated teams over its history versus its actual count of five. If the cull rate is correct, it says that the league has seen just as many undefeated teams as it should have.

The only caveat I would make is that the second-most likely undefeated candidate in the sixteen-game era, the 1985 Chicago Bears, did not go undefeated because of a perfect storm of bad conditions in their famous Monday Night Football loss at Miami. Chicago was starting a backup quarterback on the road in one of the most hostile environments in the NFL. They were also facing Dan Marino in his prime and had the added bonus of the 1972 Dolphins firing up both the crowd and the current Dolphin team.

If all of those factors hadn't piled up against Chicago, it is quite likely that they would have beaten Miami and finished that season undefeated. If the Bears had run the table, the NFL would have one more undefeated regular-season team than would be expected.

In conclusion, this study shows three things. First, the NFL is not seeing a dearth of unbeaten teams because of free agency and the salary cap. Over its history, the league has seen nearly as many teams finish the regular season with zero wins as the percentages say it should have, no matter what the league's labor circumstances happen to be at the time.

Second, the primary reason there has been a reduction in undefeated teams is that the longer schedule significantly raised the bar of what it takes to go undefeated. The move from a twelve- to a sixteen-game schedule reduced the expected undefeated percentage for an .813 team by 43 percent.

The third and possibly most important point of this analysis is that the numbers seem to be mixed as to whether we will have to wait another thirty-five years for an unbeaten team. I say this because there are some trends that suggest the league is in an era where more unbeaten teams might be expected.

For example, fifteen of the fifty-four .813+ teams since 1978 have occurred in the past five years. Six of those teams finished the season with a record of 14–2 or better, which is a phenomenal pace that has only been matched one other time in the sixteen-game era (1983–1986). It can't be stated for certain why the league is going through an era of high win–percentage teams, but the trend does suggest that there are more undefeated candidates in today's NFL than is typical.

These things tend to be cyclical, though, so the bottom line is probably this: if we don't see another unbeaten team in the next five years, a new talent cycle will begin, and regular-season perfection won't be seen for a long time. It could very well be at least twenty to twenty-five years before another team gets a shot at this type of immortality, or maybe even longer if the regular season is expanded to seventeen games.

In other words, you may want to remember the 2007 Patriots after all, because you might not see another team like it for a long time.

PART TWO

STATISTICAL REVIEWS

4

Does the Creampuff Diet Work for NFL Teams?

Over the past few years, it seems that Super Bowl winners have come from rather weak divisions. Indianapolis in 2006 had two young and not very strong division opponents in Tennessee and Houston. Pittsburgh in 2005 had two 6–10 teams in their division. None of New England's division opponents in 2003 and 2004 posted a winning record over that two-year period. The 2007 Giants were something of an exception to this, but all in all this seems to be a strong tendency of Super Bowl champions of late.

Those trends would lend credence to the idea that facing a weak group of division foes is the way to go, but how strong or weak were those divisions in the grand scheme of the NFL? And what does NFL playoff history say about the benefits of playing in a strong or weak division? Is it better to build up a good record against subpar opponents, or does having to climb a divisional mountain against good competition make a team more apt to win in the postseason?

In order to find this out, I compiled a list of the record of every division in every season from 1970 to 2007. I then ran the winning percentages for each division and ranked them according to their overall winning percentage. After that, I compiled the total number of playoff wins for each division and sorted those by playoff win type (wild-card playoff win, divisional playoff win, conference championship win, and Super Bowl win).

I'll cover the overall numbers later in this chapter, but I want to start the review by going over the trends that have occurred during these thirty-seven seasons. I have divided these seasons into four different eras. These are:

- 1970–1977: Three division winners/one wild-card qualifier per conference era
- 1978–1989: Three division winners/two wild-card qualifiers per conference era
- 1990–2001: Three division winners/three wild-card qualifiers era
- 2002–today: Four division winners/two wild-card qualifiers era

I calculated the win percentage for each era with the ties counting as a half-win/half-loss (with those totals being tabulated under the Win-Tie [WT] column).

There are some very interesting trends in each period, so let's take a look at each of them.

1970–1977: Three Division Winners/ One Wild-Card Qualifier Era

What is most notable about this time frame is that teams in weak divisions tended to do much better than teams in strong divisions, at least early on. The Colts won the Super Bowl in 1970 despite playing in a division that finished fifth out of six divisions in win percentage. Miami repeated that feat in 1972 and 1973. In the case of the Dolphins, their division was actually the weakest during that two-year span. To give you a better idea of how noncompetitive the AFC East was during those two seasons, only one of Miami's division opponents posted a winning record in that time.

DIVISION WIN PERCENTAGE BY YEAR

DIVISION	W	L	T	WT	WIN %	WIN % RANK	WC	DIV	CONF	SUPER BOWL	TOTAL PLAYOFF WINS
1970											
NFC Central	34	22	0	34	60.7%	1	n/a	0	0	0	0
NFC East	36	32	2	37	52.9%	2	n/a	1	1	0	2
AFC West	25	23	8	29	51.8%	3	n/a	1	0	0	1
NFC West	25	26	5	27.5	49.1%	4	n/a	1	0	0	1
AFC East	30	38	2	31	44.3%	5	n/a	1	1	1	3
AFC Central	23	32	1	23.5	42.0%	6	n/a	0	0	0	0
1971											
AFC West	28	24	4	30	53.6%	T1	n/a	0	0	0	0
NFC West	28	24	4	30	53.6%	T1	n/a	1	0	0	1
NFC Central	28	25	3	29.5	52.7%	3	n/a	0	0	0	0
NFC East	34	33	3	35.5	50.7%	4	n/a	1	1	1	3
AFC East	33	36	1	33.5	47.9%	5	n/a	2	1	0	3
AFC Central	23	32	1	23.5	42.0%	6	n/a	0	0	0	0
1972											
AFC Central	30	26	0	30	53.6%	T1	n/a	1	0	0	1
NFC Central	29	25	2	30	53.6%	T1	n/a	0	0	0	0
NFC East	35	33	2	36	51.4%	3	n/a	2	1	0	3
AFC West	27	27	2	28	50.0%	4	n/a	0	0	0	0
AFC East	33	36	1	33.5	47.9%	5	n/a	1	1	1	3
NFC West	23	30	3	24.5	43.8%	6	n/a	0	0	0	0
1973											
NFC West	31	25	0	31	55.4%	1	n/a	0	0	0	0
AFC Central	28	26	2	29	51.8%	2	n/a	0	0	0	0
AFC West	25	25	6	28	50.0%	3	n/a	1	0	0	1
NFC Central	26	27	3	27.5	49.1%	4	n/a	1	1	0	2
AFC East	34	36	0	34	48.6%	5	n/a	1	1	1	3
NFC East	31	36	3	32.5	46.4%	6	n/a	1	0	0	1
1974											
NFC East	37	33	0	37	52.9%	1	n/a	0	0	0	0
AFC West	29	26	1	29.5	52.7%	2	n/a	1	0	0	1
AFC East	36	34	0	36	51.4%	3	n/a	0	0	0	0
AFC Central	28	27	1	28.5	50.9%	4	n/a	1	1	1	3
NFC Central	27	29	0	27	48.2%	5	n/a	1	1	0	2
NFC West	24	32	0	24	42.9%	6	n/a	1	0	0	1
1975											
AFC Central	36	20	0	36	64.3%	1	n/a	1	1	1	3
NFC East	38	32	0	38	54.3%	2	n/a	1	1	0	2

(continued)

DIVISION WIN PERCENTAGE BY YEAR *(continued)*

DIVISION	W	L	T	WT	WIN %	WIN % RANK	WC	DIV	CONF	SUPER BOWL	TOTAL PLAYOFF WINS
1975 *(continued)*											
AFC East	34	36	0	34	48.6%	3	n/a	0	0	0	0
NFC Central	27	29	0	27	48.2%	4	n/a	0	0	0	0
AFC West	24	32	0	24	42.9%	5	n/a	1	0	0	1
NFC West	23	33	0	23	41.1%	6	n/a	1	0	0	1
1976											
AFC Central	34	22	0	34	60.7%	1	n/a	1	0	0	1
NFC East	38	32	0	38	54.3%	2	n/a	0	0	0	0
NFC Central	29	26	1	29.5	52.7%	3	n/a	1	1	0	2
AFC East	33	37	0	33	47.1%	T4	n/a	0	0	0	0
AFC West	33	37	0	33	47.1%	T4	n/a	1	1	1	3
NFC West	28	41	1	28.5	40.7%	6	n/a	1	0	0	1
1977											
AFC Central	31	25	0	31	55.4%	1	n/a	0	0	0	0
NFC East	38	32	0	38	54.3%	2	n/a	1	1	1	3
AFC West	37	33	0	37	52.9%	3	n/a	2	1	0	3
AFC East	35	35	0	35	50.0%	4	n/a	0	0	0	0
NFC West	25	31	0	25	44.6%	5	n/a	0	0	0	0
NFC Central	30	40	0	30	42.9%	6	n/a	1	0	0	1

The trend of winning a weak division being a key to winning a Super Bowl continued for the most part in this era, as two of the next four Super Bowl winners came from divisions that ranked fourth.

There are two other items of note for this period. First, number 6 division winners won only four playoff games, and none of those was any higher than a divisional playoff–level win. Second, number 1 division winners won only one Super Bowl. That was also the only conference championship won by number 1 division teams in this era. Number 1 division winners won only two other playoff games during this era, and in five seasons the number 1 division winners won zero playoff games. It simply did not pay to be the winner of the hardest division in the NFL at this time.

1978–1989: Three Division Winners/
Two Wild-Card Qualifiers Era

If winning the strongest division didn't pay from 1970 to 1977, it did pay during this time frame. Teams from the number 1, number 2, and number 3 divisions won nine of the eleven Super Bowls covered. Clubs from the number 4 and number 5 divisions won one Super Bowl each, and the number 6 division teams won zero Super Bowls.

The lower division winners did find it a bit easier to win conference titles during this period, but even that level of accomplishment was weighted toward teams from stronger divisions. Seven of the eleven conference championship teams that lost the Super Bowl came from the number 1, number 2, or number 3 divisions. Three of the other four came from the number 4 and number 5 divisions, and only one came from the number 6 division.

The losing trend for playoff teams from the number 6 division again was not merely relegated to the lack of Super Bowl or conference championship wins. Teams from the last-place division won only six playoff games during this time. In six of these seasons, playoff teams from the number 6 division failed to win a single playoff game.

The 1982 season is not included due to the league going with a conference playoff method instead of a divisional playoff method because of the players' strike.

DIVISION WIN PERCENTAGE BY YEAR

DIVISION	W	L	T	WT	WIN %	WIN % RANK	WC	DIV	CONF	SUPER BOWL	TOTAL PLAYOFF WINS
1978											
AFC Central	36	28	0	36	56.3%	1	1	2	1	1	5
AFC West	41	39	0	41	51.3%	T2	0	0	0	0	0
NFC East	41	39	0	41	51.3%	T2	0	1	1	0	2
AFC East	40	40	0	40	50.0%	4	0	0	0	0	0
NFC West	30	34	0	30	46.9%	5	1	1	0	0	2
NFC Central	35	43	2	36	45.0%	6	0	0	0	0	0

(continued)

DIVISION WIN PERCENTAGE BY YEAR *(continued)*

DIVISION	W	L	T	WT	WIN %	WIN % RANK	WC	DIV	CONF	SUPER BOWL	TOTAL PLAYOFF WINS
1979											
AFC West	47	33	0	47	58.8%	1	0	0	0	0	0
AFC Central	36	28	0	36	56.3%	2	1	2	1	1	5
NFC East	43	37	0	43	53.8%	3	1	0	0	0	1
AFC East	39	41	0	39	48.8%	4	0	0	0	0	0
NFC Central	34	46	0	34	42.5%	5	0	1	0	0	1
NFC West	25	39	0	25	39.1%	6	0	1	1	0	2
1980											
AFC Central	37	27	0	37	57.8%	1	0	0	0	0	0
AFC West	42	38	0	42	52.5%	2	1	2	1	1	5
AFC East	40	40	0	40	50.0%	3	0	0	0	0	0
NFC East	39	41	0	39	48.8%	4	1	2	1	0	4
NFC West	30	34	0	30	46.9%	5	0	0	0	0	0
NFC Central	35	43	2	36	45.0%	6	0	0	0	0	0
1981											
NFC East	46	34	0	46	57.5%	1	1	1	0	0	2
AFC West	42	38	0	42	52.5%	2	0	1	0	0	1
AFC Central	32	32	0	32	50.0%	3	0	1	1	0	2
NFC Central	38	42	0	38	47.5%	4	0	0	0	0	0
NFC West	30	34	0	30	46.9%	5	0	1	1	1	3
AFC East	35	43	2	36	45.0%	6	1	0	0	0	1
1983											
NFC East	42	36	2	43	53.8%	1	0	1	1	0	2
NFC West	34	30	0	34	53.1%	2	1	1	0	0	2
AFC East	42	38	0	42	52.5%	T3	0	0	0	0	0
AFC West	42	38	0	42	52.5%	T3	1	2	1	1	5
AFC Central	28	36	0	28	43.8%	T5	0	0	0	0	0
NFC Central	35	45	0	35	43.8%	T5	0	0	0	0	0
1984											
AFC West	51	29	0	51	63.8%	1	1	0	0	0	1
NFC West	36	28	0	36	56.3%	2	0	1	1	1	3
NFC East	44	35	1	44.5	55.6%	3	1	0	0	0	1
AFC East	36	44	0	36	45.0%	4	0	1	1	0	2
NFC Central	31	48	1	31.5	39.4%	5	0	1	0	0	1
AFC Central	25	39	0	25	39.1%	6	0	1	0	0	1

(continued)

DIVISION WIN PERCENTAGE BY YEAR *(continued)*

DIVISION	W	L	T	WT	WIN %	WIN % RANK	WC	DIV	CONF	SUPER BOWL	TOTAL PLAYOFF WINS
1985											
AFC West	45	35	0	45	56.3%	1	0	0	0	0	0
NFC East	42	38	0	42	52.5%	2	1	0	0	0	1
AFC East	41	39	0	41	51.3%	3	1	2	1	0	4
NFC Central	39	41	0	39	48.8%	4	0	1	1	1	3
NFC West	30	34	0	30	46.9%	5	0	1	0	0	1
AFC Central	27	37	0	27	42.2%	6	0	0	0	0	0
1986											
NFC West	34	28	2	35	54.7%	1	0	0	0	0	0
AFC West	43	37	0	43	53.8%	T2	0	1	1	0	2
NFC East	42	36	2	43	53.8%	T2	1	2	1	1	5
AFC Central	33	31	0	33	51.6%	4	0	1	0	0	1
AFC East	36	44	0	36	45.0%	5	1	0	0	0	1
NFC Central	34	46	0	34	42.5%	6	0	0	0	0	0
1987											
NFC West	34	26	0	34	56.7%	1	0	0	0	0	0
AFC Central	31	29	0	31	51.7%	2	1	1	0	0	2
AFC East	38	37	0	38	50.7%	T3	0	0	0	0	0
NFC East	38	37	0	38	50.7%	T3	0	1	1	1	3
AFC West	36	38	1	36.5	48.7%	5	0	1	1	0	2
NFC Central	32	42	1	32.5	43.3%	6	1	1	0	0	2
1988											
AFC Central	37	27	0	37	57.8%	1	1	1	1	0	3
AFC East	44	35	1	44.5	55.6%	2	0	1	0	0	1
NFC West	35	29	0	35	54.7%	3	0	1	1	1	3
NFC East	37	43	0	37	46.3%	4	0	0	0	0	0
NFC Central	36	44	0	36	45.0%	5	1	1	0	0	2
AFC West	34	45	1	34.5	43.1%	6	0	0	0	0	0
1989											
NFC West	37	27	0	37	57.8%	1	1	2	1	1	5
AFC Central	35	28	1	35.5	55.5%	2	1	1	0	0	2
AFC West	40	39	1	40.5	50.6%	3	0	1	1	0	2
NFC East	39	41	0	39	48.8%	4	0	0	0	0	0
NFC Central	38	42	0	38	47.5%	5	0	0	0	0	0
AFC East	34	46	0	34	42.5%	6	0	0	0	0	0

1990–2001: Three Division Winners/ Three Wild-Card Qualifiers Era

During the early part of this era, teams from the very strong NFC East won most of the Super Bowls, so that led to another top-heavy Super Bowl win representation. Nine of the twelve Super Bowl winners came from the number 1, number 2, or number 3 divisions. Two Super Bowl champs came from the number 4 division.

What is most notable about this era is that teams from weaker divisions were starting to accomplish more in the playoffs. Nine of the non–Super Bowl winning conference champions came from the number 4, number 5, or number 6 divisions. In addition, the 1999 Rams became the first postmerger Super Bowl winner from a number 6 division.

My guess as to why the weaker divisions started fielding more playoff winners at this time would have been quite simply that the increase in wild-card spots meant that the weaker divisions now had more representation in the playoffs. This doesn't seem to have been the case, however, as shown by the following table detailing wild-card qualifier distribution by division rank for each era:

DIVISION RANK	1970–1977	1978–1989	1990–2001
1	4	13	24
2	3	11	13
3	3	7	11
4	2	3	14
5	2	7	8
6	2	3	2

During 1970–1977, there were a total of sixteen wild-card teams. Ten of these, or 62.5 percent, came from the top three divisions. During 1978–1989, the total of wild-card teams from divisions 1 through 3 increased to 70.4 percent. During 1990–2001, that percentage dropped to 66.7 percent, but that percentage was still higher than the 1970–1977 percentage. All in all, the percentage of wild-card teams coming from the weaker divisions has stayed at about the same mark

DIVISION WIN PERCENTAGE BY YEAR

DIVISION	W	L	T	WT	WIN %	WIN % RANK	WC	DIV	CONF	SUPER BOWL	TOTAL PLAYOFF WINS
1990											
NFC East	45	35	0	45	56.3%	1	1	1	1	1	4
AFC West	43	37	0	43	53.8%	2	0	1	0	0	1
NFC West	32	32	0	32	50.0%	3	0	1	0	0	1
AFC East	39	41	0	39	48.8%	4	1	1	1	0	3
AFC Central	30	34	0	30	46.9%	5	1	0	0	0	1
NFC Central	35	45	0	35	43.8%	6	1	0	0	0	1
1991											
NFC East	47	33	0	47	58.8%	1	1	1	1	1	4
NFC West	34	30	0	34	53.1%	2	1	0	0	0	1
AFC West	42	38	0	42	52.5%	3	1	1	0	0	2
NFC Central	38	42	0	38	47.5%	4	0	1	0	0	1
AFC East	36	44	0	36	45.0%	5	0	1	1	0	2
AFC Central	27	37	0	27	42.2%	6	1	0	0	0	1
1992											
NFC West	38	26	0	38	59.4%	1	0	1	0	0	1
NFC East	43	37	0	43	53.8%	2	2	1	1	1	5
AFC Central	33	31	0	33	51.6%	3	0	0	0	0	0
AFC West	38	42	0	38	47.5%	4	1	0	0	0	1
AFC East	37	43	0	37	46.3%	5	1	2	1	0	4
NFC Central	35	45	0	35	43.8%	6	0	0	0	0	0
1993											
AFC West	44	36	0	44	55.0%	1	2	1	0	0	3
NFC East	42	38	0	42	52.5%	2	1	1	1	1	4
NFC Central	40	40	0	40	50.0%	3	1	0	0	0	1
AFC Central	31	33	0	31	48.4%	4	0	0	0	0	0
AFC East	38	42	0	38	47.5%	5	0	1	1	0	2
NFC West	29	35	0	29	45.3%	6	0	1	0	0	1
1994											
NFC Central	43	37	0	43	53.8%	1	2	0	0	0	2
AFC West	42	38	0	42	52.5%	2	0	1	1	0	2
AFC East	41	39	0	41	51.3%	3	1	0	0	0	1
NFC East	39	41	0	39	48.8%	4	0	1	0	0	1
NFC West	31	33	0	31	48.4%	5	0	1	1	1	3
AFC Central	28	36	0	28	43.8%	6	1	1	0	0	2
1995											
AFC West	46	34	0	46	57.5%	1	0	0	0	0	0
NFC Central	45	35	0	45	56.3%	2	1	1	0	0	2

(continued)

59

DIVISION	W	L	T	WT	WIN %	WIN % RANK	WC	DIV	CONF	SUPER BOWL	TOTAL PLAYOFF WINS
NFC West	41	39	0	41	51.3%	3	0	0	0	0	0
AFC East	37	43	0	37	46.3%	T4	2	1	0	0	3
NFC East	37	43	0	37	46.3%	T4	1	1	1	1	4
AFC Central	34	46	0	34	42.5%	6	0	1	1	0	2
1996											
AFC West	44	36	0	44	55.0%	1	0	0	0	0	0
NFC East	42	38	0	42	52.5%	2	1	0	0	0	1
NFC Central	40	40	0	40	50.0%	3	0	1	1	1	3
AFC East	39	41	0	39	48.8%	T4	0	1	1	0	2
AFC Central	39	41	0	39	48.8%	T4	2	1	0	0	3
NFC West	36	44	0	36	45.0%	6	1	1	0	0	2
1997											
NFC Central	45	35	0	45	56.3%	1	2	1	1	0	4
AFC Central	43	36	1	43.5	54.4%	2	0	1	0	0	1
AFC West	41	39	0	41	51.3%	3	1	1	1	1	4
NFC West	38	42	0	38	47.5%	4	0	1	0	0	1
AFC East	37	43	0	37	46.3%	5	1	0	0	0	1
NFC East	34	43	3	35.5	44.4%	6	0	0	0	0	0
1998											
AFC East	44	36	0	44	55.0%	1	1	1	0	0	2
NFC Central	43	37	0	43	53.8%	2	0	1	0	0	1
AFC West	42	38	0	42	52.5%	3	0	1	1	1	3
NFC West	40	40	0	40	50.0%	4	1	1	1	0	3
NFC East	36	44	0	36	45.0%	5	1	0	0	0	1
AFC Central	35	45	0	35	43.8%	6	1	0	0	0	1
1999											
AFC East	49	31	0	49	61.3%	1	1	0	0	0	1
NFC Central	43	37	0	43	53.8%	2	1	1	0	0	2
AFC West	40	40	0	40	50.0%	3	0	0	0	0	0
AFC Central	47	49	0	47	49.0%	4	1	2	1	0	4
NFC East	36	44	0	36	45.0%	5	1	0	0	0	1
NFC West	33	47	0	33	41.3%	6	0	1	1	1	3
2000											
NFC Central	44	36	0	44	55.0%	1	0	1	0	0	1
AFC East	43	37	0	43	53.8%	2	1	0	0	0	1
AFC Central	48	48	0	48	50.0%	3	1	1	1	1	4
NFC East	39	41	0	39	48.8%	4	1	1	1	0	3
AFC West	37	43	0	37	46.3%	T5	0	1	0	0	1
NFC West	37	43	0	37	46.3%	T5	1	0	0	0	1

(continued)

DIVISION WIN PERCENTAGE BY YEAR *(continued)*

DIVISION	W	L	T	WT	WIN %	WIN % RANK	WC	DIV	CONF	SUPER BOWL	TOTAL PLAYOFF WINS
2001											
AFC East	41	39	0	41	51.3%	T1	0	1	1	1	3
NFC Central	41	39	0	41	51.3%	T1	1	0	0	0	1
NFC West	41	39	0	41	51.3%	T1	0	1	1	0	2
AFC Central	49	47	0	49	51.0%	4	1	1	0	0	2
AFC West	38	42	0	38	47.5%	T5	1	0	0	0	1
NFC East	38	42	0	38	47.5%	T5	1	1	0	0	2

during each era. That may be a sign that the distance between the weaker teams and stronger teams had been closing over these three periods.

2002–2007: Four Division Winners/ Two Wild-Card Qualifiers Era

This era only has six seasons behind it, so that doesn't make for the largest sample size, but there are a couple of trends that are already starting to show up.

First, teams from the number 1, number 2, and number 3 divisions have won all six Super Bowls during this period. As much as that might seem to indicate that a team has to come from a strong division to win, it may be more due to the greater impact one team can have in a four-team division. Prior to the eight-division/four-team split, most of the divisions had at least five teams (and all of them did from 1995 to 2001). With that many teams in a division, it is much harder for one great team to pull up the overall strength of the division.

In the new setup, all the division has to do is total somewhere between 34 and 37 wins to have a good chance of finishing in the top three. If the top team wins twelve games, then the other teams have to total 22 to 25 wins. If one of those teams wins nine or ten games, the other two only have to win somewhere between 12 and 16 games. If the

DIVISION WIN PERCENTAGE BY YEAR

DIVISION	W	L	T	WT	WIN %	WIN % RANK	WC	DIV	CONF	SUPER BOWL	TOTAL PLAYOFF WINS
2002											
NFC South	37	26	1	37.5	58.6%	1	1	1	1	1	4
AFC West	36	28	0	36	56.3%	2	0	1	1	0	2
AFC East	35	29	0	35	54.7%	3	1	0	0	0	1
NFC East	34	30	0	34	53.1%	4	0	1	0	0	1
AFC South	31	33	0	31	48.4%	5	0	1	0	0	1
NFC West	29	35	0	29	45.3%	6	1	0	0	0	1
AFC North	28	35	1	28.5	44.5%	7	1	0	0	0	1
NFC North	25	39	0	25	39.1%	8	0	0	0	0	0
2003											
AFC East	36	28	0	36	56.3%	1	0	1	1	1	3
AFC South	34	30	0	34	53.1%	2	2	1	0	0	3
NFC West	33	31	0	33	51.6%	3	0	0	0	0	0
AFC West	31	33	0	31	48.4%	T4	0	0	0	0	0
NFC East	31	33	0	31	48.4%	T4	0	1	0	0	1
NFC North	31	33	0	31	48.4%	T4	1	0	0	0	1
NFC South	31	33	0	31	48.4%	T4	1	1	1	0	3
AFC North	29	35	0	29	45.3%	8	0	0	0	0	0
2004											
AFC East	37	27	0	37	57.8%	1	1	1	1	1	4
AFC North	36	28	0	36	56.3%	2	0	1	0	0	1
AFC West	34	30	0	34	53.1%	3	0	0	0	0	0
AFC South	33	31	0	33	51.6%	4	1	0	0	0	1
NFC East	31	33	0	31	48.4%	T5	0	1	1	0	2
NFC South	31	33	0	31	48.4%	T5	0	1	0	0	1
NFC North	29	35	0	29	45.3%	7	1	0	0	0	1
NFC West	25	39	0	25	39.1%	8	1	0	0	0	1
2005											
AFC West	36	28	0	36	56.3%	T1	0	1	0	0	1
NFC East	36	28	0	36	56.3%	T1	1	0	0	0	1
AFC North	34	30	0	34	53.1%	3	1	1	1	1	4
NFC South	33	31	0	33	51.6%	4	1	1	0	0	2
AFC South	32	32	0	32	50.0%	5	0	0	0	0	0
NFC North	29	35	0	29	45.3%	6	0	0	0	0	0
AFC East	28	36	0	28	43.8%	T7	1	0	0	0	1
NFC West	28	36	0	28	43.8%	T7	0	1	1	0	2

(continued)

DIVISION WIN PERCENTAGE BY YEAR (continued)

DIVISION	W	L	T	WT	WIN %	WIN % RANK	WC	DIV	CONF	SUPER BOWL	TOTAL PLAYOFF WINS
2006											
AFC East	35	29	0	35	54.7%	1	1	1	0	0	2
AFC South	34	30	0	34	53.1%	T2	1	1	1	1	4
AFC West	34	30	0	34	53.1%	T2	0	0	0	0	0
AFC North	33	31	0	33	51.6%	4	0	0	0	0	0
NFC East	32	32	0	32	50.0%	5	1	0	0	0	1
NFC North	30	34	0	30	46.9%	6	0	1	1	0	2
NFC South	29	35	0	29	45.3%	T7	0	1	0	0	1
NFC West	29	35	0	29	45.3%	T7	1	0	0	0	1
2007											
AFC South	42	22	0	42	65.6%	1	1	0	0	0	1
NFC East	40	24	0	40	62.5%	2	1	1	1	1	4
NFC North	35	29	0	35	54.7%	3	0	1	0	0	1
AFC North	32	32	0	32	50.0%	4	0	0	0	0	0
AFC East	28	36	0	28	43.8%	5	0	1	1	0	2
NFC South	27	37	0	27	42.2%	6	0	0	0	0	0
AFC West	26	38	0	26	40.6%	T7	1	1	0	0	2
NFC West	26	38	0	26	40.6%	T7	1	0	0	0	1

top team wins 14 games, as was the case twice with New England when the AFC East finished number 1 during a Super Bowl year, the rest of the division only has to win 20 to 23 games among them.

The second trend in the new league divisional format is the continuation of teams from the lower-ranking divisions winning more often in the playoffs. Five of the six non–Super Bowl winning conference champions came from the number 4 through number 7 divisions.

Another trend that has continued is that playoff participants from the worst division in the NFL are still not winning in the playoffs very often. Teams from the number 8 division have won only one playoff game during this time frame, and that was a wild-card win by St. Louis over their division rival Seattle.

Now that we've looked at each era individually, let's take a look at the overall picture.

DIVISION PLACE	W	L	T	WT	WIN %	TOTAL PLAYOFF WINS	WC	DIV	CONF	SUPER BOWL	POINT TOTAL
1	1,635	1,256	15	1,642.5	56.5%	68	21	25	13	9	146
2	1,393	1,193	10	1,398	53.9%	74	19	31	15	9	162
3	1,295	1,209	22	1,306	51.7%	56	11	23	14	8	131
4	1,447	1,515	14	1,454	48.9%	62	16	27	14	5	132
5	1,216	1,413	6	1,219	46.3%	55	12	25	13	5	121
6	962	1,263	20	972	43.3%	27	8	14	4	1	52
7	223	288	1	223.5	43.7%	10	6	3	1	0	15
8	79	113	0	79	41.1%	1	1	0	0	0	1

This point total column places a weight on each playoff win—one point for a wild-card win, two points for a divisional playoff win, three points for a conference championship win, and four points for a Super Bowl win.

The most obvious overall trend is that teams from the top three divisions win many more Super Bowls than teams from weaker divisions. Twenty-six of the thirty-seven Super Bowl champions in this time came from the top trio of divisions. Forty-two of the seventy-four conference champions also came from the top three divisions. (There are only thirty-seven champions because the 1982 season did not have divisional play.)

The other obvious trend is something that was pointed out in each individual era: teams from the worst division tend to perform terribly in the playoffs. What is surprising in the overall totals is how fast the drop-off is from the number 5 to the number 6 team. Number 6 teams have just over half as many total playoff wins and divisional wins as the number 5 teams. They also have only four conference championships to the number 5 division's eight, and one Super Bowl win to the number 5 division's five. I imagine those totals will start getting closer now that the number 6 division team is actually only the third worst team, but this does illustrate how fast the drop-off can be between a good playoff team and a poor one.

If I had to explain why it is that great teams tend to come from strong divisions, I would point to something that happened to the

Raiders in the late 1960s. Oakland's offensive linemen were having trouble blocking Buck Buchanan, the Chiefs' dominant pass-rushing defensive tackle. Al Davis decided that he needed to get some bulk in front of Buchanan. The Raiders drafted Gene Upshaw to fill that spot and he was obviously the answer to their problem.

The moral to this story is that if the Raiders hadn't been faced with the problem of stopping Buchanan, they might have tried to get by with a lesser player at left guard. Well, knowing how Al Davis and John Madden valued offensive linemen, they might have gone out and drafted Upshaw anyway, but the point is that big matchup problems call for big matchup solutions, so Upshaw had to be drafted.

Teams that don't have as many big matchup problems might not have the same sense of urgency to make major personnel upgrades. Players are often said to play to the level of their competition, but I think teams tend to build to the level of their competition as well.

That may be the reason the 1980s Bears didn't win more championships. From 1984, when the Bears' greatness first started becoming evident, through 1992, the highest divisional place that the NFC Central finished a season with was fourth (in 1985 and 1991). The division finished with the fifth-lowest winning percentage three times during this span and finished sixth four times. That means that the Bears were playing in the weakest, or next to weakest, division seven times in nine years.

My theory on this is that although Chicago was certainly a very talented team, they didn't have to do very much to keep dominating their division. This very possibly may have lulled the team into thinking that they were better than they really were. While the Giants, Redskins, and 49ers all had tough division opponents breathing down their necks during this time, the Bears really only had to deal with the Vikings on a consistent basis.

Since Minnesota won ten or more games only two times during this span, and since Chicago beat them twelve out of seventeen times at one point (if the second game in 1983 is counted), the Vikings were not really on the Bears' radar screen. Chicago didn't have to keep up with strong competition during the regular season and built their team accordingly. They could win the NFC Central with Doug Flutie filling in for an injured Jim McMahon, but they weren't going to beat Washington in the playoffs with Flutie behind center.

This type of thing might also explain the failure of the 1970s Rams to win the big one. Los Angeles dominated the NFC West for most of that decade, winning the division for seven straight years at one point. In four of those years, the NFC West finished in sixth place among the divisions, and it was fifth in two other years. Atlanta, New Orleans, and San Francisco simply weren't going to prepare the Rams for their playoff games against Dallas and Minnesota.

Maybe the best way to summarize this section is by comparing the win percentage of a division with the number of playoff wins the division racked up.

NUMBER OF PLAYOFF WINS	WINS	LOSSES	TIES	WT	WIN %
0	2,094	2,153	28	2,108	49.3%
1	2,575	2,640	35	2,592.5	49.4%
2	1,540	1,558	12	1,546	49.7%
3	1,112	1,087	10	1,117	50.6%
4	651	580	1	651.5	52.9%
5	278	232	2	279	54.5%

The above table shows a correlation between winning playoff games and coming from a strong division. The teams that tend to win the most playoff games come from the toughest divisions. That as much as anything shows that the creampuff diet really does not work that well for NFL teams.

5

Does It Take an Elite
Running Back to Win
a Super Bowl?

There are conflicting mind-sets when it comes to the value of a running back in building a Super Bowl–caliber team. Al Davis subscribes to the theory that an elite ball carrier is not necessary in putting together a championship roster. Since Davis's teams won two Super Bowls with Clarence Davis, Mark van Eeghen, and Kenny King in the backfield, his claim certainly has some backup.

On the other hand, many people believe in building around strong running backs. The Houston Texans took a boatload of grief in the 2006 NFL draft when they did not select Reggie Bush with the number 1 overall pick. Bush was the nearly unanimous choice as the best player in that draft, but many in the press said the Texans blew their championship chances by skipping him.

So which side is right? What does NFL history say about Super Bowl teams and elite running backs? I ran some studies to find out.

First, let's define what is meant by elite running back. I usually keep the bar fairly high for "elite" players, but for this study I'll lower it a bit. I am doing that because we really don't need to know if the running back was an all-time great, but rather whether he was considered among the best in the league for that particular season. If the player is in the Hall of Fame, made an All-Pro team, or made the Pro Bowl in the Super Bowl season, I will list him as a potentially elite player. Let's start by listing all of the starting running backs for Super Bowl–winning teams along with a notation of if they met any of the elite criteria.

STARTING RUNNING BACKS

SUPER BOWL	YEAR	RUNNING BACK	HOF?	ALL-PRO?	PRO BOWL?	Y IN ANY CATEGORY
			SUPER BOWL–WINNING TEAMS			
I	1966	Jim Taylor	Y	Y	N	Y
II	1967	Donny Anderson	N	N	Y	Y
III	1968	Matt Snell	N	Y	Y	Y
IV	1969	Mike Garrett	N	Y	N	Y
V	1970	Norm Bulaich	N	N	Y	Y
VI	1971	Duane Thomas	N	N	N	N
VII	1972	Larry Csonka	Y	Y	Y	Y
VIII	1973	Larry Csonka	Y	Y	Y	Y
IX	1974	Franco Harris	Y	Y	Y	Y
X	1975	Franco Harris	Y	Y	Y	Y
XI	1976	Clarence Davis	N	N	N	N
XII	1977	Tony Dorsett	Y	Y	Y	Y
XIII	1978	Franco Harris	Y	Y	Y	Y
XIV	1979	Franco Harris	Y	Y	Y	Y
XV	1980	Mark van Eeghen	N	N	N	N
XVI	1981	Ricky Patton	N	N	N	N
XVII	1982	John Riggins	Y	N	N	Y
XVIII	1983	Marcus Allen	Y	N	Y	Y
XIX	1984	Roger Craig	N	N	Y	Y
XX	1985	Walter Payton	Y	Y	Y	Y
XXI	1986	Joe Morris	N	Y	N	Y
XXII	1987	Timmy Smith	N	N	N	N
XXIII	1988	Roger Craig	N	Y	Y	Y
XIV	1989	Roger Craig	N	Y	N	Y
XXV	1990	Ottis Anderson	N	N	N	N
XVI	1991	Earnest Byner	N	Y	N	Y

(continued)

STARTING RUNNING BACKS *(continued)*

SUPER BOWL	YEAR	RUNNING BACK	HOF?	ALL-PRO?	PRO BOWL?	Y IN ANY CATEGORY
		SUPER BOWL–WINNING TEAMS *(continued)*				
XVII	1992	Emmitt Smith	I	Y	Y	Y
XVIII	1993	Emmitt Smith	I	Y	Y	Y
XXIX	1994	Ricky Watters	N	Y	Y	Y
XXX	1995	Emmitt Smith	I	Y	N	Y
XXXI	1996	Dorsey Levens/Edgar Bennett	N/N	N/N	Y/N	Y
XXXII	1997	Terrell Davis	N	Y	Y	Y
XXXIII	1998	Terrell Davis	N	Y	N	Y
XXXIV	1999	Marshall Faulk	I	Y	Y	Y
XXXV	2000	Jamal Lewis	I	N	N	N
XXXVI	2001	Antowain Smith	I	N	N	N
XXXVII	2002	Michael Pittman	I	N	N	N
XXXVIII	2003	Antowain Smith	I	N	N	N
XXIX	2004	Corey Dillon	I	N	N	N
XL	2005	Jerome Bettis	I	N	N	N
XLI	2006	Joseph Addai	I	N	N	N
XLII	2007	Brandon Jacobs	I	N	N	N
		SUPER BOWL–LOSING TEAMS				
I	1966	Mike Garrett	N	Y	Y	Y
II	1967	Hewitt Dixon	N	Y	Y	Y
III	1968	Tom Matte	N	N	Y	Y
IV	1969	Dave Osborn	N	N	Y	Y
V	1970	Duane Thomas	N	N	N	N
VI	1971	Larry Csonka	Y	Y	Y	Y
VII	1972	Larry Brown	N	Y	N	Y
VIII	1973	Chuck Foreman	N	N	Y	Y
IX	1974	Chuck Foreman	N	Y	Y	Y
X	1975	Robert Newhouse	N	N	N	N
XI	1976	Chuck Foreman	N	Y	Y	Y
XII	1977	Otis Armstrong	N	N	N	N
XIII	1978	Tony Dorsett	Y	Y	N	Y
XIV	1979	Wendell Tyler	N	N	N	N
XV	1980	Wilbert Montgomery	N	N	N	N
XVI	1981	Pete Johnson	N	Y	N	Y
XVII	1982	Andra Franklin	N	Y	N	Y
XVIII	1983	John Riggins	Y	Y	N	Y
XIX	1984	Tony Nathan/Woody Bennett	N/N	N/N	N/N	N
XX	1985	Craig James/Tony Collins	N/N	N/N	N/N	N
XXI	1986	Gerald Willhite	N	Y	N	Y

(continued)

STARTING RUNNING BACKS (continued)

SUPER BOWL	YEAR	RUNNING BACK	HOF?	ALL-PRO?	PRO BOWL?	Y IN ANY CATEGORY
		SUPER BOWL–LOSING TEAMS (continued)				
XXII	1987	Sammy Winder	N	N	N	N
XXIII	1988	Ickey Woods	N	Y	N	Y
XXIV	1989	Bobby Humphrey	N	N	Y	Y
XXV	1990	Thurman Thomas	Y	Y	Y	Y
XXVI	1991	Thurman Thomas	Y	Y	Y	Y
XXVII	1992	Thurman Thomas	Y	Y	Y	Y
XXVIII	1993	Thurman Thomas	Y	Y	N	Y
XXIX	1994	Natrone Means	N	Y	N	Y
XXX	1995	Bam Morris	N	N	N	N
XXXI	1996	Curtis Martin	I	Y	N	Y
XXXII	1997	Dorsey Levens	I?	Y	N	Y
XXXIII	1998	Jamal Anderson	I?	Y	N	Y
XXXIV	1999	Eddie George	I?	Y	Y	Y
XXXV	2000	Tiki Barber	I	N	N	N
XXXVI	2001	Marshall Faulk	I	Y	Y	Y
XXXVII	2002	Charlie Garner	I	N	N	N
XXXVIII	2003	DeShaun Foster	I	N	N	N
XXXIX	2004	Brian Westbrook	I	N	N	N
XL	2005	Shaun Alexander	I	Y	N	Y
XLI	2006	Thomas Jones	I	N	N	N
XLII	2007	Laurence Maroney	I	N	N	N

("I" indicates that the player is currently ineligible for the Hall of Fame.)

Fourteen of the forty-one Super Bowl starters have no rankings in any of the three categories. The only caveat to this is that it could be said that Jamal Lewis, Corey Dillon, and Jerome Bettis were elite-level running backs. Take them out and it would equate to ten out of thirty-eight nonelite running backs on Super Bowl–winning teams.

I do think these numbers do illustrate a trend but I wanted to see more evidence of it. I decided to look at the Super Bowl losers to see how many of their running backs could be considered elite.

Fourteen of these backs do not meet the elite requirement, although again there is a caveat in that Tiki Barber and possibly Brian Westbrook could be considered elite. Take those two out and it equals twelve out of thirty-nine conference champions without top-level ball carriers. Just as with the Super Bowl champions, the trend in this area is toward nonelite running backs, as four of the last six Super Bowl–losing teams have not been blessed with a great player to carry the rock.

Now let's add the totals from both the winners and the losers columns up and see how they compare.

ERA	GREAT RUNNING BACK STARTS	NUMBER OF AVAILABLE STARTS	PERCENTAGE OF STARTS
Super Bowls I–XXXV	55	70	78.6%
Super Bowls XXXVI–XLII	5	14	35.7%
Total	60	84	71.4%

This would seem to give the Davis argument some legs, especially the Super Bowl XXXVI–XLII numbers. If nearly one-third of all of the Super Bowl participants haven't needed elite running backs, and the trend is leaning strongly in the nonelite direction, it should provide ample evidence that the Texans may not have made a mistake in passing over Bush after all.

PART THREE

A LOOK AT
THE COACHING
PROFESSION

6

The Darwinism of the Coaching Forest

When I started breaking down game tapes for a living, after a while I began to notice that the philosophical differences between coaches went even deeper than I had always thought it did. It was then that I started to go about trying to find a better way to understand and organize those philosophies.

The method I decided to use was something I drew from the game Dungeons and Dragons (D&D). My friends and I played a lot of D&D in high school and many parts of the game stuck with me. In this case, the game's concept of alignments came to mind when I started analyzing coaching mind-sets in greater depth.

A D&D alignment has two axes. The first axis represents the character's moral leaning: good, neutral, or evil. The second axis represents the character's general attitude toward how to implement those morals: lawful, chaotic, or neutral.

A player has to pick one alignment from each axis group, and the combination of those two alignments defines the character's overall life philosophy. For example, if a character is lawful good, he believes not only in behaving as a good person, but also in the rule of law as being the best way to go about achieving the greater good. A chaotic good character, on the other hand, would be classified as more of a "hippie" type that believes in man's overall goodness but also wants as little oversight from authority figures as possible. The multitude of alignment combinations means that you can create a philosophy to match up with pretty much any kind of character you want to play.

Coaching Alignments—the First Axis: Personnel or Scheme

When I started trying to categorize coaching philosophies, I soon realized that they also had two axes.

The first axis choice for a coach is whether he is a personnel coach or a scheme coach. The easiest way to describe the difference between a personnel coach and a scheme coach is that a scheme coach will try to beat his opponents with his coaching, while a personnel coach will try to beat his opponents with his players. The best way to illustrate this might be to use the examples of Bobby Bowden and Steve Spurrier.

Bobby Bowden is a personnel coach. His philosophy at Florida State over the past twenty-plus years has been to outrecruit his opponents and thus have a greater supply of talented athletes at his disposal. Bowden then uses these athletes in a game of attrition by rotating his talented starters and equally talented second-stringers into the game throughout the first half. Over the years, the Seminoles' opponents were often able to keep up with Florida State during the first two quarters of games because they had nearly as many talented frontline starters as did the 'Noles.

Once the second half rolled around, however, Florida State's opponents would start to wear down. They weren't able to rotate their backups into the game because those players simply weren't good enough to beat the Seminoles' second-stringers. Once their opponent's starters wore down, Florida State would then have relatively fresh starters and backups going against winded opposition. That is the main reason they dominated the second halves of games and won ten games a year for fourteen straight seasons.

Contrast that to Steve Spurrier's approach. Spurrier was able to get plenty of talented players at Florida, but recruiting was never his strong suit. In fact, it could probably be said that Spurrier's success-to-recruiting ratio was greater than that of any other coach in college football. Just consider that when Rex Grossman first met Spurrier, he informed the coach that he had been voted Mr. Football in Indiana the previous year. Spurrier reportedly responded, "We don't recruit Indiana." It didn't matter to Spurrier that Grossman was a talented quarterback. He simply didn't have a lot of interest in selling players on his program.

What Spurrier could do as well as anyone else in the NCAA, though, was offensive play calling. He knew that if he had at least relatively equal talent to his opponent, he would be able to outsmart the other coaches enough times to win plenty of games. This was especially true during his early days at Florida. The SEC defensive coaches used fairly simplistic game plans back in the late 1980s and early 1990s, and Spurrier knew he could definitely out-play-call this group. That is what makes him the quintessential scheme coach.

Coaching Alignments—the Second Axis: Athletic or Hitter

The second alignment axis has to do with the level of physicality a coach preaches to his players. By physicality, I mean the amount of emphasis a coach places on having his team administer bodily pain to the other team.

Many coaches believe that football is a battle of physical will and that only the toughest teams will be capable of surviving this battle. These types of coaches are labeled with a hitter alignment.

A coach who places little emphasis on pounding the other team into submission and instead believes in beating his opponent with athleticism has an athletic alignment.

I'll use another college coaching example to further illustrate the difference between these two styles. Paul "Bear" Bryant was absolutely a hitter coach. His autobiography repeatedly stresses his belief in this philosophy. He didn't necessarily believe his team had to be bigger than their opponents, but they had to be tough as rawhide and want to hit all day long. It's the reason Bryant ran a training camp like Junction, as only the toughest of the tough were going to gut their way through that hellhole.

Contrast that philosophy to that of one of Bryant's coaching rivals, Georgia Tech's Bobby Dodd. Dodd was the type of coach who ran practices that were very light on hitting. He didn't believe in winning at all costs and would never have even thought of running a camp as strenuous as Junction. He believed in execution, fundamentals, and winning the game in a clean, sportsmanlike way. In other words, he wanted to win via an athletic contest, not a tough-man competition.

Alignments Are Not Dogma

Whenever I have tried to explain the coaching alignments system to someone, the questions I always get revolve around how the alignments put a coach in too limiting of a box. For instance, Bowden without a doubt relied on personnel during Florida State's glory years, but at the same time it cannot be forgotten that during his early years in Tallahassee he was known as a riverboat gambler (the Puntrooskie play against Clemson being the best example of that).

My answer to this is twofold. First, when any coach lacks player talent, he will invariably turn into a scheme coach. A personnel coach trying to run a personnel system with second-rate players will be an unemployed personnel coach before long. Bowden's early teams did not have the talent level of the better schools on their schedules, and he therefore had to be as creative as possible in his schemes to try to make up for that lack of talent.

The real test for a coach is whether he relies on personnel or scheme methods when he has the option to pick between the two. In Bowden's case, he was initially a scheme coach due to circumstance. When the circumstances changed, he immediately transformed into a personnel coach, so that's why he gets the personnel label.

Second, the alignments are not intended to be hard-and-fast rules. In the D&D game, for example, a chaotic good character could have a vain streak that might override his alignment in certain situations. In the same way, although Spurrier would usually go with a scheme mind-set, if Florida went into a game situation where they had the contest won, Spurrier wasn't averse to switching to a very simple play-calling mode and just pounding the ball to run the clock down. That is a personnel technique, but it doesn't make Spurrier a personnel coach.

Alignment Combinations

There are four different alignment combinations: personnel/hitter, personnel/athletic, scheme/hitter, and scheme/athletic.

Generally speaking, personnel coaches tend to lean toward the hitter alignment, and scheme coaches tend to lean toward athletic alignment. The reason for this is quite simply that a head coach only has so many hours in a day. Of the many things he can do for his team, his contributions tend to largely be one of two things: play calling or motivation.

Football can be a terribly complex game, especially the play-calling aspect. If a head coach wants to focus his energies on the play-calling side of the ledger, he won't have much time to do motivation. Because of this, he will usually tend toward players who are self-starters and can do many things well, and those kinds of players are the backbone of the athletic alignment.

The personnel coach, on the other hand, is trying to win by having bigger, faster, and stronger players, so he will usually spend most of his energy trying to find those kinds of players. Once he gets them, he will try to maximize their potential by encouraging them to use their size and speed to full advantage. That usually means hitting and a lot of it.

Hitting hurts, though, so personnel coaches typically spend most of their time trying to get their teams to increase their pain threshold. Doing this requires a lot of motivational effort on the coach's part, and thus leaves little time for a personnel coach to be extremely creative in his play calling. Another way to put it is that personnel coaches manage their players' psyches rather than managing the playbook.

The Upside of Each Alignment

Personnel—An effective personnel coach with superior personnel will almost always be a successful coach. No matter how much play-calling expertise his opponent may have, the game of football still comes down most of the time to which team has the better players. Any coach is likely to win if he has better talent, but the personnel coach thrives in this type of environment. He may not be an expert in game plans, but he does know enough to put his best players in situations to make plays.

Scheme—A scheme coach will not be as good as a personnel coach in adapting his system to his talent. In fact, in many cases a scheme coach will not adapt his system at all (I'll get into that more in a bit). What the scheme coach is an expert at, though, is finding ways to make his scheme mask his players' weaknesses. A scheme coach is also typically very good at getting his players to function as a single unit. All coaches desire this, but scheme coaches are especially good at getting that to happen. They have very specific roles for their players and are experts at finding players to fit those roles.

Hitter—As I mentioned in the previous section, hitter coaches often specialize in player motivation. They usually have a good idea as to how much pain and suffering the other team can take before quitting. They know that hitting is not something that wins games in the first quarter but rather has a cumulative effect. Because of this, hitter coaches also tend to be very persistent. Many more times than not, they are also among the best halftime speakers.

Athletic—The upside to a coach with an athletic alignment is that he will tend to get the most out of any player he is given. Personnel, scheme, and hitter coaches typically want only certain types of players and will usually do away with those who don't fit into their mind-set. Athletic coaches, on the other hand, are very good at identifying what a player can do for their team and finding a way to utilize those skills. Athletic coaches also tend to get longer careers out of their players because they don't wear them down.

The Downside of Each Alignment

Personnel—The downside to the personnel alignment is that if the team doesn't have the athletes, either due to injuries or bad recruiting/drafting, they simply won't win the game.

The other negative to a personnel team is that they don't tend to absorb injuries well. Because the personnel team is not set up to mask weaknesses as effectively as a scheme team, when they are hit with injuries, they have to try to beat their opponents with inferior players in unfavorable matchup situations.

Personnel coaches are usually acutely aware of this. Nothing illustrates that better than Bowden's approach to recruiting. There have been multiple occasions on signing day over the past few years where it looked like Florida State wasn't going to be able to sign the blue-chip players they were aiming for.

Whenever Bowden's coaches or recruiters would get worried about this and inquire as to whether they should try to sign some of the red-chip players instead, Bowden would always say no. This was a risky recruiting ploy because if the Seminoles didn't get the elite blue-chippers and passed on signing the red-chippers, they could end up without any of the high-end players.

The reason Bowden never varied from the recruiting plan is that he knew his personnel scheme would only work with top-level personnel. If the Seminoles ended up with a bunch of red-chip players, they would not be able to implement Bowden's attrition-focused game plans. This would force Bowden and his staff to become scheme coaches, and they were not set up to win that kind of game.

Scheme—The main downside of scheme coaches is that they can be somewhat limited by their schemes. Nothing says this better than the old coaching adage that you should only try to outscheme another coach if your team isn't as talented as his.

The reason for this is that schemes tend to limit the uses of talent. For example, a coach will often call zone defenses more frequently if his club has injuries in their secondary. The zone coverage limits the amount of ground each player has to cover and therefore limits the amount of damage a second-rate backup can inflict on the team.

The downside to a zone defense is that if the team has talented players, the coverage can limit the things those players can do. For example, a great cornerback might end up staying on his side of the zone defense instead of following the other team's best wide receiver all around the field. Another way to put this is that personnel coaches are usually able to get their best players involved in plays more often, whereas scheme coaches can't do that as well.

An additional downside to being a scheme coach is that, all other things being relatively equal, he will lose more than his share of games to a personnel coach. There are many cases that provide proof of this, including the Bowden-Spurrier series.

Bowden and Spurrier faced off fourteen times in twelve seasons, with Bowden winning the series 8-5-1. Spurrier's teams were very physically talented, but they probably were slightly behind the Seminoles in overall talent during most of those games. Spurrier's lack of interest in recruiting and his strong belief in his play calling was the main reason the Gators were just a bit behind Florida State in the talent area.

Spurrier's play-calling prowess was offset by Mickey Andrews's defensive coaching prowess. Florida State also had an excellent offensive play caller in Mark Richt, so the Seminoles could keep up with Spurrier's offensive genius in most cases. In other words, Spurrier couldn't out-coach Bowden's staff and therefore his teams often lost because they didn't have quite the personnel firepower of FSU.

Athletic—The downside of the athletic approach is that athletic teams tend to do quite poorly against hitter teams. The Dodd-Bryant example illustrates this quite well.

Bryant was rather dismissive of Dodd in his autobiography by recounting a time when he told his team that Georgia Tech would hit hard but not hit hard all of the time. He also said Tech didn't play tough all the time because they didn't live tough like the Crimson Tide did, and he claimed that Tech's players were afraid of Alabama's players. Since Dodd's teams had a 2–7 record against Bryant's teams, the Bear's claims obviously had some ring of truth to them.

The reason that athletic teams can't handle hitter teams is the simple fact that they aren't used to being hit. Since the athletic team typically views the contest as a game and not warfare (as hitter teams often do), they simply aren't willing to go quite as far to win.

Hitter—There are two downsides to being a hitter coach. The first, that it is very difficult and time-consuming to develop hard-hitting players, I already discussed a bit earlier.

The second downside to hitter coaches is when they are faced with an opponent that won't give in. Hitter coaches sell to their teams that if they just keep pounding on the opposition, that team will eventually quit. When the opponent doesn't quit, the hitter team can go through a period of not only self-doubt but also of doubt in their coach.

This is even more serious than it sounds because this doubt doesn't usually go away quickly. It's the kind of thing that if it happens once, the players will always have it in the back of their minds that it could happen again. Lombardi and Bryant both had to face some type of this team doubt during their careers, and it took a very deft approach on their parts to hold the team together. Lesser motivators can lose their teams, however, so this is obviously the biggest danger of being a hitter coach.

A History of Coaching Alignments in the NFL

In the early days of the NFL, nearly every head coach subscribed to the personnel philosophical alignment. The reason for this is that most of the coaches back then were hired because of their playing background.

This was especially true with the league's top coaches. George Halas, Curly Lambeau, and Jimmy Conzelman were all player/coaches for the first nine years of their careers. Steve Owen played for eight years prior to taking over as the Giants coach, and he had two years as a player/coach in New York. Ray Flaherty also had eight seasons as a player before taking over the Redskins' coaching reins.

One of the main reasons for hiring player/coaches back then was that for many years coaches were prohibited from calling plays from the sidelines. It thus behooved a team to have a coach in the huddle. Even so, this meant that teams were picking the best coaching types from among the players, so a person with a lot of brains and little brawn was not going to make the coaching cut back then.

The first signs of change in this approach came in 1944 when the NFL revoked the no coaching from the sideline rule. Once this occurred, the value of scheme management skills in coaches started showing up almost immediately. Greasy Neale, one of the great play-calling innovators in NFL history, had been coaching Philadelphia for three seasons up to that point and his record was a meager 9-21-2. His Eagles ran off a 7-1-2 record in 1944, in part due to Neale's increased ability to utilize his scheme management prowess. It wasn't just a one-year fluke, either, as Neale posted a 54-22-3 record in the seven seasons following the rule change.

Even with the increased value of schemes in pro coaching, the league was still dominated by coaches with largely personnel-based alignments. For all of Paul Brown's scheme prowess, he was still a personnel coach. When he had Otto Graham and a group of terrific receivers and pass blockers, his Cleveland teams mostly lived by the pass. Once Graham retired and Cleveland drafted Jim Brown, Coach Brown relied more on his running attack. Add Brown to the group of Buddy Parker, Weeb Ewbank, and Vince Lombardi and it becomes clear that personnel coaches were still ruling the roost through the end of the 1960s.

The first major battle of the personnel and scheme coaching trees in the NFL started in the 1970s. This battle is best illustrated by the contrast between two coaches: Don Shula and Tom Landry.

Shula is, in my mind, the ultimate personnel coach. He certainly had his preferences when it came to how to build a team, but no coach in NFL history adapted better to his personnel than Shula did.

The story has been told a thousand times about how Shula adapted to the varying skills of his quarterbacks over the years, but I believe his adaptability is just as evident in the way he handled his running game and defense, especially early in his career. When Shula took over in Baltimore, the Colts' most notable runners were Tom Matte and Lenny Moore, both of whom were halfbacks. Moore and/or Matte remained the Colts' big-name ball carriers for the rest of Shula's Baltimore tenure, but take a look at the division of halfback/fullback carries for the Colts during that time:

YEAR	HALFBACK	FULLBACK
1963	160	181
1964	222	188
1965	202	210
1966	149	247
1967	189	223
1968	241	164
1969	259	122

Baltimore bounced from a halfback-oriented run offense to a fullback-oriented run offense on a very frequent basis. In 1963, this happened because Moore was banged up and not playing quite up to his previous standard. When he found his groove in 1964, Shula had no problem switching back to using him so much that he led the league with sixteen touchdowns. When Moore started slowing down and Matte had to play quarterback in 1965, Shula went back to the fullbacks. A couple of years later when Matte was able to carry more of the load, Shula returned to the halfback game.

This trend continued in Miami. When Shula took over the Dolphins, he inherited a backfield that included fullback Larry Csonka and half-backs Jim Kiick and Mercury Morris. Csonka was obviously the best of that group, as he is the only Hall of Famer of the three, but take a look at the fullback/halfback carry division for the Dolphins from 1970 to 1974:

YEAR	HALFBACK	FULLBACK
1970	251	193
1971	241	195
1972	354	234
1973	225	265
1974	268	263

For the first couple of years, the two halfbacks got more total carries, but Csonka still nearly equaled their carry output.

In 1972, Bob Griese was injured in week 5 and Miami had to carry on with Earl Morrall as their passer. Shula knew that he wasn't going to win it all by having Morrall throw the ball a lot, so the best strategy would be to lean on his ball carriers more. Since Csonka was already fairly tapped out, Shula leaned more heavily on Kiick and Morris. When Griese returned to the lineup in 1973 and Kiick wasn't able to handle as much of the ball-carrying load, Shula went back to the fullback-centric run game. That was only a one-year change, however, as the addition of Benny Malone in 1974 allowed the halfback position to once again take over the top spot in Shula's game planning.

The key to all of this is that it didn't matter to Shula what position his best runner played. If the halfbacks were better, Shula gave them the ball. If there was more talent at the fullback position, that's where the ball was going. As obvious as this solution sounds, believe me when I tell you there are scheme coaches out there who would not have handled these situations in a similar manner. Shula was a personnel coach, though, and was more than willing to adapt his game plans and systems to his talent.

Shula also showed his skill as a personnel coach in how he handled his defensive schemes. When he took over in Baltimore, he inherited a 4–3 scheme. He had been a defensive back in a 4–3 defense for seven years and ran the 4–3 scheme as the Lions defensive coordinator before taking the Colts head coaching job. By the time he got to Miami, Shula had seventeen professional seasons' worth of experience either playing in or coaching a 4–3 front.

When he got to Miami, Shula still ran the 4–3 defense as a base front, but in 1971 the Dolphins acquired Bob Matheson. Matheson was a tweener player, a bit undersized to be a defensive end but also a bit too large to be a linebacker. Instead of forcing Matheson to play either position exclusively, Shula and defensive coordinator Bill Arnsparger decided to use Matheson as both an end and a linebacker. They would put Matheson in the game on passing downs and either have him rush the passer or drop back into coverage. He disguised his intentions before the snap so the offense wouldn't know how to account for him.

This type of deception is incredibly common in today's NFL, but it was groundbreaking back then. Shula found a way to utilize a tweener player in a way that really hadn't been done before. This eventually led him to look for more of the Matheson-tweener types. His success in finding these kinds of players was the primary reason the Dolphins eventually switched to a 3–4 front a few years later. Shula once again proved his willingness to adapt to his players' skills no matter what type of scheme changes it required.

Contrast Shula's personnel approach with Tom Landry's scheme approach. Landry believed in the value of his systems and they way they allowed his team to manipulate pre-snap keys (the formation or set variations that can give away an offensive or defensive unit's intentions).

Landry's systems were built around disguising and/or busting these keys. His offense was incredibly complex, with excessive shifts and formation changes made just before the snap, so much so that a defense would find it very hard to determine exactly what the Cowboys were going to do.

Dallas's Flex defense was also key-oriented. Landry's defensive linemen were supposed to play off of the line a bit and read the offensive keys on the run. This led some to say that Dallas didn't get as much as

they could have out of their defensive line because they had them playing on train tracks. Nevertheless, Landry was a firm believer in the value
of reading keys and thus kept his Flex system in place. This overriding
belief in his system shows that Landry was more concerned with his
ability to outsmart the other coaches via play calling than he was about
finding ways to better utilize his individual players' skills.

The Shula/Landry scheme/personnel philosophical differences were
also quite evident in the way they affected each of their front office's
approach to stocking the roster.

Because the Shula system was so adaptable to a player's skills, the
Dolphins could be more flexible in the types of players they would take.
Another way to put this is that since Shula could work with either
tweener types or perfect physical fits, their personnel department had
many more options to choose from. Since most teams avoided tween-
ers, that gave Miami the ability to dip deeper into the talent pool to fill
their needs.

The Cowboys front office was the exact opposite of this. Dallas more
than any other team during the Landry years was an organization that
was not going to lower its physical standards on draft day. Landry
believed so strongly in the value of his systems that he was not the type
of coach to whom a personnel department could give a tweener, no
matter how talented that tweener was.

This is because Landry needed players to fit into his system. The
Cowboys front office wouldn't have drafted an undersized player like
Joe Washington because his skills were not the kind that Landry's system could effectively utilize. Washington was a talented running back
who had a very productive career with the Chargers, Colts, and Redskins, but those teams had to adjust their offenses to utilize his unique
skills. Landry had such a firm belief in the value of his offensive system
that the thought of adjusting it to fit an atypical player such as Washington simply didn't register with him.

None of this is meant as a pejorative to Landry. He simply believed
in the value of his systems as they were set up. Landry figured that if
you had bigger, stronger, and faster players and won the key recogni-

tion battles, you would win the games. Changing his system to adapt to uniquely talented players would take away some of the system's value in key disguising/busting, and he didn't think it was worth it to go down that road.

If the contrast between Shula and Landry illustrates the battle between the personnel and scheme alignments, the contrast between Shula and Chuck Noll shows the clash between the athletic and hitter mind-sets.

Shula never placed much emphasis on having his teams physically dominate their opponents, but instead focused on other attributes. On defense he believed in the value of pursuit and having players in the proper position to make plays. He wanted intelligent players who knew where they were supposed to be on the field at all times and valued that over the ability to deliver a blow.

On offense Shula believed in out-executing the other team. He wanted strong offensive linemen, but he also wanted them to be able to execute many different types of blocks. Nothing illustrates this better than the Super Bowl VIII video where Shula goes over the multiple types of run blocks that the Dolphins linemen used to dominate what looked to be a much more physically talented Vikings defensive line.

Noll, on the other hand, was a firm believer in the value of beating on your opponent until he decided to quit. Offensively, the Steelers did value quickness, especially in their offensive line, but their linemen were also powerhouses. Jim Haslett went so far as to accuse those Steelers teams of pioneering steroid use. Steve Courson, a guard who played for Pittsburgh from 1978 to 1983, admitted to using steroids and thus provides some corroboration for that claim.

As much as the Steelers offense liked to be hitters, Pittsburgh's defense was even more brutal. There are so many instances of this that it reads almost like a rap sheet: Golden Richards getting his ribs broken by Mel Blount in Super Bowl X. The NFL Films clips showing Joe Greene getting pissed at that Philadelphia offensive lineman and then hitting the guy. The other NFL Films clip with Greene where he gets in a fight with the entire Cleveland team. Jack Lambert running all the way downfield to get a hit in on a Bengals linebacker after that player hit a Pittsburgh quarterback near/at the out-of-bounds marker. Blount beating up on receivers so much that the rules committee was finally forced to adopt the five-yard chuck rule in 1978.

The most telling story about the Steelers defense was the time when someone said to Noll that he sure was fortunate to have put together a group of intimidating defenders. Noll replied that it wasn't happenstance at all, and that Pittsburgh looked for just those kinds of defensive players. It was that kind of brawn that separated the Steelers from the Dolphins and is a likely reason Pittsburgh, and not Miami, became the dynasty team of the 1970s.

The Last of a Dying Breed

As long as there was a team with a huge personnel and toughness advantage like the 1970s Steelers ruling the roost, scheme coaches were going to be hard pressed to carve out a niche in the NFL coaching forest.

Although nobody knew it at the time, those Steelers teams turned out to be the apex of the personnel/hitter era. Once Pittsburgh fell off the championship perch, the NFL was in one of those periods between dynasties. In previous eras, that would mean that either a mini-dynasty or a couple of one-year-wonder teams would win for few years until the next personnel juggernaut came along.

This dynamic changed at the end of the 1970s for a couple of reasons. First, the NFL had seen a league-wide proliferation of advanced scouting techniques that led to a more even distribution of college talent information. Once these systems made their way throughout the league, personnel coaches and talent administrators were finding it harder and harder to build an edge via the personnel method. If ever there was a going to be a time that a scheme coach was going to be able to expand the influence of the scheme coaching tree, this was it.

Enter Bill Walsh. In his early 49ers days, Walsh had one of the worst collections of players in the league, and maybe in league history. He knew he was going to have to outthink the opposition in order to make up for the lack of physical talent, so he implemented his highly advanced play-calling system.

It took a couple of years, but by 1981 the 49ers personnel department had improved the roster to make it much more competitive. Even so, that team didn't have anywhere near the talent that Walsh's later 49ers teams did, so he had to spend more time working on game plans. The extra time he had to spend on play calling meant that he couldn't focus as much on motivating his players to outhit the other team. Add the two up and it means that in his early days Walsh was definitely a scheme/athletic coach.

The most notable part of Walsh's coaching tenure was how he was eventually able to turn his team, or more specifically his defense, into a scheme/hitter group. Landry was one of the league's first successful scheme/hitter coaches, but as I mentioned earlier, the Cowboys always had superior physical talent. Just look at some of Dallas's defensive linemen over the years: Harvey Martin, Randy White, Jethro Pugh, Bob Lilly, and Too Tall Jones. Those players were big enough and talented enough that Landry could have easily coached a personnel-based defensive scheme and still won more than his share of games.

Walsh's teams were not hitters on the scale of the 1970s Steelers or Cowboys, or even of the 1980s Giants or Bears, but he was able to get his team to play a very hard-nosed style of football. Maybe the best way to put it is that Walsh was able to get a team that should have been a scheme/athletic team to go toe to toe with the great hitter teams of the day. For proof, take a look at the 49ers' record against top-notch hitter teams from 1981 through 1988:

YEAR	OPPONENT	SCORE	W/L
1981	at Washington	30–17	W
1981	vs. Dallas	45–14	W
1981	at Pittsburgh	17–14	W
1981	vs. New York Giants/NFC Wild Card	38–24	W
1981	vs. Dallas/NFC Championship	28–27	W
1982	vs. Los Angeles Raiders	17–23	L
1983	at Chicago	3–13	L

(continued)

(continued)

YEAR	OPPONENT	SCORE	W/L
1983	vs. Dallas	42–17	W
1983	at Washington/NFC Championship	21–24	L
1984	vs. Washington	37–31	W
1984	at New York Giants	31–10	W
1984	vs. Pittsburgh	17–20	L
1984	vs. New York Giants/NFC Divisional	21–10	W
1984	vs. Chicago/NFC Championship	23–0	W
1985	at Los Angeles Raiders	34–10	W
1985	vs. Chicago	10–26	L
1985	at Washington	35–8	W
1985	vs. Dallas	31–16	W
1985	at New York Giants/NFC Wild Card	3–17	L
1986	at Washington	6–14	L
1986	vs. New York Giants	17–21	L
1986	at New York Giants/NFC Divisional	3–49	L
1987	vs. Chicago	41–0	W
1988	at New York Giants	20–17	W
1988	at Chicago	9–10	L
1988	vs. Los Angeles Raiders	3–9	L
1988	at Chicago/NFC Championship	28–3	W

The 49ers were 16–11 when facing the toughest hitter teams of Walsh's tenure. They started off 5–0 in 1981 when the league didn't have as dominant a group of hitter teams as it did a few years later, but an 11–11 record after that is still a great overall mark against physical clubs for a team that was supposed to be a finesse group.

As great as Walsh's influence was, however, the scheme tree was still in a fight for its life during the 1980s. Even though Walsh was supplying the football world with a number of head coaching candidates from his assistant coaching ranks, he was being matched coach for coach by the great personnel coaches of the 1980s, Bill Parcells and Joe Gibbs. Once Jimmy Johnson, a personnel coach if ever there was one, started sending his coaches into the world in the early 1990s, the personnel tree looked like it was still going to be the dominant tree in the NFL coaching forest.

The Defection

That all changed when Bill Belichick jumped from the personnel tree to the scheme tree. This type of alignment change is all but unheard of in coaches. As I pointed out earlier, a personnel coach will sometimes lean on schemes when his players are hurt, but as soon as he gets healthy personnel back, he'll revert back to his personnel ways. Scheme coaches will also sometimes scale back their schemes if the personnel on their team aren't able to implement the schemes, but you can be sure they will fall back on their old ways as soon as their players are properly trained.

Belichick had always been a creative defensive coordinator, but as innovative as his defensive strategies were, he was still working under a personnel coach in Parcells. Parcells and Belichick both believed in the value of hitters, so that part of their coaching philosophies meshed, but Parcells was undoubtedly not a scheme coach.

In one of his autobiographies, Parcells talks about how some coaches seem to get away from doing the things that their team does well in an effort to show off their play calling. Parcells used a pitching analogy to illustrate his thoughts on the matter. If your fastball is getting them out, just keep throwing the fastball until you retire all twenty-seven batters. Parcells has also been quoted as saying that play calling is probably the most overrated part of football. Those two things show not only that he is not a scheme coach, but he also has a certain level of contempt for the scheme approach.

We now know that Belichick has a scheme/hitter coaching alignment, but because he adjusted so well to the personnel/hitter alignment of Parcells, he wasn't seen as a scheme type of coach. I believe that Belichick even tried to be a personnel/hitter coach when he took over in Cleveland and that is part of the reason his tenure there was so disappointing.

I also believe that when Belichick was slated to take over the Jets head coaching job after Parcells retired, he knew that Parcells would insist on the organization's scouting group taking on a personnel/hitter mind-set in drafting players. Belichick had to know that he didn't want to be a personnel/hitter coach and that the only way he would be able to adopt his scheme/hitter philosophy would be to leave Parcells's shadow.

There was no way to know it at the time, but Belichick's move to the scheme tree was the step that allowed that tree to take over as the dominant one. The personnel tree still has more than its share of adherents, including Marty Schottenheimer, Norv Turner, Herm Edwards, Jack Del Rio, and Jeff Fisher. Even so, the personnel coaches are winning fewer and fewer Super Bowls. Take a look:

SUPER BOWL	WINNING COACH	SCHEME/PERSONNEL ALIGNMENT
I	Vince Lombardi	Personnel/Hitter
II	Vince Lombardi	Personnel/Hitter
III	Weeb Ewbank	Personnel/Athletic
IV	Hank Stram	Scheme/Hitter
V	Don McCafferty	Personnel/Hitter
VI	Tom Landry	Scheme/Hitter
VII	Don Shula	Personnel/Athletic
VIII	Don Shula	Personnel/Athletic
IX	Chuck Noll	Personnel/Hitter
X	Chuck Noll	Personnel/Hitter
XI	John Madden	Personnel/Hitter
XII	Tom Landry	Scheme/Hitter
XIII	Chuck Noll	Personnel/Hitter
XIV	Chuck Noll	Personnel/Hitter
XV	Tom Flores	Personnel/Hitter
XVI	Bill Walsh	Scheme/Athletic
XVII	Joe Gibbs	Personnel/Hitter
XVIII	Tom Flores	Personnel/Hitter
XIX	Bill Walsh	Scheme/Hitter
XX	Mike Ditka	Personnel/Hitter
XI	Bill Parcells	Personnel/Hitter
XXII	Joe Gibbs	Personnel/Hitter
XXIII	Bill Walsh	Scheme/Hitter
XXIV	George Seifert	Scheme/Hitter
XV	Bill Parcells	Personnel/Hitter
XXVI	Joe Gibbs	Personnel/Hitter
XXVII	Jimmy Johnson	Personnel/Hitter
XXVIII	Jimmy Johnson	Personnel/Hitter
XXIX	George Seifert	Scheme/Hitter

(continued)

(continued)

SUPER BOWL	WINNING COACH	SCHEME/PERSONNEL ALIGNMENT
XXX	Barry Switzer	Personnel/Hitter
XXXI	Mike Holmgren	Scheme/Athletic
XXXII	Mike Shanahan	Scheme/Athletic
XXXIII	Mike Shanahan	Scheme/Athletic
XXXIV	Dick Vermeil	Personnel/Hitter
XXXV	Brian Billick	Personnel/Hitter
XXXVI	Bill Belichick	Scheme/Hitter
XXXVII	Jon Gruden	Scheme/Athletic
XXXVIII	Bill Belichick	Scheme/Hitter
XXXIX	Bill Belichick	Scheme/Hitter
XL	Bill Cowher	Scheme/Hitter
XLI	Tony Dungy	Scheme/Athletic
XLII	Tom Coughlin	Personnel/Athletic

Personnel coaches have won twenty-five of the forty-two Super Bowls, but they have only won four of the past fourteen. The plain fact is that scheme coaches are winning more and more often.

One of the main reasons the scheme tree is proliferating is that there are more scheme coaches populating the coaching forest with their adherents. Tony Dungy is almost single-handedly doing this by operating a virtual pipeline of successful scheme coaches in Lovie Smith, Herm Edwards, Mike Tomlin, and Rod Marinelli among others.

That isn't the only reason that the scheme tree is getting larger. The NFL is a copycat league, so teams are now much more willing to hire a scheme coach than they were in the past.

It is also much easier for a coach to sell his play-calling abilities than it is to sell his motivational skills. Play calling is a skill that can largely be attributed to one person via quantifiable statistics. If an offensive coordinator has his unit at the top of the league in yards gained or points scored, he can point to that as proof of his play-calling prowess and thus seemingly prove his worth.

Play-calling value is also appealing to assistant coaches because that trait doesn't put the assistant as much at odds with the players, other coaches, or potentially the general manager or owner as the personnel or hitter alignments might. A strong-willed personnel-oriented assistant coach who shows himself to be a dominant personality may rub a team's management the wrong way, especially if that team's GM/owner wants a coach who will be malleable. Coaches with lower-key personalities aren't as likely to be perceived a threat since they can be overruled easily.

Having said this, I think that the personnel tree is poised to make a comeback for a number of reasons. The first is that the Belichick coaching tree is the hardest one to proliferate. Scheme/hitter alignments are the rarest around because they put more strain on coaches than any other type of alignment. Not only does the coach have to get the players to increase their pain thresholds, he also has to outthink his opponents. Any of Belichick's assistants who try to put his scheme/hitter coaching alignment into play are going to be hard pressed to match his success in it because of how difficult it is to specialize in both areas.

This shows up in the win-loss record of the Belichick coaching tree. Romeo Crennel's Cleveland tenure has improved of late, but the jury is definitely still out on his long-term head coaching prowess. Kirk Ferentz and Charlie Weis both have respectable college coaching records (or should I say Weis did until this past year), but that doesn't help proliferate the professional scheme/hitter coaching tree. Nick Saban did a decent job in his first year in Miami but then ran out of town as fast as he could when the Alabama job came open after his second year with the Dolphins. Eric Mangini is the only Belichick disciple to make the playoffs as a pro coach, and he followed that season up with a 4–12 record the next year. No Belichick disciple at this point looks like he has the chops to keep the tree alive.

The second reason personnel coaches will make a comeback is if scheme/hitter coaches aren't winning and teams still want to tap into the benefits of advanced play calling, scheme/athletic coaches will start to come into vogue. This is already happening, as Dungy's tree expansion shows, and it is a ready-made formula for personnel coaching success.

I say this because, as was mentioned earlier in this chapter, the downside to scheme/athletic teams is that they tend to fare very poorly against either personnel/hitter or scheme/hitter teams. For proof of this, just consider how Dungy's teams have fared in the playoffs. Most of Dungy's playoff losses were against Philadelphia, New England, or Pittsburgh, and all three of those teams were of the personnel or scheme/hitter alignment.

This isn't to knock Dungy's coaching prowess but rather to point out that the Colts' method of team building has a significant weakness. One of the main reasons athletic teams struggle against hitters is that they tend to be smaller than their opponents. They often sacrifice size for athleticism or durability, and when they are faced with a group of larger players, they simply don't match up well.

That is really the primary reason that the scheme coaching tree could take a backseat. Teams are going to focus on the scheme/athletic teams' weakness of not being able to handle a punch in the mouth. Dallas and San Diego have both recently shown that a front office can still build an effective personnel/hitter team. Once a club comes up with a great set of hard-hitting personnel and pairs it up with a coach who knows how to effectively use the personnel, that team will eclipse the scheme/athletic clubs for league dominance. That will start the evolution of coaching trees in an entirely new direction, and thus continue the Darwinism of the coaching forest.

7

Do Coaches Have a Ten-Year Shelf Life?

Al Davis has often expressed a theory he has about head coaches in the NFL. He believes that coaches have an effective shelf life of approximately ten years. After that length of time, or so the theory goes, a coach will lose his effectiveness for a number of reasons. His best players will typically be leaving due to age, any leftover players will begin to tune him out, his opponents will start to catch up to his game planning, and fatigue will set into both the coach and his staff.

That sounds good in theory, but what is the historical backup for it? Do coaches tend to falter after a decade at the helm?

It turns out that there is some evidence to support this theory. Take a look at the track record of some of the best coaches in NFL history:

- Don Shula started his coaching career in Baltimore in 1963. He had a run of near championship wins with the Colts in the 1960s but couldn't quite get them over the championship hump. He then went to Miami and finally got that monkey off his back with a win in Super Bowl VII in 1972, which was his tenth season as a head coach. The Dolphins followed this up with another Super Bowl win the following season.

At that point, Shula had coached for eleven seasons. He had ten playoff wins in that time and his teams appeared in five NFL championship games/Super Bowls, winning two of them. Shula was only forty-three years old at that time, so he was still quite young and seemingly should have had many championships left. It didn't turn out that way. Shula coached for twenty-two more seasons. He had nine playoff wins and appeared in two Super Bowls in that part of his career, which is a good showing, but it pales in comparison to his first eleven seasons.

- Joe Gibbs began coaching the Redskins in 1981, won his last championship in 1991, and quit in 1992, by which time it was obvious that Washington was on a downward trend and would need retooling. Gibbs's record during his second tenure in the nation's capital certainly did not come close to measuring up to his first run there.

- Hank Stram started coaching the Chiefs in 1960 and won his Super Bowl in 1969, his tenth season. Stram coached seven more seasons in the NFL but never won another playoff game after the Super Bowl IV win.

- Chuck Noll took over the Steelers in 1969, won his last Super Bowl in the 1979 season, and never won another conference championship after that. In fact, his teams only won two playoff games in his last twelve years of coaching.

- Even low-key Bud Grant, a man known for keeping football in the proper perspective (he once went hunting during one of his team's Super Bowl bye weeks), wasn't immune to the effects of the ten-year rule. He started coaching the Vikings in 1967 and won his last conference championship in 1976, his tenth season. His teams had only two playoff wins in his last eight years.

As convincing as those cases might be, however, when I initially ran the numbers to see what effect the ten-year mark had on a coach's track record, they seemed to tell a different story. The following tables show the record of every coach who patrolled the sidelines for more than ten seasons. The first table details their record for the first ten years.

WT stands for wins/ties, or the number of wins if ties are counted as half-wins and added to wins.

COACHING RECORDS: YEARS 1–10

COACH	TOTAL # OF SEASONS	REGULAR SEASON					POSTSEASON					CHAMP APP	CHAMP WON
		W	L	T	WT	WIN %	W	L	T	WT	WIN %		
George Allen	12	97	38	5	99.5	71.1%	2	6	0	2.0	25.0%	1	0
Bill Belichick	13	89	71	0	89.0	55.6%	10	1	0	10.0	90.9%	3	3
Paul Brown	25	105	17	4	107.0	84.9%	9	3	0	9.0	75.0%	10	7
Jimmy Conzelman	15	53	32	14	60.0	60.6%	0	0	0	0.0	0.0%	0	1
Don Coryell	14	89	49	1	89.5	64.4%	3	6	0	3.0	33.3%	0	0
Tom Coughlin	12	85	75	0	85.0	53.1%	4	5	0	4.0	44.4%	0	0
Bill Cowher	15	99	61	0	99.0	61.9%	6	7	0	6.0	46.2%	1	0
Mike Ditka	14	101	51	0	101.0	66.4%	6	6	0	6.0	50.0%	1	1
Tony Dungy	12	102	58	0	102.0	63.8%	5	8	0	5.0	38.5%	0	0
Weeb Ewbank	20	64	60	2	65.0	51.6%	2	0	0	2.0	100.0%	2	2
Jeff Fisher	14	88	62	0	88.0	58.7%	5	4	0	5.0	55.6%	1	0
Tom Flores	12	85	67	0	85.0	55.9%	8	3	0	8.0	72.7%	2	2
Joe Gibbs	16	101	51	0	101.0	66.4%	12	4	0	12.0	75.0%	3	2
Sid Gillman	18	73	55	2	74.0	56.9%	1	4	0	1.0	20.0%	5	1
Bud Grant	18	98	38	4	100.0	71.4%	8	8	0	8.0	50.0%	4	0
Dennis Green	13	97	62	0	97.0	61.0%	4	8	0	4.0	33.3%	0	0
Forrest Gregg	11	70	76	0	70.0	47.9%	2	2	0	2.0	50.0%	1	0
George Halas	40	84	31	19	93.5	69.8%	0	0	0	0.0	0.0%	0	1
Mike Holmgren	16	99	61	0	99.0	61.9%	9	6	0	9.0	60.0%	2	1
Chuck Knox	22	91	51	1	91.5	64.0%	4	7	0	4.0	36.4%	0	0
Joe Kuharich	11	56	69	3	57.5	44.9%	0	0	0	0.0	0.0%	0	0
Curly Lambeau	33	71	28	14	78.0	69.0%	0	0	0	0.0	0.0%	0	2
Tom Landry	29	67	65	6	70.0	50.7%	1	4	0	1.0	20.0%	0	0
Marv Levy	17	74	69	0	74.0	51.7%	3	3	0	3.0	50.0%	1	0
Ted Marchibroda	12	75	79	0	75.0	48.7%	2	4	0	2.0	33.3%	0	0
Jim Mora	15	91	68	0	91.0	57.2%	0	4	0	0.0	0.0%	0	0
Dick Nolan	11	69	70	5	71.5	49.7%	2	3	0	2.0	40.0%	0	0
Chuck Noll	23	88	53	1	88.5	62.3%	11	4	0	11.0	73.3%	3	3
Steve Owen	23	73	39	9	77.5	64.0%	2	3	0	2.0	40.0%	5	2
Bill Parcells	19	92	66	1	92.5	58.2%	8	4	0	8.0	66.7%	2	2
Jack Pardee	11	86	68	0	86.0	55.8%	1	5	0	1.0	16.7%	0	0
Buddy Parker	15	72	43	5	74.5	62.1%	3	1	0	3.0	75.0%	3	2

(continued)

COACHING RECORDS: YEARS 1–10 (continued)

COACH	# OF SEASONS	REGULAR SEASON					POSTSEASON					CHAMP APP	CHAMP WON
		W	L	T	WT	WIN %	W	L	T	WT	WIN %		
Bum Phillips	11	78	69	0	78.0	53.1%	4	3	0	4.0	57.1%	0	0
Dan Reeves	23	90	61	1	90.5	59.5%	6	5	0	6.0	54.5%	3	0
Lou Saban	16	61	65	5	63.5	48.5%	2	1	0	2.0	66.7%	2	2
Marty Schottenheimer	21	94	56	1	94.5	62.6%	5	8	0	5.0	38.5%	0	0
George Seifert	11	113	47	0	113.0	70.6%	10	5	0	10.0	66.7%	2	2
Mike Shanahan	15	89	59	0	89.0	60.1%	7	2	0	7.0	77.8%	2	2
Buck Shaw	12	73	48	5	75.5	59.9%	1	1	0	1.0	50.0%	1	0
Don Shula	33	105	30	5	107.5	76.8%	7	5	0	7.0	58.3%	4	2
Hank Stram	17	87	48	5	89.5	63.9%	5	2	0	5.0	71.4%	3	2
Norm Van Brocklin	13	48	82	7	51.5	37.6%	0	0	0	0.0	0.0%	0	0
Dick Vermeil	15	76	73	0	76.0	51.0%	6	4	0	6.0	60.0%	2	1
Dave Wannstedt	11	81	79	0	81.0	50.6%	2	3	0	2.0	40.0%	0	0
George Wilson	12	60	66	6	63.0	47.7%	2	0	0	2.0	100.0%	1	1
Sam Wyche	12	71	88	0	71.0	44.7%	3	2	0	3.0	60.0%	1	0
Totals	773	3,810	2,654	131	3,875.5	58.8%	193	164	0	193.0	54.1%	71	44

The next table covers years eleven and beyond for these coaches.

COACHING RECORDS: YEARS 11-PLUS YEARS

COACH	# OF SEASONS	REGULAR SEASON					POSTSEASON					CHAMP APP	CHAMP WON
		W	L	T	WT	WIN %	W	L	T	WT	WIN %		
George Allen	2	19	9	0	19.0	67.9%	0	1	0	0.0	0.0%	0	0
Bill Belichick	3	38	10	0	38.0	79.2%	5	3	0	5.0	62.5%	1	0
Paul Brown	15	108	87	5	110.5	55.3%	0	5	0	0.0	0.0%	2	0
Jimmy Conzelman	5	34	31	3	35.5	52.2%	1	1	0	1.0	50.0%	2	1
Don Coryell	4	22	34	0	22.0	39.3%	0	0	0	0.0	0.0%	0	0
Tom Coughlin	2	18	14	0	18.0	56.3%	4	1	0	4.0	80.0%	1	1
Bill Cowher	5	50	29	1	50.5	63.1%	6	2	0	6.0	75.0%	1	1
Mike Ditka	4	20	44	0	20.0	31.3%	0	0	0	0.0	0.0%	0	0
Tony Dungy	2	25	7	0	25.0	78.1%	4	1	0	4.0	80.0%	1	1
Weeb Ewbank	10	66	69	5	68.5	48.9%	2	1	0	2.0	66.7%	1	1
Jeff Fisher	4	27	37	0	27.0	42.2%	0	1	0	0.0	0.0%	0	0
Tom Flores	2	12	20	0	12.0	37.5%	0	0	0	0.0	0.0%	0	0
Joe Gibbs	6	53	43	0	53.0	55.2%	5	2	0	5.0	71.4%	1	1
Sid Gillman	8	49	44	5	51.5	52.6%	0	1	0	0.0	0.0%	1	0
Bud Grant	8	60	58	1	60.5	50.8%	2	4	0	2.0	33.3%	0	0

(continued)

COACHING RECORDS: 11-PLUS YEARS (continued)

COACH	# OF SEASONS	REGULAR SEASON					POSTSEASON					CHAMP APP	CHAMP WON
		W	L	T	WT	WIN %	W	L	T	WT	WIN %		
Dennis Green	3	16	32	0	16.0	33.3%	0	0	0	0.0	0.0	0	0
Forrest Gregg	1	5	9	1	5.5	36.7%	0	0	0	0.0	0.0	0	0
George Halas	30	234	117	12	240.0	66.1%	6	3	0	6.0	66.7%	8	5
Mike Holmgren	6	58	38	0	58.0	60.4%	4	5	0	4.0	44.4%	1	0
Chuck Knox	12	95	96	0	95.0	49.7%	3	4	0	3.0	42.9%	0	0
Joe Kuharich	1	2	12	0	2.0	14.3%	0	0	0	0.0	0.0	0	0
Curly Lambeau	23	155	104	8	159.0	59.6%	3	2	0	3.0	60.0%	5	4
Tom Landry	19	183	97	0	183.0	65.4%	19	12	0	19.0	61.3%	5	2
Marv Levy	7	69	43	0	69.0	61.6%	8	5	0	8.0	61.5%	3	0
Ted Marchibroda	2	12	19	1	12.5	39.1%	0	0	0	0.0	0.0	0	0
Jim Mora	5	34	38	0	34.0	47.2%	0	2	0	0.0	0.0	0	0
Dick Nolan	1	0	12	0	0.0	0.0	0	0	0	0.0	0.0	0	0
Chuck Noll	13	105	95	0	105.0	52.5%	5	4	0	5.0	55.6%	1	1
Steve Owen	13	78	61	8	82.0	55.8%	0	5	0	0.0	0.0	3	0
Bill Parcells	9	80	64	0	80.0	55.6%	3	4	0	3.0	42.9%	1	0
Jack Pardee	1	1	9	0	1.0	10.0%	0	0	0	0.0	0.0	0	0
Buddy Parker	5	32	32	4	34.0	50.0%	0	0	0	0.0	0.0	0	0
Bum Phillips	1	4	8	0	4.0	33.3%	0	0	0	0.0	0.0	0	0
Dan Reeves	13	102	105	1	102.5	49.3%	5	4	0	5.0	55.6%	1	0
Lou Saban	6	34	34	2	35.0	50.0%	0	1	0	0.0	0.0	0	0
Marty Schottenheimer	11	106	70	0	106.0	60.2%	0	5	0	0.0	0.0	0	0
George Seifert	1	1	15	0	1.0	6.3%	0	0	0	0.0	0.0	0	0
Mike Shanahan	5	49	31	0	49.0	61.3%	1	3	0	1.0	25.0%	0	0
Buck Shaw	2	17	7	0	17.0	70.8%	1	0	0	1.0	100.0%	1	1
Don Shula	23	223	126	1	223.5	63.9%	12	12	0	12.0	50.0%	3	1
Hank Stram	7	44	49	5	46.5	47.4%	0	1	0	0.0	0.0	0	0
Norm Van Brocklin	3	18	18	0	18.0	50.0%	0	0	0	0.0	0.0	0	0
Dick Vermeil	5	44	36	0	44.0	55.0%	0	1	0	0.0	0.0	0	0
Dave Wannstedt	1	1	8	0	1.0	11.1%	0	0	0	0.0	0.0	0	0
George Wilson	2	8	18	2	9.0	32.1%	0	0	0	0.0	0.0	0	0
Sam Wyche	2	13	19	0	13.0	40.6%	0	0	0	0.0	0.0	0	0
Totals	313	2,424	1,958	65	2,456.5	55.2%	99	96	0	99.0	50.8%	43	20

(On a side note, a number of the 11-plus-years successes came from coaches getting title wins in their 11th and 12th seasons, so much so that I almost changed the study to one of years 1–12 and then 13-plus. I didn't do it for two reasons. First, the rule of thumb that is quoted is always 10 years, not 11 or 12, and the idea is to test the validity of the conventional wisdom as it is given. The second reason is that changing the cutoff point to 13-plus years would have reduced the number of coaches reviewed from forty-six to thirty, and I thought the study would have more validity with the larger sample size.)

The difference in regular-season winning percentage between the two lists is only 3.6 percent, which equates to just over ½ of a win every season in a sixteen-game schedule. The ratio of championship appearances to seasons coached on a per-year basis was in favor of the 1–10-years column but not by as much as I might have thought going into this study. In their first 10 seasons, these coaches averaged one championship appearance for every 6–7 years coached, whereas in the 11-plus-years portion of their careers, these coaches averaged a championship game appearance every 7–8 years. The title wins to years coached ratio was weighted heavily in the 1–10-years direction, with title wins for every 10–11 seasons on that side of the ledger versus a title win for every 16 years coached in seasons 11 and up.

Those championship numbers certainly aren't dramatic enough to definitively illustrate a sudden coaching drop after 10 years, but a good portion of the championship success in the 11-plus-years area is due to Halas, Lambeau, and Landry. Eighteen of the forty-three championship appearances and eleven of the twenty title wins belong to Halas, Lambeau, and Landry. Those three account for zero championship game appearances and three title wins in years 1–10 (Halas and Lambeau won their titles in the pre–championship game era), so if they were removed from both sides, it would dramatically alter the ratio of championship game appearances and title wins between the two columns. The 1–10-years ratios of championship appearances and title wins would stay basically the same (6 years for appearances, 10–11 years for wins), but the 11-plus-years ratio would jump to 10 years for appearances and 27 years for wins. This strongly indicates that if an owner wants to win a championship, he will be very hard pressed to do it with a veteran coach.

The only thing that troubles me about this analysis is that in some cases there are reasons why a coach was either more or less effective as his career went on that probably had little or nothing to do with his actual coaching effectiveness.

Take Paul Brown's for instance. Brown's record is somewhat distorted by the fact that his tenth year happened to dovetail with Otto Graham's last year of playing quarterback for him. With Graham as his quarterback, Brown's record was 105-17-4 (a win percentage of .849) and he won seven AAFC/NFL championships. Brown's Cleveland record without Graham was 53-31-3 (a win percentage of .626) and he only coached in one other playoff game sans Graham, a title loss to Detroit in 1957. Brown's Cincinnati teams achieved success faster than any other expansion team up to that point, but they also had no playoff success. In fact, as incredible as it might sound, in his last thirteen seasons of coaching, Paul Brown did not win a single playoff game. Was that due to his coaching being less effective, or was it a simple matter of going from having one of the best quarterbacks of all time to having more average quarterbacks?

The flip side of this is Tom Landry. Landry started his coaching career in 1960 and had five straight losing seasons. The Cowboys owner, Clint Murchison, was convinced that Landry was a quality coach, so instead of firing him, he gave him a ten-year contract extension.

Landry was able to get things turned around, but five years later the Cowboys were once again in a tough spot. They had managed only one win in four playoff appearances and were being crowned the team that couldn't win the big one. There were and are a good number of owners who would have thrown in the towel on a coach in that situation, but Murchison once again stuck it out with Landry. Landry rewarded Murchison's faith with five championship appearances and two title wins in the following years. Again I ask the question, was it a matter of Landry being a better coach later in his career, or was it because he got a second and third chance that a lot of coaches wouldn't have received?

The Brown and Landry examples may be compelling, but if two all-time great coaches are the most valid exceptions to the rule, it probably means that the rule is generally accurate. The numbers show that in this matter, Al Davis is right.

8

Marty Schottenheimer: Hall of Famer?

If you want to stir up an argument among Browns, Chiefs, and Chargers fans, try asking them if they think Marty Schottenheimer did enough in his coaching career to warrant induction into the Pro Football Hall of Fame. The immediate knee-jerk reaction of most of these fans would likely be that of course he doesn't belong in the Hall of Fame. They would point out that although he had a lot of regular-season success, Schottenheimer never won a Super Bowl and never even coached in one.

Is that the correct tack to take on grading career immortality for coaches? Or, more specifically, what exactly does it take to put a coach into Canton? Schottenheimer's career may or may not be over, but in the event that it is, these queries leave us with one overarching question: did he do enough to warrant inclusion in the Hall of Fame?

I think the first place to start with this question is to determine what the de facto standards are for Hall of Fame coaches. The system I will use to determine this is identical to the system I used in determining the dynastic impact of teams (see chapter 2). To review, that system rewards the following accomplishments:

- Have a winning season
- Post a .600 record, .700 record, .800 record, and so on
- Make the playoffs
- Win secondary-level playoff games
- Win the conference championship
- Win the league championship

A winning season nets a coach one point. A coach is also awarded half a point for each step up the incremental winning percentage success ladder his team climbs. For example, if the coach posts a 12–4 record (.750 winning percentage), he receives one point for a winning season, half a point for posting a .600-plus record, and another half a point for posting a .700-plus record.

A coach is awarded a point for making the playoffs, regardless of what level of the playoffs his team achieved. For a win in the wild-card round, a coach will be awarded one point. A win in a divisional or second-round playoff game (or in a play-in tiebreaker game during the 1930s–1960s) nets a coach two points. For winning a conference championship game, the coach will be awarded three points. These three points are also awarded to coaches whose teams appeared in an AFL or NFL championship game prior to the advent of conference championship games. Winning a league championship gives a coach four points.

The idea behind the system is to award an ever-increasing number of points for the largest accomplishments. I placed much more value on winning championships than on anything else, simply because the Hall of Fame nominating committees seem to do the same. In Schottenheimer's case, the goal of the system is to give him a reasonable amount of credit for putting together so many playoff teams without overvaluing that accomplishment.

So how do his accomplishments measure up? Is he one of the top coaches of all time? Let's start this review by taking a look at the top twenty coaches on the list (with Hall of Famers listed in bold).

RANK	COACH	.500+	.600	.700	.800	.900	1.0	P/O	WC WIN	DIV P/O WIN	CONF WIN	CHAMP WIN	TOTAL
1	**George Halas**	34	28	20	8	3	2	8	2	0	8	7	126.50
2	**Paul Brown**	20	18	14	9	5	1	15	0	1	12	7	124.50
3	**Don Shula**	27	23	17	6	3	1	19	3	8	7	2	119.00
4	**Tom Landry**	20	17	14	3	0	0	18	2	11	5	2	102.00
5	**Curly Lambeau**	25	19	13	6	2	0	5	0	0	4	6	86.00
6	**Chuck Noll**	15	10	7	2	0	0	12	1	7	4	4	79.50
7	**Steve Owen**	14	13	9	5	1	0	10	0	0	8	2	70.00
8	**Joe Gibbs**	12	10	5	3	0	0	10	4	5	4	3	69.00
9	**Vince Lombardi**	10	8	5	3	1	0	6	1	0	6	5	63.50
10	Bill Belichick	8	7	4	3	1	1	7	3	5	4	3	60.00
11	Mike Holmgren	14	7	3	3	0	0	12	5	4	3	1	58.50
12	**Bud Grant**	12	8	7	5	0	0	12	1	5	4	0	57.00
13	Bill Parcells	11	9	4	2	0	0	9	2	4	3	2	54.50
T14	Bill Cowher	11	9	3	2	1	0	10	3	6	2	1	53.50
T14	Dan Reeves	12	9	4	2	0	0	9	1	6	4	0	53.50
16	**Bill Walsh**	7	7	3	3	1	0	7	0	4	3	3	50.00
T17	**Ray Flaherty**	9	7	6	3	1	0	6	0	0	6	2	49.50
T17	**Marv Levy**	10	7	5	3	0	0	8	2	5	4	0	49.50
19	**John Madden**	10	9	6	3	2	0	8	0	7	1	1	49.00
20	George Seifert	8	8	5	4	0	0	7	1	5	2	2	48.50

Every coach in the top nine is already in the Hall of Fame. Of the next eleven coaches on the list, only five are Hall of Famers (Grant, Walsh, Flaherty, Levy, and Madden), but it is very likely that Holmgren, Parcells, and Belichick will all be inducted as well. Very strong cases could also be made for Cowher and Reeves, especially considering that Cowher will likely resume his NFL coaching career in the near future. The only coach in the top twenty who likely won't be inducted is George Seifert, and that is mostly due to the 49ers organization getting the bulk of the credit for his success.

So that's nineteen out of the top twenty coaches who either are or very likely will be Hall of Famers. Can you guess who the next coach on the list is? Yep, it's none other than Marty Schottenheimer. Here are coaches 21–40 on the list:

RANK	COACH	.500+	.600	.700	.800	.900	1.0	P/O	WC WIN	DIV P/O WIN	CONF WIN	CHAMP WIN	TOTAL
21	Marty Schottenheimer	15	11	5	3	0	0	13	2	3	0	0	45.50
22	Tony Dungy	10	9	5	2	0	0	10	4	3	1	1	45.00
T23	Chuck Knox	13	10	6	2	0	0	11	3	4	0	0	44.00
T23	Mike Shanahan	9	7	4	3	0	0	7	1	3	2	2	44.00
25	**Sid Gillman**	10	8	5	1	0	0	6	0	0	5	1	42.00
26	**Hank Stram**	11	6	4	2	0	0	5	0	1	3	2	41.00
27	Buddy Parker	10	9	5	1	0	0	3	1	0	3	2	38.50
28	Jimmy Johnson	7	4	2	1	0	0	6	3	2	2	2	37.50
T29	**Mike Ditka**	8	8	4	2	1	0	7	1	3	1	1	36.50
T29	**Weeb Ewbank**	7	5	4	0	0	0	4	0	0	3	3	36.50
31	Tom Flores	6	5	3	1	0	0	5	2	2	2	2	35.50
T32	**Jimmy Conzelman**	10	8	5	3	1	0	2	0	0	2	2	34.50
T32	**Greasy Neale**	7	5	4	3	1	0	3	1	0	3	2	34.50
T34	**George Allen**	12	10	7	1	1	0	7	0	1	1	0	33.50
T34	Dick Vermeil	7	6	3	2	0	0	6	1	2	2	1	33.50
36	Tom Coughlin	6	5	1	1	0	0	7	3	3	1	1	32.50
37	Blanton Collier	7	7	5	0	0	0	5	0	2	2	1	32.00
38	Jim Lee Howell	7	3	3	1	0	0	3	1	0	3	2	31.50
T39	Andy Reid	6	6	3	1	0	0	6	3	4	1	0	31.00
T39	Buck Shaw	10	8	4	2	0	0	2	0	1	2	1	31.00

Schottenheimer may be on the cusp of the top twenty, but it does seem that the fifty-point total is the magic number for automatic induction. Of the Hall of Fame coaches in the above list who didn't reach that mark, some had to wait many years for induction (e.g., Stram and Allen), while others had playing careers that added to their coaching accomplishments (Ditka and Conzelman). Neale was somewhat lucky in that when he was inducted in 1969, most of the early coaching greats had already been honored and the newer breed hadn't been coaching long enough to put any candidates above him. Gillman was honored as much for his coaching innovations as for his record.

Schottenheimer has yet to reach that fifty-point total, so at this point he would be considered on the precipice of making the grade on that basis alone. Even if he does stick around and can reach the fifty-point mark, however, there are two other issues his candidacy will have to overcome.

The first is that there are too many other potential coaching Hall of Fame nominees who have multiple championships on their résumés to go along with similar point totals to Schottenheimer's. Buddy Parker has 38.5 points and won two championships in the 1950s, beating Paul Brown's dynasty teams for both titles. Jimmy Johnson has 37.5 points and won two titles with one of the greatest teams of all time. In addition, it would not be a stretch to think that voters could also give Johnson a good amount of credit for the Super Bowl Dallas won after he left. Tom Flores won two Super Bowls in four years and in many ways had a similar career to his Raiders coaching counterpart (and Hall of Famer) John Madden.

The second problem for Schottenheimer is that the coach his record most closely resembles is Chuck Knox. Knox was the Schottenheimer of the 1970s, taking most of his teams to the playoffs and some of them to conference title games, but, just like Marty, he could never even get his team over the conference championship hump. Knox's career totals are nearly identical to Schottenheimer's in every way and Knox has received almost no voter support in his Hall of Fame candidacy. If this precedent is any indicator, Schottenheimer will not be a Hall of Famer.

If there is one Hall of Fame coach whose record could possibly play in Schottenheimer's favor, it would be George Allen. Allen is similar to Schottenheimer in that he had plenty of winning regular-season records while his postseason record was atrocious.

I knew going into this that Allen had limited postseason success, but I never realized it was quite as bad as it turned out to be. Allen's teams made the playoffs seven times. Six of those times, they didn't win even one playoff game. The only time Allen had any playoff success was in 1972. His first playoff win that year came against the one-year-wonder Packers in the divisional round. The Redskins followed up that win by beating the Cowboys, Allen's most hated rivals, in the 1972 NFC Championship Game. Allen's antipathy for Dallas was something that he passed along to his team, and his players approached the game like it was a grudge match. That approach was a primary reason why Washington won the game 26–3.

Allen's playoff teams never again faced an opponent as weak as Green Bay or one they hated as much as Dallas. That means that when it came to facing playoff teams that were just as strong as Washington but that didn't generate the hate the Cowboys did, Allen was never able to pilot his team to even one win. His lack of playoff success does seem to present a very favorable precedent for Schottenheimer.

The downside to Allen as a precedent is that his compelling personality was a big part of the reason he was inducted. His idiosyncrasies included eating a diet that largely consisted of vanilla ice cream and peanut butter and sometimes being paranoid on a Nixonian scale. These traits were well documented and seemed to make him a more accessible character. Allen was also a man whose commitment to the coaching dream was so intense that he came across as a somewhat tragic figure when he couldn't notch the big-game wins. In addition, his nomination was strengthened by his reputation as a coaching innovator whose credits include popularizing (although not creating) the nickel defense and hiring the first special teams coach in NFL history. Schottenheimer is not known as an innovator and he lacks the personality quirks and the tragedy angle, so he probably won't get in on Allen's pass.

Another hurdle in Schottenheimer's candidacy may be the candidacy of Dan Reeves. Reeves was a contemporary of Schottenheimer's and his Broncos teams were directly responsible for Schottenheimer's Browns not making the Super Bowl. Reeves has four conference championships on his résumé and the sum total of his achievements is quite similar to Bud Grant's and Marv Levy's, two Hall of Famers. Given all of those facts, as long as Reeves is a candidate and not an enshrinee, it is next to impossible to say that Schottenheimer should be voted in.

So what is the bottom line for Marty to get inducted? I think it boils down to three things. The first is to get Dan Reeves inducted in Canton as quickly as possible. The second is for Schottenheimer to put some distance between himself and Chuck Knox.

The third would be for Schottenheimer to coach at least one team that makes a Super Bowl appearance. That would immediately distinguish his record from Knox's and make his playoff record more than equal to George Allen's. If he were to win a Super Bowl, Schotten-heimer would then be over the "can't win the big one" hump. Even if he lost a Super Bowl, it would be helpful because it would give him at least some of the potential tragedy angle.

If both of the first two things occur, I think Schottenheimer prob-ably has a 50–50 chance of induction. A Super Bowl win would make him a shoo-in and a loss would probably increase his chances to at least 70–30. If none of them occur, it is almost a cinch that the only gold jacket Schottenheimer will be wearing is one he buys at the local Men's Wearhouse.

9

It Takes a Coaching Acorn to Build a Coaching Tree

There are many arguments presented to explain why blacks are seemingly underrepresented in the NFL's head coaching ranks. The most prevalent of these is that since the player population of the NFL is about 70 percent black, the coaching demographic should be similar or identical.

The idea that the pro coaching ranks should be filled with blacks because of the ratio of black to white players derives from the assumption that coaches are generally drawn from a pool of ex-professional ball players. Sportswriters will often write about this at length, mostly to state their opinion of this being proof, or at least a smoking gun, of the NFL's hidden racism.

I don't want to be too hard on others in the media, but my biggest issue with the writers who push this premise is that none of them (or at least none who I have ever seen) ever asks the question that is most central to their premise: what is the percentage of ex-NFL players in the NFL coaching ranks? There is an assumption that a high percentage of coaches are former players, but what do the numbers say?

To find this out, I ran a three-year study (2004–2006) on the coaching backgrounds of every head coach, offensive/defensive coordinator, and assistant coach in the league. I wanted to see what percentage of each segment of coaches had NFL playing experience, so the only criterion was that the coach had to have spent at least a portion of one season as a player on an NFL roster. Being drafted or participating in a training camp did not count. It also had to be an NFL roster, so coaches who had professional experience in other leagues (CFL, USFL, etc.) were not counted as having NFL experience.

The raw numbers for the study are listed below.

COACHING BACKGROUND

TEAM	TOTAL NO. OF COACHES	NO. OF COACHES W/NFL EXPERIENCE	HEAD COACH	OFF COOR	DEF COOR
			2004		
BAL	20	5	N	Y	N
BUF	16	6	Y	Y	Y
CIN	17	3	N	N	Y
CLE	19	5	N	Y	N
DEN	18	7	N	Y	N
HOU	17	1	N	N	N
IND	16	6	Y	N	N
JAX	17	8	Y	Y	N
KC	21	6	N	N	N
MIA	18	4	N	N	N
NE	14	3	N	N	N
NYJ	18	4	Y	N	N
OAK	18	8	N	Y	N
PIT	13	8	Y	Y	Y
SD	17	4	Y	N	N
TEN	15	4	Y	N	N
ARI	17	4	N	N	N
ATL	18	3	N	N	N
CAR	16	5	N	Y	N
CHI	17	8	N	N	Y
DAL	15	3	N	Y	N
DET	18	5	N	Y	Y
GB	18	4	N	N	N
MIN	16	6	Y	N	Y

(continued)

TEAM	TOTAL NO. OF COACHES	NO. OF COACHES W/NFL EXPERIENCE	HEAD COACH	OFF COOR	DEF COOR
2004 *(continued)*					
NO	19	4	Y	N	N
NYG	17	3	N	Y	Y
PHI	18	2	N	N	Y
STL	18	4	N	N	N
SF	19	1	N	N	N
SEA	16	6	N	N	Y
TB	19	2	N	N	N
WSH	20	4	N	Y	N
Total	555	146	9	12	8
% of Total		26.3%	28.1%	37.5%	25.0%
2005					
BAL	19	4	N	N	N
BUF	15	6	Y	Y	Y
CIN	17	2	N	N	N
CLE	17	7	N	Y	N
DEN	21	8	N	Y	N
HOU	17	1	N	N	N
IND	17	6	Y	N	N
JAX	18	6	Y	N	N
KC	21	6	N	N	N
MIA	20	3	N	N	N
NE	14	1	N	N/A	N
NYJ	17	4	Y	N	N
OAK	19	8	N	Y	N
PIT	13	8	Y	Y	Y
SD	18	6	Y	N	N
TEN	16	4	Y	N	N
ARI	17	5	N	N	N
ATL	19	4	N	N	N
CAR	15	3	N	Y	N
CHI	16	6	N	N	Y
DAL	14	3	N	Y	N
DET	18	5	N	N	Y
GB	18	3	N	N	N
MIN	16	7	Y	N	Y
NO	18	6	Y	N	N

(continued)

COACHING BACKGROUND *(continued)*

TEAM	TOTAL NO. OF COACHES	NO. OF COACHES W/NFL EXPERIENCE	HEAD COACH	OFF COOR	DEF COOR
		2005 *(continued)*			
NYG	18	3	N	Y	Y
PHI	18	1	N	N	Y
STL	19	5	N	N	N
SF	19	2	N	N	N
SEA	16	6	N	N	Y
TB	19	1	N	N	N
WSH	20	5	N	Y	N
Total	559	145	9	9	8
% of Total		25.9%	28.1%	28.1%	25.0%
		2006			
BAL	19	5	N	N	N
BUF	18	4	Y	N	N
CIN	17	2	N	N	N
CLE	17	7	N	Y	N
DEN	21	7	N	Y	N
HOU	16	5	Y	N	N
IND	17	6	Y	N	N
JAX	18	6	Y	N	N
KC	19	7	Y	N	N
MIA	20	3	N	Y	N
NE	13	1	N	N	N
NYJ	20	9	N	N	N
OAK	19	8	Y	N	N
PIT	13	8	Y	Y	Y
SD	17	4	Y	N	N
TEN	16	4	Y	N	N
ARI	17	5	N	N	N
ATL	20	6	N	N	N
CAR	17	3	N	Y	N
CHI	19	6	N	N	Y
DAL	15	3	N	N	N
DET	19	3	N	N	N
GB	19	7	N	N	N
MIN	22	4	N	N	N
NO	17	3	Y	Y	N

(continued)

COACHING BACKGROUND *(continued)*

TEAM	TOTAL NO. OF COACHES	NO. OF COACHES W/NFL EXPERIENCE	HEAD COACH	OFF COOR	DEF COOR
		2006 *(continued)*			
NYG	19	3	N	Y	Y
PHI	17	2	N	N	Y
STL	20	4	N	N	Y
SF	18	3	N	N	N
SEA	20	6	N	N	N
TB	19	2	N	N	N
WSH	20	5	N	Y	N
Total	578	151	10	8	5
% of Total		26.1%	31.3%	25.0%	15.6%

The percentage listed under the "number of coaches with NFL experience" column indicates the percentage of the total coaching ranks that were made up of ex-NFL players. The percentage at the bottom of the Head Coach, Offensive Coordinator, and Defensive Coordinator columns indicates the percentage of each of those jobs that was held by an ex-NFL player.

The first item of note is that the percentage of ex-NFL players in the NFL coaching ranks held quite steady at just around 26 percent for each of the three seasons. There were plenty of coaching changes in the league during this time, so this wasn't a matter of a lack of staff changes limiting coaching movement during the test period.

The second item of note is that very few of the ex-player coaches were big-name players. Many of them played for two seasons or less, and more than a few gained their NFL experience as replacement players during the 1987 strike-shortened season. Many of the coaches also gained their experience at least twenty to thirty years ago, if not more. Given the major changes the league has seen during that time, it isn't a stretch to think some of these coaches would be hard-pressed to use that experience as a way to effectively connect with today's players.

One thing that I was surprised by was the relative lack of value of an NFL playing career on becoming a head coach or a coordinator.

Head coaches and offensive coordinators over this period had NFL playing experience about 30 percent of the time, or only 4 percent more often than any other coach. Having NFL experience didn't seem to be helpful at all when it came to being a defensive coordinator, as only 20 percent of defensive coordinators over this time were NFL alumni.

The 26 percent ex-player composition among the NFL coaching ranks clearly shows that it isn't necessary to have played the game if you want to pursue a coaching career. The one thing that does seem necessary for a prospective NFL coach is to have a college coaching background, as the percentage of coaches who started their coaching career at the NFL level is usually between 18 and 20 percent. That percentage may actually be a bit misleading, as many of the coaches who start at the pro level are strength and conditioning coaches who will not be moving up the coaching ladder. If the nonpositional coaches were removed, the percentage would be much lower.

What this study shows is that the ex-player/coach angle really isn't a valid way to argue for more black coaches. Since 74 percent of the coaches have zero NFL playing experience and 80-plus percent come from collegiate coaching backgrounds, it would seem that the best way to get more black NFL coaches would be to get more black coaches in the college ranks.

Or, to put it another way, the coaching-tree acorns are not going to be found in the ex-players' forest. They are going to be found in the collegiate coaching forest.

PART FOUR

HISTORICAL ICONOCLASM

10

Who Are the Best Hall of Fame Candidates?

Nothing seems to work fans up more than the Hall of Fame advocacy of their favorite players. These fans often start player advocacy movements that are one of the main reasons why the Hall of Fame voters take so much grief every year.

I think a lot of this grief is quite unfair given the overall strength of the Hall of Fame inductees over the years. All one has to do is look at the multitude of undeserving nominees in Cooperstown to appreciate how well the voting process for the Pro Football Hall of Fame has worked.

Having said that, there are more than a few players for whom a very strong case could be made for induction into Canton. The Hall's voters have done a fairly solid job of working their way through some of these players, but there are others whose record is equally as strong who haven't been inducted. What I would like to do here is try to identify the most deserving of the uninducted candidates.

As is the case with the rest of the research in this book, I applied a form of objective methodology in an effort to find the very best of the best. I don't and didn't want this to be a subjective advocacy on my part, but rather a more objective look at which players' records say they are the most deserving of the honor.

The primary goal in choosing a methodology to determine the best available candidates was to try to ensure that it selected candidates who were not going to lower the bar for future inductees. I am of the mindset that once any honorary voting process reaches a certain level of maturity, as the Pro Football Hall of Fame's certainly has, a rule of thumb for future honorees should be that they make the overall accomplishment body of the inducted at least as strong, and hopefully stronger, than when they entered. This shouldn't be a hard-and-fast rule, as there will always be a few induction-worthy exceptions, but by and large a candidate shouldn't be chosen for the Hall unless he meets that requirement.

The methodology I chose in this case revolves around All-Pro nominations. I chose All-Pros as the primary criterion because it is the most difficult honor for a player to achieve. Being picked for an All-Pro team isn't like being picked for the Pro Bowl, which may be the most overrated honor in all of sports. It's not just that many players make the Pro Bowl as second or third alternates because a starter can't participate in the game due to an injury. The Pro Bowl is also the honor about which it is said that if you get overlooked for a deserving pick early in your career, you shouldn't worry because you'll get a pick that you didn't deserve later in your career. Those two nomination aberrations made it fairly easy to eliminate the Pro Bowl as an effective Hall of Fame criterion.

The trouble with using All-Pro picks is that over the years there have been anywhere between two and nine All-Pro teams each season. My remedy for this is to use the consensus All-Pro picks as designated by *The ESPN Pro Football Encyclopedia*. The editors of that book compiled a list of all of the major All-Pro teams for each season and tracked whether a player was a first, second, or third All-Pro selection. The team-level awards were given weighted point totals that rewarded a higher team selection. The editors then awarded the consensus pick to the player with the most points at his position.

Since the Hall of Fame is intended to honor only the best of the best, I decided to place a very heavy bonus weight on the consensus All-Pro achievement. Getting picked for any All-Pro team was worth one point, but getting a consensus All-Pro earned a player three bonus points.

The next step after choosing the achievement bar was to see how the current base of inductees measures up using that bar. There are currently 212 Hall of Famers, all of whom had at least one All-Pro nomination. Those players had a total of 4,170 points in this system, or an average of 19.7 points per player. The players also had 905 consensus All-Pro nominations among them, or an average of 4.3 per player.

Averages for the player totals can be thrown off by some of the inductees who got in on either the strength of their coaching careers (e.g., George Halas, Jimmy Conzelman), or had playing careers that were legendary for reasons other than All-Pro picks (e.g., Jim Thorpe, Red Grange). Because of this, I also decided to review the median totals for each group. The median in system points was 19, but it was right on the precipice of the 20-point total. The median for consensus All-Pro nominations was four. The combination of both comparison types made me choose a 20-point benchmark as the starting point for selecting the highest-value nominees for Canton.

There were two potential downsides to weighing the All-Pro nominations in this manner. The first is that this system doesn't weigh the relative value of the non-consensus years. What I mean by this is that if a player gets one All-Pro vote in a season and another player gets three All-Pro votes, and neither is the consensus All-Pro pick, they still both only get one point. My counter to this would be that while some players would pick up incremental value from this, if you have to add a bunch of small incremental values to better justify a player's greatness, the player's candidacy is probably wanting at some level.

The second downside is if a player's career dovetails with one of the all-time greats at his position. For example, if a linebacker spent the best years of his career trying to compete with Dick Butkus or Lawrence Taylor for All-Pro spots, he would be hard-pressed to gain points in this measurement. The good news on this front is that the Hall of Fame voters tend to be very sensitive to this type of situation. There are numerous middle linebackers in the Hall who played at the same time as Butkus, just as there are many running backs from Jim Brown's era who were granted Hall of Fame status. The only player I found who was negatively impacted in this system by such an occurrence was Derrick Thomas. I still believe the odds are quite good that Thomas will get inducted into the Hall soon enough, so his exclusion from this table doesn't concern me that much.

With no further ado, here are the players who scored 20 points or more in this system. Please keep in mind that this list does not include players who aren't eligible yet due to being retired for less than five seasons.

RANK	PLAYER	ALL-PRO	CONSENSUS	POINTS
1	Bruce Smith	12	8	36
2	Jim Tyrer	10	8	34
3	Randall McDaniel	11	6	29
T4	Rod Woodson	9	6	27
T4	Ray Guy	9	6	27
T6	Lavvie Dilweg	8	6	26
T6	Larry Grantham	11	5	26
8	Mick Tingelhoff	7	6	25
9	Mac Speedie	6	6	24
T10	Johnny Robinson	8	5	23
T10	Al Wistert	8	5	23
T12	Bruno Banducci	7	5	22
T12	Dave Grayson	7	5	22
T12	Bob Talamini	7	5	22
T15	Dick Barwegan	6	5	21
T15	Dermontti Dawson	6	5	21
T15	Ox Emerson	6	5	21
T15	Jimmy Patton	6	5	21
T19	Mel Gray	8	4	20
T19	Jim McMillen	5	5	20
T19	Del Shofner	5	5	20
T19	Steve Wisniewski	8	4	20
T19	Riley Matheson	8	4	20

I didn't plan it out this way, but there are two things that I like about this list. The first is that it turned out players from every era in NFL history. The second is that many of these players don't have the advantage of being touted by a vocal advocacy group. Their career records say they are deserving of being considered, but because in many cases they lack such a group, they often aren't being as strongly considered as some others are.

Even though these candidates' All-Pro point totals say they should be inducted, an All-Pro total does not necessarily a Hall of Fame candidate make (as Master Yoda might say). Let's take a closer look at each of these players' histories to see how strong their candidacy really is.

1. **Bruce Smith: Defensive end, 1988–1999 Buffalo Bills, 2000–2002 Washington Redskins**

Smith is a sure-fire first ballot shoo-in for the 2009 Hall of Fame class.

2. **Jim Tyrer: Offensive tackle, 1961–1973 Dallas Texans/Kansas City Chiefs, 1974 Washington Redskins**

Out of all of the candidates on this list, Tyrer is easily the one who would cause the most controversy were his name to be brought before the Hall's voters. From an on-the-field standpoint, Tyrer is a no-brainer Hall of Famer. He is generally regarded as the best run-blocking tackle in AFL history and was on the first team All-Time AFL squad.

The reason Tyrer isn't in the Hall of Fame already is that on September 15, 1980, depressed over some recent financial setbacks, he shot and killed his wife and then committed suicide.

I am of a mixed mind-set on the Tyrer candidacy because someone very close to me suffered from depression late in her life and eventually committed suicide. Anytime I think back on this person, I try to remember the good times we had as opposed to the very sad end. That thought makes me lean toward inducting Tyrer, as it would celebrate the good parts of his life.

The flip side of this obviously is that Tyrer didn't just commit suicide; he also killed someone. While I understand why this should keep Tyrer out of the Hall of Fame, I will ask this question. If O. J. Simpson had been found guilty of double murder in the criminal trial, would his Hall of Fame candidacy have been revoked? My understanding of the situation is that it would not have been revoked no matter what the outcome of the trial turned out to be. The Hall's belief is that once a player has been inducted, he cannot be removed from the Hall because of off-the-field incidents. In the O.J. case, what the Hall is essentially saying is that his on-field accomplishments are the only things that should be considered.

If that's the case, then why should Tyrer not be viewed by the same set of rules? Shouldn't the Hall's voters be precluded from taking any off-field incidents into account? Does it really matter if Tyrer killed someone before his induction and Simpson after his? Is the Hall's eye all-seeing before the induction and completely blind after it?

The answer, in my view, is that of course the voters should be precluded from taking off-field incidents into account. In fact, they did overlook the incident one time in Tyrer's case. His last season in the NFL was 1974, so he was eligible for induction consideration starting with the 1980 voting. He obviously didn't make the Hall in the 1980 voting and he wasn't even a finalist that year.

In the 1981 voting, however, Tyrer was a finalist. I don't know if he was named a finalist before or after the tragedy. When I contacted the Hall to try to find out when the 1981 finalist list was compiled, I was told that the voters created the list in secret back then and the compilation date was therefore unknown.

In the long run, though, it doesn't really matter when the list was compiled. If it was before the incident, the voters left Tyrer's name on the list even after he murdered someone. If it was after, the voters still thought enough of his accomplishments to overlook his postcareer issues.

That means that at one time, the voters were willing to grade Tyrer based on his on-field accomplishments. If they were willing to do it once, why can't they do it again? It would be very tough for the voters to put Tyrer in the Hall in today's climate when the NFL is going through more than a small amount of bad off-field PR due to player run-ins with the law. At some point, though, they should adopt a consistent approach with regards to off-field incidents and put Tyrer in Canton.

Bottom line: In my book, it is only the on-field accomplishments that matter when it comes to Hall of Fame voting. Tyrer deserves induction.

3. Randall McDaniel: Offensive guard, 1988–1999 Minnesota Vikings, 2001 Tampa Bay Buccaneers

The primary reason that McDaniel is not yet in the Hall of Fame is that he has only been eligible for induction for two seasons. McDaniel had eleven All-Pro nominations over his career and every eligible player with that many nominations has been inducted into the Hall.

Bottom line: McDaniel deserves induction and his wait for the honor will not be very long.

T4. Ray Guy: Punter, 1973–1986 Oakland/Los Angeles Raiders

That Guy has not yet been inducted into the Hall of Fame should be seen as something of an embarrassment for the Hall of Fame voters. Guy is one of only five eligible players with a combination of at least nine All-Pros and six consensus All-Pros who is not in the Hall. Two of the other four are Smith and Woodson, who will almost certainly be first-ballot Hall of Famers. The other pair of noninductees are Tyrer and McDaniel, and obviously both of them should already have been inducted.

If that wasn't enough reason to put Guy into Canton, consider this. There were fifty-eight players elected to the NFL's 75th Anniversary All-Time team. Fifty-four of those players are already in the Hall of Fame. Of the four not in the Hall, two are not currently eligible (Jerry Rice and Rod Woodson). The only two eligible players on the 75th Anniversary All-Time team who are not inducted in Canton are Guy and Billy "White Shoes" Johnson. There is no reason Guy should not be seen as being equal to the rest of the players on that list, so that is another reason to consider him induction-worthy.

Some Hall of Fame voters might argue that a punter should not be inducted into the Hall because, after all, he's just a punter. That argument makes little sense, because the punter position has been deemed valuable enough to receive every other accolade the media can offer. The punter position has received All-Pro recognition since 1964 and it has also been a position on every All-Decade team since the 1960s. If punters are worthy enough to be voted on for the Pro Bowl, All-Pro, All-Decade, and All-Time teams, why isn't the most decorated punter of all time worthy of receiving the highest honor in the sport?

The other argument against Guy has come from *Sports Illustrated*'s Paul "Dr. Z" Zimmerman. Zimmerman contends that Guy's career numbers are not good enough to warrant his entry into the Hall.

While I understand where Zimmerman is coming from on this front, there are two retorts I would make. First, punting statistics are difficult to put into context because of two factors: field position and coverage units.

Field position limits the amount of yards a punter can try to kick for. Nothing illustrates this limitation better than the career punt averages for the best punters of all time. There is not even a one-yard distance difference between the punter with the fifth best gross average (Todd Sauerbrun, 43.99 yards) of all time and the punter with the twenty-fourth best average (Josh Miller, 43.08 yards).

Dr. Z's workaround for this is to look at net punting averages and point out that Guy's numbers in this arena were not up to Hall of Fame par. I might have been inclined to agree with him until I spoke with an NFL special teams coach about this very subject.

I asked the coach about the punter's role in coverage and he said that the only thing that is asked of the punter is to get enough hang time. He said as long as the punter gets four seconds of hang time on a 40-yard punt or five seconds on a 50-yard punt, then that should be sufficient for the coverage units to get downfield. Hang time was never an issue for Guy so unless it can be shown that he was lacking in that area, the net punting argument does not hold water in my view.

The second retort is the last and most important point I could make in Guy's favor. Dr. Z's statistics notwithstanding, almost all of his contemporaries disagreed with his assessment of Guy's punting prowess. There didn't seem to be any doubt in their minds, either, as in every consensus All-Pro season, Guy was named first-team on all of the All-Pro teams that picked punters. As much as I respect Dr. Z's opinion in football matters, the overwhelming opinion of the football writing community in Guy's day was that he was by far and hands down the best punter in the league. If that doesn't say Hall of Famer, I don't know what does.

Bottom line: It won't be long before Guy will have to be nominated by the Seniors Committee instead of by the Selection Committee. Since there are so many other viable senior candidates on the list today, the voters should put Guy into Canton before that point.

T4. Rod Woodson: Cornerback/Safety/Kick returner, 1987–1996 Pittsburgh Steelers, 1997 San Francisco 49ers, 1998–2001 Baltimore Ravens, 2002–2003 Oakland Raiders

Woodson is another first-ballot Hall of Famer who is almost certain to get inducted with the 2009 class.

T6. Lavvie Dilweg: End, 1926 Milwaukee Badgers, 1927–1934 Green Bay Packers

Dilweg's All-Pro nominations make a great case for his Canton candidacy, but they might not even be the strongest argument in his favor. Dilweg is one of only eighteen players who were named to the NFL's 1920s All-Decade team. Sixteen of the other players on that team are in Canton. Add these two factors together and it becomes clear that Dilweg's entry into the Hall would raise the induction bar level for everyone else. That alone is a great reason to put him in.

Bottom line: Dilweg might have trouble getting nominated by the Seniors Committee because candidates from the 1920s and 1930s historically haven't made the list that often. That has been changing of late, so it could bode well for Dilweg. I believe an argument could be made that Dilweg is the strongest senior candidate available, and he most certainly deserves induction.

T6. Larry Grantham: Linebacker, 1960–1972 New York Titans/Jets

Grantham's reputation suffers in part from his being an All-Pro during the AFL's early days. While I can understand some of the hesitance of voters to give equal credit to some of the AFL's early All-Pros, that shouldn't apply to Grantham for one reason. He was still being voted to the All-Pro team well after the AFL was close to a parity level with the NFL. Grantham was a consensus AFL All-Pro from 1960 to 1964 and most football historians would probably concur with the idea that the AFL was quite close to a parity level with the NFL by 1964. If that is the case, Grantham was proving that his early All-Pro nominations were not a fluke.

The best argument against Grantham is that his later All-Pro nominations were mostly on the second All-Pro team. Even with that caveat, it shows that he kept up a quality level of performance for eleven seasons. Add that to his early level of dominance and it shows why he is worthy of serious Hall of Fame consideration.

Bottom line: This is a tough call. Grantham has a good case, but in all honesty there are many other players who have stronger candidacies than him, including a good number from the AFL. Until some of those players are voted in, Grantham should be passed over.

8. Mick Tingelhoff: Center, 1962–1978 Minnesota Vikings

Tingelhoff is one of my personal favorites for induction. From 1964 to 1969, he was easily the best center in the NFL. He was the consensus All-Pro in each of these years and most of the time it wasn't even a very close race.

He would already be a Hall of Famer were it not for Super Bowl IV. The Vikings faced the Chiefs and Tingelhoff had to face off against Kansas City's monster tackles, Curley Culp and Buck Buchanan. Tingelhoff's listed weight was only 237 pounds, so speed was his game. Culp and Buchanan were both giants (Culp was 6'2", 265 pounds, Buchanan 6'7", 270 pounds), and Tingelhoff was simply not big or strong enough to handle these two.

Tingelhoff's reputation took a hit in that game from which it never recovered. But to paraphrase a famous saying, one game does not a career make. Super Bowl IV should not have dulled the luster of over a half decade worth of dominance to the extent that Tingelhoff be denied induction.

Bottom line: Tingelhoff is a great candidate on many levels, and the Seniors Committee should put him on their short list.

9. Mac Speedie: End, 1946–1952 Cleveland Browns

Whenever AAFC candidates are brought up in a Hall of Fame discussion, it is almost always said that the rival league was not quite up to the standard of the NFL. The AAFC isn't even seen as being the historic equal of the AFL because the AFL had all ten of its teams absorbed into the league, while the AAFC had but three of its teams taken in. One of the AAFC teams, Baltimore, lasted only year before closing up shop, so it really ended up being only two teams. If you want to get the full sense of how minor a league the AAFC is considered by some, just know that the AAFC's win-loss records are not even included in the NFL record books.

The denigration of the AAFC's place in history is the main reason that Speedie is not in the Hall, but should that be the case? How much credit should AAFC players get for their non-NFL accomplishments?

While researching this, I happened to run across an excellent article on NFLhistory.net about this very subject and how it relates to Speedie's Hall of Fame candidacy. Andy Piascik, the article's author, does a very good job of illustrating why the AAFC should be considered a major league.

Piascik points out that the ratio of AAFC to NFL players in 1950, the first year after the AAFC teams came over to the NFL, was almost exactly the same as it was in 1949. Piascik says the NFL comprised 59 percent of the players in 1949 and 59.6 percent in 1950. That is strong evidence to support a claim that the AAFC was at least very close to being equal in overall strength.

The one area where I might be inclined to approach the issue a bit differently than Piascik is Hall of Fame representation numbers. Piascik states that the AAFC and the NFL had similar ratios of Hall of Famers when comparing the number of Hall inductees against the number of total players in each league. He then compares this figure with the ratio of the AFL/NFL Hall of Famers on rosters in 1960 to show that the AAFC was stronger at the beginning of its tenure than the AFL was at its start.

The tack I might take on this front is that Hall of Famers aren't your typical players, so therefore to compare the inductee/overall player ratio is only part of the story. Another way to approach this is to see how well the AAFC's great players are represented when compared with the NFL's great players. As I have done in the rest of this chapter, I will use a consensus All-Pro pick as a barometer of single-season greatness.

Let's start by taking a look at the consensus All-Pros in the NFL from 1946 to 1949, with players in bold being current Hall of Famers.

- 1946: Jim Benton, Jim Poole, Jim White, Al Wistert, Riley Matheson, Len Younce, **Bulldog Turner**, **Sid Luckman**, **Bill Dudley**, **Steve Van Buren**, Ted Fritsch

- 1947: Ken Kavanaugh, Mal Kutner, Al Wistert, Fred Davis, Riley Matheson, Buster Ramsey, **Bulldog Turner**, **Sid Luckman**, **Steve Van Buren**, **Bill Dudley**, Pat Harder

- 1948: Mal Kutner, **Pete Pihos**, Al Wistert, Dick Huffman, Buster Ramsey, Ray Bray, **Bulldog Turner**, **Sammy Baugh**, **Charley Trippi**, **Steve Van Buren**, Pat Harder

- 1949: **Pete Pihos**, Ed Sprinkle, **Tom Fears**, Dick Huffman, **George Connor**, Buster Ramsey, Ray Bray, Fred Naumetz, **Bob Waterfield**, **Steve Van Buren**, **Tony Canadeo**, Elmer Angsman, Pat Harder

Now compare that to the AAFC consensus All-Pros, again with Hall of Famers listed in bold:

- 1946: **Dante Lavelli**, Mac Speedie, Jack Russell, Alyn Beals, **Bruiser Kinard**, Martin Ruby, Bill Radovich, Bruno Banducci, Robert Nelson, Frankie Albert, Glenn Dobbs, Spec Sanders, **Marion Motley**

- 1947: Mac Speedie, Jack Russell, Lou Rymkus, Nate Johnson, Bruno Banducci, Dick Barwegan, Robert Nelson, **Otto Graham**, Spec Sanders, Chet Mutryn, **Marion Motley**

- 1948: Mac Speedie, Alyn Beals, Bob Reinhard, Lou Rymkus, Dick Barwegan, **Bill Willis**, Lou Saban, **Otto Graham**, Johnny Strzykalski, Chet Mutryn, **Marion Motley**

- 1949: Mac Speedie, Alyn Beals, **Arnie Weinmeister**, Lou Rymkus, John Kissell, Dick Barwegan, Visco Grgich, Lou Saban, **Otto Graham**, Chet Mutryn, Buddy Young, **Joe Perry**

Now let's add these up and see how the numbers compare. The totals below show the number of consensus All-Pros in each season, and how many of those were Hall of Famers:

YEAR/LEAGUE	CONSENSUS ALL-PROS	HALL OF FAMERS
1946 NFL	11	4
1946 AAFC	13	3
1947 NFL	11	4
1947 AAFC	11	2
1948 NFL	11	5
1948 AAFC	11	3
1949 NFL	13	6
1949 AAFC	12	3
NFL Total	46	19
AAFC Total	47	11

The NFL has 41.3 percent of its consensus All-Pros in the Hall of Fame, while the AAFC lags behind at a 23.4 percent pace. The AAFC's total also includes one year from Bruiser Kinard, an NFL great who had jumped leagues at the end of his career. Take Kinard out and the AAFC percentage drops to 21.7 percent.

That leads me to believe that the Hall is underrepresented from an AAFC point of view, probably one or two players short of where it should be.

The odd part of this is that Mac Speedie is one of the players who got the short end of this stick. Speedie was a dominant player in the AAFC and then dominated just as well when he joined the NFL, with two consensus All-Pros in the three seasons he played in the merged league.

Speedie's problem was that Paul Brown could be an extremely vindictive man when it came to players or coaches who crossed him, and Speedie definitely crossed Brown more than once. Speedie's Wikipedia entry says that he brought a skunk to camp once and named it Paul. Mac also felt he was underpaid, which was a primary reason he decided to leave the Browns and take on a higher salary with the Saskatchewan Rough Riders in the Western Interprovincial Football Union (otherwise known as the CFL). Brown is said not to have forgotten the incident, and Speedie claimed that Brown helped keep him out of the Hall by persuading voters not to vote for him.

Bottom line: With all due respect to the memory of Paul Brown, Speedie should have been put into the Hall a long time ago.

T10. Johnny Robinson: Safety, 1960–1971 Dallas Texans/Kansas City Chiefs

Robinson's case is one that makes me believe that maybe Ange Coniglio has a point about the Hall of Fame voters having it in for the AFL. Ange runs a Web site called Remember the AFL (www.remembertheAFL.com), and he has to be one of the most passionate football fans I have ever met. I don't think it is a stretch to say that to Ange the AFL-NFL war never really ended. He is constantly sending out e-mail updates and press releases covering a variety of subjects, and he is on a mission to get the NFL to celebrate the fifty-year anniversary of the AFL.

When I started to put together this chapter, I e-mailed Ange and asked him to send me a list of the top AFL Hall of Fame candidates. Ange touts many AFLers as Hall candidates, but he had Robinson first on his list, so that says a lot for how Robinson is viewed by hard-core historians.

What also says a lot for Robinson is that the AFL got screwed when it came to putting its best people into the Hall. For proof, just consider this. There are fifty people on the AFL's All-Time team. Of these fifty, only fourteen are inducted in Canton. Three of the fourteen were George Blanda, Weeb Ewbank, and Sid Gillman, all of whom had long NFL careers to go along with their AFL achievements, so it could be accurately said that only eleven out of the forty-seven AFL-heavy nominees have been inducted.

Compare that record with the NFL's 1960s All-Decade team. Of the forty players on that team, twenty-five are inducted in Canton. That's 23 percent of the best AFL players in the Hall versus 63 percent of the NFL's best players. The AFL may not have been considered an equal league talent-wise in its first couple of years, but for the bulk of its existence it was pretty damn close to the NFL. It could also be argued that by 1969 the AFL had passed the NFL as the better league, at the very least in terms of the top teams. That the Hall of Fame induction rate of NFL players during the same time frame is two and a half times higher than the AFL not only simply doesn't add up, it is a travesty.

As far as how this relates to Robinson's candidacy, let me put it this way. Robinson's All-Pro years were 1963 and 1965–1971. He had dominated the AFL during its later years when it was the NFL's equal and then carried that dominance over to his two NFL seasons. He was even a consensus All-Pro alongside the all-time great safety Larry Wilson in 1970. If Robinson was good enough to be considered on the same level as Wilson in 1970, there is no reason he should not be in the Hall of Fame today.

Bottom line: It would quite appropriate if Robinson were inducted in 2009 in conjunction with an AFL fiftieth anniversary celebration.

T10. Al Wistert: Offensive tackle, offensive guard, defensive tackle, 1943 Phil-Pitt Steagles, 1944–1951 Philadelphia Eagles

Wistert's case will start the run of great linemen of the 1930s and 1940s who deserve Hall of Fame induction. The linemen in the All-Decade team for both of these eras are sorely underrepresented in Canton. To illustrate this point, here are the induction percentages for the All-Decade offensive linemen from the 1920s to the 1980s:

- 1920s: seven out of eight offensive linemen inducted (87.5%)

- 1930s: three out of ten offensive linemen inducted (30%)

- 1940s: four out of fourteen offensive linemen inducted (28.6%)

- 1950s: four out of six offensive linemen inducted (66.6%)

- 1960s: four out of seven NFL offensive linemen inducted (57.1%) and three out of ten AFL offensive linemen inducted (30%), for a total of seven out of seventeen offensive linemen inducted (41.1%)

- 1970s: ten out of ten offensive linemen inducted (100%)

- 1980s: six out of ten offensive linemen inducted (60%)

Every other decade outside of the 1930s and 1940s has at least 40 percent of their offensive linemen inducted, so those two decades are certainly underrepresented.

They weren't the only ones. As I detailed earlier, the AFL also got the short end of the induction stick overall and this position was no different. If the AFL offensive linemen numbers were removed from the equation, the overall induction rate of All-Decade linemen from the other decades is 73 percent, or over two and a half times as high as the 1930s/1940s induction rate. That clearly shows that the Seniors Committee needs to place some emphasis on the best line candidates of those eras.

Wistert would be the best place to start to correct this. In addition to being nominated for five consecutive consensus All-Pros, he played in three consecutive championship games in 1947–1949, two of which the Eagles won. There are those that would say that Wistert benefited from playing during the war years, but three of his consensus All-Pros came in 1946–1948, after the war was over.

Bottom line: Putting Wistert in the Hall would honor his era, his position, and his team, all of which are in need of additional representation.

T10. Bruno Banducci: Offensive guard, 1944–1945 Philadelphia Eagles, 1946–1954 San Francisco 49ers

In the Mac Speedie section, I spoke of the AAFC being short two Hall of Famers. At first glance I thought that Bruno Banducci would be the second candidate. I am not so sure of that now for a couple of reasons.

The first is the seeming sparseness of his historical record. I like to consider myself a pretty knowledgeable football historian. I bought my first *NFL Record & Fact Book* when I was nine years old and wore it just about completely out. I have dozens of pro football encyclopedias in my collection and have spent hundreds of hours poring over them. I have traveled as far north as Connecticut and as far west as Washington State to comb used bookstores for old football tomes. I have football instruction manuals dating back to the 1920s and even have original copies of books written by Pop Warner and Amos Alonzo Stagg. I also have an extensive library of football videos and magazines and have been a member of the Pro Football Researchers Association on and off for about fifteen years.

All of this study has led to me to be pretty familiar with many players from many eras, but Banducci is one name that I hadn't heard of before doing this study. After I saw him on the list, I made an effort to find out more about him.

First, I went through my library and found some San Francisco 49ers history books. I perused every page of these books and could barely find a mention of Banducci. In one book, the only time Banducci's name came up was in a team photo.

I then went to Google and looked up Banducci there. Again, I found almost nothing on him. There was a Wikipedia entry that said he was a professional football player of Italian American descent, but that was about it. Even the Web sites dedicated to the 49ers would only have a mention of his name because it was on the annual rosters. Nowhere on these sites could I find a mention of great deeds by Banducci from his teammates or opponents.

The lack of mention in any of the reference material makes him come across rather like a fireman who walks out of a burning building with a child in his arms. You know he probably did something noteworthy, but without more corroboration you really can't say with specificity what it was.

The second issue is that although Banducci had five consensus All-Pro picks, even they don't speak too well for his candidacy. I say this because his first two consensus All-Pros came in 1946–1947, during the AAFC's first two seasons. As I pointed out in the Speedie comment, the AAFC should not be seen as a minor league, but as the league progressed, Banducci didn't, or at least he didn't in the All-Pro voters' eyes. He was absent from the All-Pro roster from 1948 until 1951, when he was chosen as a second team All-Pro on the UPI roster.

Fast-forward to 1952–1954 when Banducci makes three straight consensus All-Pro teams. As impressive as this showing is, I take it with a grain of salt because the 49ers added Leo Nomellini and Bob St. Clair to their offensive line right around this time. Nomellini had a Hall of Fame career as a defensive tackle but he made consensus All-Pro as an offensive tackle in 1951 and 1952. St. Clair is a Hall of Famer, so he also represented a big upgrade. That Banducci wasn't an All-Pro nominee before these two arrived and was suddenly a consensus All-Pro afterward makes me a bit leery about his credentials, especially given the lack of ancillary anecdotal evidence.

Bottom line: Add it up and I would give Banducci's candidacy a no.

T12. Dave Grayson: Cornerback/Safety, 1961–1962 Dallas Texans, 1963–1964 Kansas City Chiefs, 1965–1970 Oakland Raiders

Grayson is the Darrell Evans of the NFL. In his *New Historical Baseball Abstract,* Bill James said that Evans was the most underrated player in baseball history. The two main reasons James cites for Evans's being overlooked are:

1. He had a wide variety of skills but did not do one thing exceptionally well.

2. A good amount of his value came from "undocumented skills," or things that cannot be tracked by statistics.

James points out that when a player can't hang his hat on a few items of note, it is often hard for the public and press to remember his accomplishments over the long term. Had Evans been more of a home run hitter or a defensive wizard, his accomplishments would have stayed in baseball fans' collective memory much longer.

Grayson's candidacy suffers from similar issues in that he changed both teams and positions in midcareer. He made his first All-Pro team in 1963 with Kansas City as a cornerback. He then notched a consensus All-Pro for the Chiefs in 1964, also at cornerback.

Grayson moved to the Raiders in 1965 and was voted for his second and third consensus All-Pros at cornerback in 1965 and 1966. Just as his reputation as a great cornerback was being cemented, he was moved to safety, but that didn't stop him from posting consecutive consensus All-Pros at that position in 1968 and 1969.

Grayson was named to the first team AFL All-Time team, so he was certainly thought of very highly by those who saw him play. Even so, today's voters probably have trouble of knowing how to slot him. He was a great cornerback but only played there for a few years. He played for some very good Chiefs and Raiders teams but didn't stay with those teams long enough to be thought of as one of those teams' great players. When you think of the Chiefs secondary around that time, Emmitt Thomas or Johnny Robinson will come to mind before Grayson. The same thing goes for the Raiders, as Willie Brown or Jack Tatum will always be thought of before Grayson.

Unless the voters make a concerted effort to review Grayson as an individual and not as a cornerback, safety, Chief, or Raider, he'll be hard-pressed to get induction.

Bottom line: That doesn't mean Grayson should be overlooked. In my view, he would make another great AFL candidate for the 2009 fiftieth anniversary of that league.

T12. Bob Talamini: Offensive guard, 1960–1967 Houston Oilers, 1968 New York Jets

Talamini is another player who likely carries the stigma of having excelled during the AFL's formative days. The best way to illustrate that his credentials should not be looked down upon is to see which other AFL offensive linemen he was paired up with during his consensus All-Pro years. Here is the list, with current Hall of Famers in bold:

- 1962: Eldon Danenhauer, Al Jamison, **Ron Mix**, **Jim Otto**
- 1963: **Ron Mix**, Jim Tyrer, **Billy Shaw**, **Jim Otto**
- 1964: **Ron Mix**, Stew Barber, **Billy Shaw**, **Jim Otto**
- 1965: Jim Tyrer, **Ron Mix**, **Billy Shaw**, **Jim Otto**
- 1967: **Ron Mix**, Jim Tyrer, Walt Sweeney, **Jim Otto**

This shows that Talamini shouldn't be seen as one of the AFL's early-year wonders. He wasn't Eldon Danenhauer or Al Jamison. Talamini kept up with the Ron Mixes and Jim Ottos and Billy Shaws of his day. He might not have dominated for the length of time that Mix, Tyrer, and Otto did, but five consensus All-Pros is still pretty damned impressive, especially given the company he was keeping on those teams.

Bottom line: Talamini is something like Grantham in that his record is quite good, but there are others with more impressive marks. I would put Tyrer and Johnny Robinson in before Talamini.

T15. Dick Barwegan: Offensive guard, 1947 New York Yankees (AAFC), 1948–1949 Baltimore Colts (AAFC), 1950–1952 Chicago Bears, 1953–1954 Baltimore Colts

Barwegan's candidacy suffers from some of the same issues as Speedie's in that three of his five consensus All-Pros came in the AAFC. His showing in the AAFC All-Pro listing could have been even more impressive than Speedie's, however, because Barwegan played with two different teams while in the AAFC. He got his first consensus All-Pro with the Yankees in 1947 and then ran off two in a row with Baltimore in 1948 and 1949.

Barwegan then switched teams again, joining the Bears in 1950. He made consensus All-Pros with Chicago during his first two seasons there, so that makes it three teams he won that honor with.

As if that weren't impressive enough, take a look at which players Barwegan shared the consensus All-Pro honor with during his consensus years: Bruno Banducci, Bill Willis, Visco Grgich, Bill Willis again, and Lou Creekmur. Willis and Creekmur are both Hall of Famers and Banducci is on this list, so that is excellent company. Add to that Barwegan's being on the 1950s All-Decade team and it is clear that he would obviously be a great number two AAFC candidate to go along with Speedie.

Bottom line: He shouldn't go in before Speedie. Once that happens, Barwegan would be a great candidate for his era.

T15. Dermontti Dawson: Center, 1988–2000 Pittsburgh Steelers

I don't have a lot to say about Dawson's candidacy because he has only been available for voter discussion for three seasons as of this writing. His credentials are such that the odds are quite good that he will likely be voted in very soon.

Bottom line: He'll be in Canton shortly.

T15. Ox Emerson: Guard/Center, 1931–1937 Portsmouth Spartans/Detroit Lions, 1938 Brooklyn Dodgers

Emerson in some ways is to the 1930s what Wistert and Banducci were to the 1940s. He is one of the great guards in an era that is underrepresented. Emerson was a consensus All-Pro pick for five consecutive seasons. He was also a member of the 1930s All-Decade team and played in two NFL championship games, winning one with Detroit in 1935.

Bottom line: Emerson is not only a viable candidate, but he is probably the last of the viable 1930s candidates. At some point the voters should put him in and effectively close out the voting on players from that era.

T15. Jimmy Patton: Safety, 1955–1966 New York Giants

Patton may be the most overlooked player from the Giants' 1950s championship teams. He was named consensus All-Pro every season from 1958 to 1962.

Possibly the best way to put Patton's five consecutive consensus All-Pro nominations into perspective is to see how that accomplishment matches up against the safeties currently inducted in Canton. Here is the list.

SAFETY	ALL-PRO	CONSENSUS
Jack Christiansen	6	5
Ken Houston	12	5
Paul Krause	9	3
Yale Lary	8	5
Emlen Tunnell	8	4
Larry Wilson	8	6
Willie Wood	10	5

(Ronnie Lott and Mel Renfro are also Hall of Famers who played safety, but since they split their time between safety and cornerback, I didn't include them in this comparison.)

As impressive as Patton's six All-Pros/five consensus showing seems on the face of it, it really doesn't fare that well when compared to these all-time greats. Patton would rank last in All-Pros and only in front of two players in the consensus column.

Bottom line: It is very hard to back a player's candidacy when it would lower the bar of excellence for his position, and that is what inducting Patton would do. Because of this, I have to give his candidacy a no.

T19. Mel Gray: Kick returner, 1986–1988 New Orleans Saints, 1989–1994 Detroit Lions, 1995–1997 Houston/Tennessee Oilers, 1997 Philadelphia Eagles

With as many strong candidates as there are on this list, it is going to be exceptionally hard to make a case for putting in a pure special teams player like Gray, especially with Ray Guy still not having been inducted. Nevertheless, Gray's eight All-Pros and four consensus picks do set him apart from just about every other special teams player not named Guy.

On a side note, the biggest impact on Gray's candidacy could come from Steve Tasker. Tasker had seven All-Pros during his career. Since only a couple of the All-Pro teams in *The ESPN Pro Football Encyclopedia* had a spot for a special teams specialist, that position wasn't considered one that would have a consensus pick. Tasker did win five first-team All-Pro spots, though, and in my mind that should probably count as a consensus All-Pro. If his picks were seen in that light, he would have 22 points in this list, which would rank him tied for twelfth, or ahead of Gray.

Bottom line: Gray was a very good player, but I think the consensus would be that Tasker was a better special teams player. Gray's candidacy will have to wait for Tasker rather than the other way around.

T19. Jim McMillen: Guard, 1924–1928 Chicago Bears

McMillen's case is strong in some areas and weak in others. He was an All-Pro in every season that he played, so that is a huge strength. But the fact that he played only five seasons limits his induction chances. The reason McMillen ended his career on top is that he decided to devote all of his energies to working on his highly successful professional wrestling career. You could say McMillen was the Rock or Stone Cold of his day, as he was a championship-level performer in the squared circle.

No matter his reasons for leaving, McMillen's overall accomplishments may leave him just a bit short. He didn't make the 1920s All-Decade team, so that is a point against him. How much his lack of nomination on that team had to do with resentment over the large amount of money he made in the ring (he actually helped George Halas bankroll his effort to take over the Bears from Ed Sternaman) cannot be determined. Nevertheless, unless it can be argued that McMillen was a Gale Sayers type of comet-across-the-sky player, he really can't be considered a viable Hall of Fame candidate. Since it can't be said for certain that he was that kind of player, it pretty much cinches that he doesn't qualify under the Sayers exception.

Bottom line: McMillen deserves to be remembered but is not really worthy of a bust.

T19. Del Shofner: End/Defensive back, 1957–1960 Los Angeles Rams, 1961–1967 New York Giants

The best way to put Shofner's five consensus All-Pro nominations into perspective is to see how he matches up in that category against the eighteen modern-era wide receivers in the Hall of Fame today.

WIDE RECEIVER	ALL-PRO	CONSENSUS
Lance Alworth	7	7
Pete Pihos	8	5
Paul Warfield	8	4
Raymond Berry	6	3
Fred Biletnikoff	6	2
Tom Fears	5	2
Elroy "Crazylegs" Hirsch	4	2
Dante Lavelli	6	2
James Lofton	6	2
Lynn Swann	3	2
Michael Irvin	3	1
Steve Largent	8	1
Bobby Mitchell	5	1

(continued)

(continued)

WIDE RECEIVER	ALL-PRO	CONSENSUS
Art Monk	3	1
John Stallworth	2	1
Charley Taylor	10	1
Charlie Joiner	2	0
Don Maynard	5	0
Tommy McDonald	4	0

Since one of Pihos's consensus All-Pros came as a defensive end, it can be accurately stated that Shofner has more consensus All-Pro picks at wide receiver than all but one current Hall of Famer. In fact, since there are no other wide receivers on this top twenty list, Shofner actually has more consensus All-Pros than any other wide receiver currently eligible for induction. His history shows a consistent record of excellence that, when combined with his affiliation with a championship-caliber team, makes a compelling case for his induction.

Bottom line: Putting Shofner in the Hall would raise the bar for future candidates, and that is always a good thing. Put him in.

T19. Steve Wisniewski: Offensive guard, 1989–2001 Oakland/Los Angeles Raiders

The case for Wisniewski's Hall of Fame candidacy is nearly identical to Dermontti Dawson's in that he has only been a candidate for a very short time. The only thing that might keep him from being inducted would be his reputation as a do-anything-to-win type of player. That didn't keep him from racking up plenty of All-Pro recognition, though, so the odds are quite good that won't keep him out of the Hall, either.

Bottom line: Wisniewski shouldn't go in before Randall McDaniel or Dermontti Dawson, but he should be the very next in line after those two.

T19. Riley Matheson: Guard, 1939–1942 Cleveland Rams, 1943 Detroit Lions, 1944–1947 Cleveland/Los Angeles Rams

For Matheson's nomination, I once again turn to the NFLhistory.net article by Andy Piascik. Piascik points out that most of Matheson's best seasons came when the war depleted NFL rosters. He also says that the guard position was hit especially hard, as Aldo Forte, Ray Bray, Buster Ramsey, Russ Letlow, Dick Barwegan, and Len Younce, some of the best guards of the era, missed a combined seventeen seasons due to military service. Piascik says that because Matheson's All-Pro credentials were boosted due to the war, his candidacy is not quite as strong as it would seem on its face.

Piascik's comments remind me of a comment my brother Scott made about the Beatles a few years ago that I have never forgotten. Scott had recently spoken with some people who thought that some of the Beatles' songs should be noted as having been written by an individual rather than by the band as a whole. For example, "Yesterday" was pretty much written entirely by Paul McCartney. To those people, it wasn't really a Beatles tune but rather a Paul McCartney song performed by the Beatles.

Scott thought this line of thinking to be nonsense since the band had decided long ago that their songs were a collective effort. It's fine to note that McCartney wrote most, if not all, of the song, but since McCartney saw it as a Beatles song back then, who are we to say that it isn't a Beatles song today?

I kind of think along those same lines when it comes to diminishing the All-Pro picks during the war years. While I understand that the war did prevent a number of good players from competing for All-Pro honors, isn't the idea of the award to honor the players who did play? Should we engage in this type of revisionist history of saying that even though the voters said Matheson was one of the best players of that year, we know better than to think he was that good?

Maybe another way to look at this is by asking a hypothetical question: what if the United States' involvement in World War II lasted six or seven years instead of four, and thus prevented the Barwegans and Ramseys and Younces of the world from ever resuming their careers? Would we then say that Matheson shouldn't be a Hall of Famer because he wasn't ever able to play against what should have been the best competition of his day? Wouldn't that be just a bit presumptuous of us?

One should also remember how Matheson performed after the war ended. He was a consensus All-Pro in both 1946 and 1947. And who did he share the consensus honors with in those years? Len Younce and Buster Ramsey, both of whom were on Piascik's list of players that Matheson didn't have to beat out during the war years. How can we presume that Matheson would not have been able to compete with those two during the war when he did just that after the war?

The answer is we can't.

Bottom line: Matheson's career achievements are more than adequate to justify his entry in the Hall.

In addition to the Hall's honor rolls being short on offensive guards and AFL players, this list shows that the Raiders are also underrepresented in Canton. Oakland's management and players often claim there is a conspiracy against them in many levels around the NFL. Sometimes I think they are making mountains out of molehills when they say this, but the Raiders do have a valid point when it comes to this. Their four candidates (Guy, Grayson, Wisniewski, and Woodson) tie them with Dallas/Kansas City for the highest number of candidates on this list. That probably doesn't qualify as a conspiracy, but it sure is a noticeable pattern.

Those are just the players whose records suggest that they should receive strong consideration for induction. There are numerous coaches with similar résumé levels. Let's take a look at eight of these coaches and see how their candidacies stack up.

1. Buddy Parker: Head coach, 1949 Chicago Cardinals, 1951–1956 Detroit Lions, 1957–1964 Pittsburgh Steelers

The Hall of Fame case for Parker is very strong. He took Detroit to three straight NFL championship games in 1952–1954. The Lions played all three of those games against the Browns and beat them twice.

Those two wins put Parker on a very elite list. He is the only Hall of Fame–eligible coach other than Bill Parcells who has at least three championship game appearances and two title wins and isn't in the

Hall. Parcells will certainly be inducted in the near future, so Parker will soon be the only coach with that negative distinction.

As if the dual championships weren't enough, Parker was one of the few coaches who were able to win consistently against Paul Brown in the early 1950s. Parker had a 4–1 record against Brown during his Detroit tenure, so he obviously had the great coach's number, or at least he did while he was in Motown.

Parker's accomplishments don't end there. He left the Lions prior to the 1957 season and took over in Pittsburgh. As I detail in the Art Rooney Sr. piece elsewhere in the book, the Steelers at that time were one of the worst-run organizations in the NFL. Despite this, Parker was able to guide Pittsburgh to a 51-47-6 record in his eight seasons there.

Just think about that for a moment. Only one Steelers coach prior to Parker had a winning record, and that was Jock Sutherland with a 13-10-1 mark. Only one Steelers coach had even won as many as twenty games before Parker came on board. Parker won only five fewer games than the previous five Pittsburgh coaches combined, and it took those coaches twelve seasons to do so. The Steelers had only posted four winning seasons in their entire history prior to Parker, and he put up three winning seasons in only eight years.

Parker even did so well that he led Pittsburgh to what amounted to a playoff game in 1963. The Steelers played the Giants in the last week of the season. New York had a 10–3 record and Pittsburgh a 7-3-3 mark, but because ties were not counted in the conference standings, the Steelers would be the Eastern Conference champs if they could top the Giants. New York won the game 33–17, but in some ways that contest could be seen as the high-water mark of the Pittsburgh club up to that point in its history.

So why isn't Parker in the Hall of Fame right now? When I asked around about this, I was told that part of the reason may be that the Lions of the 1950s were said to be riddled with gambling influences (see the chapter on Bert Bell for additional information on this).

If that is what is holding the Hall's voters back on his induction, I don't understand it. First, Parker won two titles despite having a quarterback who was alleged to have shaved points on a regular basis. Shouldn't that say a lot for Parker's abilities instead of saying anything against them?

Second, Parker left Detroit under some very mysterious circumstances, something that seems to be held against him. I don't understand why this would be. Dan Moldea's 1989 book *Interference* is an exceptionally detailed look at the influence of organized crime on professional football. It says a number of things about gambling and the 1950s Lions, but not once, literally not one time, does Moldea say that Parker had anything to do with the gambling. I don't know this for a fact, but it is fairly easy to imagine that Parker left when he did because the gambling influences on the team were getting to be too much. Parker did trade for Layne when he made the move to Pittsburgh, but unless and until someone comes out and says that he was helping the gamblers, this reason simply cannot be accepted as good enough to keep him out of Canton.

Bottom line: Barring any new evidence on the gambling front, Parker deserves a bronze bust.

2. Clark Shaughnessy: Head coach, 1948–1949 Los Angeles Rams, assistant coach/consultant for numerous teams

One of the issues I have with the Hall of Fame voters in general is there are certain types of candidates they won't induct. I'm not talking about guards or safeties or guys from the 1930s in this case. I'm talking about officials and assistant coaches.

I know some of you are probably saying to yourselves "Officials? KC wants to talk about inducting referees into the Hall of Fame? Is he nuts?!" My reply to that is, why not? The voters have already inducted Hugh "Shorty" Ray, the NFL's supervisor of officials from 1938 to 1952. Ray instituted a number of changes designed to speed up and streamline game play and officiating, so he certainly had a huge positive impact on the game and deserved a spot in the Hall.

Ray's induction obviously set a precedent for supervisors, but I believe the honor should also be passed along to game-level officials. Baseball started inducting umpires into Cooperstown in 1953, and eight of its arbiters have been afforded Hall of Fame honors during this time. Given the positive impact that referees like Jim Tunney or Jerry Markbreit, two men whose strong officiating style helped maintain the flow of many an important contest, had on the game, the voters would do just as well to include them in pro football's ultimate honor.

Another group that I firmly believe should be included in the Hall of Fame is assistant coaches. This may also seem anathema to some, but there are plenty of reasons why assistant coaches should be honored.

The first and best reason is that assistant coaches have a history of impacting big games. How much credit do you think Joe Gibbs would give to Richie Petitbon for his defensive coaching prowess during the Redskins' Super Bowl years? Or to Joe Bugel for his offensive line coaching acumen?

You could ask the same question about Bill Walsh and his offensive line coach Bobb McKittrick. Or Mike Ditka and Buddy Ryan in Chicago. Or Joe Collier for what he was able to do with Denver's defense during their AFC championship years. Or Don Shula and Monte Clark. Or Shula and Bill Arnsparger.

There is also a bit of hypocrisy when it comes to crediting assistant coaching impact. When the pro–George Allen group wanted to strengthen his somewhat weak Hall of Fame candidacy, they made a lot of noise about Allen's days as the Bears defensive coordinator. I don't know that his days in Chicago were the deciding factor in Allen's eventual induction, but I do ask why he gets any credit for that if the lifetime assistants seem to get no credit for comparable achievements.

Allen isn't the only Hall of Fame head coach whose assistant days are highly noted, either. Bill Walsh rightfully receives a lot of credit for the offensive innovations he made while serving as an assistant in Cincinnati. Sid Gillman served as an assistant coach in Philadelphia for only a couple of seasons, yet Ron Jaworski credits him with much of his success. And Bill Belichick's days as a defensive coordinator under Bill Parcells are certain to get a lot of play when Belichick is eventually up for induction.

If the voters want to honor the most deserving assistant coach first, Shaughnessy would be the man to start with. It is not a stretch to say that he was the most influential assistant coach in NFL history. His playbook innovations are still being used around the league today: T formation, man in motion, varied use of the flanker. All contemporary NFL offenses can trace their beginnings back to the Shaughnessy man-in-motion T formation.

He also was the creator of much of modern football's jargon. The post, corner, arrow, and streak routes all owe their semantic lives to Shaughnessy. They aren't the only terms, either, as Shaughnessy was also responsible for terms such as deuce and trips formations and the nickel defense, among others.

The main reason Shaughnessy is not in the Hall already is that his head coaching tenure was limited (14-7-3 in two seasons). The secondary reason is the same reason the other assistants are being kept out: the voters don't want the Hall to become a gold watch for NFL coaching lifers.

That mind-set is not the way that honoring the great assistant coaches should be viewed. Shaughnessy's influence on the way the game is played was so great that it wouldn't be an act of charity to give him Hall of Fame status. It would be an act of acknowledging the immense impact he had on the NFL and set a very appropriate precedent for future assistant coaching Hall of Fame candidates.

Bottom line: Shaughnessy is the best of the special-case nominations and more than deserving of induction.

3. Tom Flores: Head coach, 1979–1987 Oakland/Los Angeles Raiders, 1992–1994 Seattle Seahawks

Flores is another candidate who may be being held back by his Raiders connection. Flores ranks thirty-first on the coaches' point total list (see chapter 8). There are thirteen non–Hall of Fame coaches ahead of him on that list. But Flores has more championship wins than six of those coaches and just as many title wins as five others. On that basis alone, he deserves strong consideration for the Hall.

One of the knocks against Flores is that he was just a caretaker for a team that was really run by Al Davis. Some players and organization types who were in the Raiders organization during Flores's era would disagree with that statement, however. They say that Flores had to take a greater hand in running things due to Davis having to spend more time with court battles. Flores also did this when Davis tended to his wife after she suffered a concurrent heart attack and stroke in 1979. The Davis angle also kept John Madden out for a long time, but the Hall's voters saw their way around that in 2006, so there is precedence for looking past that when reviewing Raiders coaches.

Another black mark on Flores's career seems to be his tenure in Seattle. He posted a 14–34 record in three seasons running the show for the Seahawks, and that was seen as confirmation by some that he really was just one of Al Davis's puppets.

To anyone who says that, I would point out some comparative points about Flores's career as compared to Hall of Famer Marv Levy's. Marv Levy didn't have to go through much if any of "the organization did it all" crap when he was voted into the Hall a mere four years after he retired. Bill Polian did a fantastic job of stocking the Bills roster with a ton of great players, just as he is doing now in Indianapolis. Levy showed a lot of leadership skill in keeping the Bills' combustible locker room together, but Flores did just as well to keep the Raiders together.

This was especially true in 1980 when Oakland lost their starting quarterback early on and had to replace him with reclamation project Jim Plunkett. A lot of teams might have fallen apart when this happened, but Flores's Raiders were able to salvage a wild-card berth and make a strong playoff run to win the Super Bowl that year.

Levy also didn't seem to have his Kansas City days held against him. Levy coached the Chiefs for five seasons prior to his Bills stint and posted a 31–42 mark. That mark included only one winning season and no playoff berths. Since that record happened before and not after his Buffalo glory days, however, the voters seemed to either forget or downplay those mediocre years when reviewing Levy's Hall of Fame nomination.

If a subpar record was overlooked for Levy, why shouldn't it be overlooked for Flores?

Bottom line: The answer is that Flores's Seattle days should be overlooked. He deserves induction.

4. Dan Reeves: Head coach, 1981–1992 Denver Broncos, 1993–1996 New York Giants, 1997–2003 Atlanta Falcons

I covered Reeves's candidacy highlights in the Marty Schottenheimer chapter, but I do want to point out a couple of other things. First, Reeves's candidacy seems to be suffering from a combination of the Bud Grant/Marv Levy (can't win the big one) and Tom Flores (someone else is responsible for your success) syndromes.

That Grant and Levy are both in the Hall bodes well for Reeves. That Reeves was able to take two teams to the playoffs without John Elway also augurs well for his candidacy. That he took one of those other teams to the Super Bowl is even more impressive.

Second, let's not forget about Reeves's playing accomplishments. He scored forty-two rushing/receiving touchdowns in his career. To put his scoring into perspective, consider that as late as 1971, he ranked thirty-fourth in career scoring in NFL history. He wasn't a dominant player, but he was voted onto two All-Pro teams in 1966 and he started in two Super Bowls. Those accomplishments alone wouldn't get him into the Hall, but they are more than worthy to add to his long list of coaching achievements.

Bottom line: The only possible reason the voters might be keeping Reeves out is that he could start his coaching career again. Joe Gibbs did that and the Hall didn't fall apart, so that is really not a very good reason to keep Reeves out. He should already have been inducted.

5. George Seifert: Head coach, 1989–1996 San Francisco 49ers, 1999–2001 Carolina Panthers

Seifert is similar to Flores in that he won two championships with a strong organization behind him.

The dissimilarity between Flores and Seifert is that Flores took over a team in transition. When John Madden retired in 1978, many other Raiders followed him, including Fred Biletnikoff and Willie Brown. After Flores took over in 1979, Oakland traded away Ken Stabler and Dave Casper as well. Flores had to make do with a reworked roster and was still able to guide his team to a Super Bowl in his second year.

Seifert took over a Super Bowl winner that had a couple of years of greatness left in it. He didn't have to contend with many personnel changes during that first year, or at least none anywhere near as significant as Flores had to deal with. If Seifert's first Super Bowl win is a bit discounted because of the circumstances, his Hall of Fame candidacy is not nearly as strong.

Bottom line: I'm not that sold on Seifert being a Hall of Fame–level coach, but I am sold that he shouldn't even be considered until Flores is voted in.

6. Lou Saban: Head coach, 1960–1961 Boston Patriots, 1962–1965 Buffalo Bills, 1967–1971 Denver Broncos, 1972–1976 Buffalo Bills

The reason I put Saban on this list is that he, like many of the other candidates here, has two championships on his résumé. That alone should put him up for consideration, but there is actually more to Saban's candidacy than just the two titles.

Saban's career accomplishments are almost identical to those of another Hall of Fame coach, that being Weeb Ewbank. Ewbank won two championships with Baltimore in the 1950s and then went on to coach the Joe Namath Jets to their Super Bowl win. On that basis, Ewbank has an edge on Saban, but in just about every other way, Saban is nearly his equal.

In sixteen seasons of AFL/NFL coaching, Saban led his teams to a 95-99-7 record. In twenty seasons of AFL/NFL coaching, Ewbank led his teams to a 130-129-7 record. Saban's teams had four playoff berths. Ewbank's teams had four playoff berths. Saban's teams made it to three championship games, the same number as Ewbank's teams. Saban posted seven winning records. Ewbank had seven winning records.

So it really boils down to that Ewbank had one more championship win than Saban did. Even if Saban is slightly behind in that department, how much does he close the gap when his two consensus All-Pro nominations as a center for the Browns in 1948–1949 are accounted for? Consensus All-Pros are a hard thing to come by, so they should count for something.

I am not saying that Saban is a hands-down Hall of Famer. On the other hand, I do think that if Ewbank did more than enough to warrant his Hall of Fame induction—and in my opinion he did—Saban did more than enough as well.

Bottom line: To look at this another way, ask yourself these two questions. If Saban had won that third championship, would he be in Canton already? If Saban had won two NFL titles instead of two AFL titles, would he be in? In my book, the answer to both of those questions is yes. On that basis, along with the favorable Ewbank comparison, Saban belongs in the Hall.

7. Jimmy Johnson: Head coach, 1989–1993 Dallas Cowboys, 1996–1999 Miami Dolphins

I am actually rather surprised at some level that Johnson isn't already in the Hall of Fame. After he led Dallas to the two Super Bowl wins in the early 1990s, he was seen as almost a football coaching god. His guarantee of a victory in the 1993 NFC Championship Game (the one where Seifert wondered if Johnson's balls were made of brass or papier-mâché) put him on a level where few coaches in NFL history had ever been. NFL Films did some positively worshipful pieces on him and even Rush Limbaugh touted Johnson's never-take-a-day-off work ethic.

Combine Barry Switzer's taking Johnson's Cowboys to a Super Bowl win with Johnson's slightly above average coaching tenure in Miami and it dulled the luster on his reputation. But he was still a key person in one of the greatest turnaround chapters in pro football history and has two rings on his hand. That should give voters more than enough justification to put him into Canton.

Bottom line: Johnson deserves induction, but he'll probably suffer the same fate as John Madden after his career. The voters seemed to hold it against Madden that he was a big-name television personality and kept him out of Canton because of it. Johnson will likely be held out for the same reason, so his induction could take a while.

8. Don Coryell: Head coach, 1973–1977 St. Louis Cardinals, 1978–1986 San Diego Chargers

Don Coryell's career could be said to be a mix of Clark Shaughnessy and George Allen.

Coryell equates to Shaughnessy because of the impact he had on the NFL's passing attack. If Bill Walsh was the progenitor of the high-percentage passing game, Coryell was the progenitor of the vertical passing game. He took the vertical passing torch from Gillman and passed it on to Joe Gibbs.

The downside to the Coryell candidacy is that he didn't win the big one. In that sense he would match up well with Allen. In fact, Coryell matches up with Allen in many ways. These include:

- Allen had 116 regular-season wins in twelve seasons of coaching. Coryell won 111 games in fourteen years on the sidelines.

- Allen's playoff record was a meager 2–7. Coryell had a less than stellar playoff record of 3–6.

- Allen got voted in because of his overall impact on the game. Coryell certainly had just as much, if not more, of an impact on the game than Allen.

As I mentioned in the Marty Schottenheimer essay, Allen's record is probably the weakest of any coach in the Hall because of his lack of postseason success. I don't normally back candidates if they don't keep the accomplishment bar as high as it currently is, and putting Coryell in would not do that.

Bottom line: Coryell only belongs in the Hall if the voters start to value the "impact on the game" candidates. Under that criterion, Coryell should not go in before Shaughnessy.

When I first ran the All-Pro numbers, I fully expected the names on that list to include many of the Hall of Fame finalists from the past few years. Being a finalist means that the player was on the final list of fifteen candidates. I have to admit to being quite surprised that Bob Kuechenberg, Art Monk, Gary Zimmerman, and L. C. Greenwood did not make the cut, as they have been finalists on many occasions.

Since those players came up short in the All-Pro area, it made me wonder even more about their qualifications. Do their overall accomplishments make them worthy of Canton? Let's take a look at some of the most popular finalists, as sorted by the number of times the player has been nominated as a finalist. (Note: two of these candidates, Art Monk and Gary Zimmerman, were voted into the Hall of Fame during the most recent election process. I decided to keep my comments on their relative nomination strengths in the book because I believe they make some valid points as to why each was inducted.)

1. Jerry Kramer: Offensive guard, 1958–1968 Green Bay Packers; finalist ten times

Kramer didn't do quite enough to make the 20-point All-Pro list mark, but he did make an All-Pro team on seven occasions and was a consensus All-Pro for three. He was also on the 1960s All-Decade team.

As impressive as those two honors are, the most notable of Kramer's accomplishments is that he was on the NFL's 50th Anniversary team. He is also the only player on the 50th Anniversary squad not to make the Hall of Fame. There were only sixteen players on that team and Kramer was the only guard, so that speaks volumes for how his accomplishments were seen as of 1969 (when that group was compiled).

Kramer's ten appearances as a Hall of Fame finalist would seem to bode well for his for his future Hall of Fame prospects. There are only five other players who have appeared as finalists ten times or more, and all five of them (Lynn Swann, Tom Mack, Carl Eller, Willie Wood, and Paul Hornung) were eventually inducted into the Hall.

That two of the players with long waits were Wood and Hornung shows that there was definitely a Lombardi Packers backlash among the Hall of Fame voters. If that wasn't enough, Kramer's literary success with the book *Instant Replay* was also likely held against him. I can only imagine that some of the writers probably thought Kramer already had enough fame because of his playing and writing careers and felt some jealousy because of it.

I would hope that the Seniors Committee would look over Kramer's accomplishments and once again recommend him for induction. I would bet that most of the new voters wouldn't hold either the Packers' greatness or Kramer's own literary fame against him the next time around.

Bottom line: The writers have given Kramer every other honor they have at their disposal. Holding him out of the Hall at this point just doesn't seem right.

2. **Art Monk: Wide receiver, 1980–1993 Washington Redskins, 1994 New York Jets, 1995 Philadelphia Eagles; finalist seven times**

Monk has one of the weakest candidacies of any Hall of Fame finalist. He had a mere three All-Pro nominations, and only one of those was a consensus pick. In fact, in one of his "All-Pro" years, Monk received only a single vote in all eight of the All-Pro teams that *The ESPN Pro Football Encyclopedia* lists. That vote wasn't even a first-team pick, as he was one of four wide receivers on the UPI second-team All-Pro list.

On the plus side, Monk was on the 1980s All-Decade team and is the only skill player other than Roger Craig on that roster not to make the Hall. He also ended his career as the all-time reception leader, so that is in his favor as well.

Even so, Monk's reception numbers were impressive in part because he started his career at the front end of an explosion in receptions by wide receivers. His numbers were high because the NFL became a passing league, and because he was one of the first receivers to put up fifteen seasons of sixteen-game schedules. He only held the all-time reception lead for three seasons, as Jerry Rice passed him in 1995.

That was the first sign of the proper historical perspective for Monk's numbers. Now that this reception explosion has more than twenty-five years of history behind it, he has dropped all the way to seventh in all-time receptions. His fall won't stop there, either, as Terrell Owens will very likely pass him for seventh by the end of the 2008 season if he keeps up his current pace. Tony Gonzalez, Torry Holt, and Randy Moss could all also pass Monk within a couple of seasons.

It isn't just that Monk is being passed over career-total-wise, either. His numbers actually aren't that comparable to the other receivers currently in the top seven as of this writing (Jerry Rice, Cris Carter, Tim Brown, Marvin Harrison, Andre Reed, and Isaac Bruce). Monk has the fewest receptions per season of any of these players. He also had only sixty-eight touchdowns, which was easily the fewest of the group and sixteen behind sixth place.

In the end, my take on the Monk nomination is that he is only a viable candidate because he held the all-time reception lead for a short time. Being the all-time reception leader is a notable accomplishment, to be sure, but there are many instances in NFL history where a career leader in the early stages of a fast-changing statistical category has been passed over for induction. Bobby Walston was the NFL's all-time scoring leader from 1961 to 1962 and no one spoke of him as being a football immortal. Verne Lewellen was the career leader in touchdowns scored for eleven seasons in the 1920s–1940s, and yet there isn't a clamoring to grant him a bust. Benny Friedman owned the record for most passing touchdowns for thirteen seasons (1929–1942), and he wasn't inducted until more than seventy years after his career ended. It isn't an automatic ticket to induction, and the Hall's voters are showing plenty of historical perspective by realizing this and not rubber-stamping Monk's nomination.

Bottom line: Monk is only a Hall candidate because of the timing of his accomplishments. I would vote no on his induction.

3. Bob Kuechenberg: Offensive guard, offensive tackle, center, 1970–1983 Miami Dolphins; finalist six times

Kuechenberg has been one of my personal favorites for induction for many years. I was actually looking forward to writing this part of the book because I figured I would be able to make a really strong case for his candidacy and hopefully have some impact on his making it into Canton.

Instead of doing that, I am afraid I have to say that his Hall of Fame prospects are not nearly as strong as I thought they would be. Kuechenberg had but five All-Pro nominations and only one of those was a consensus nomination. I was frankly also surprised to see that he did not make the 1970s All-Decade team.

The combination of these two facts shows that the voters of Kuechenberg's day thought that he was a very good but not great lineman. I don't get the sense that the writers had anything personal against him, so I have to think that their votes were simply a matter of gauging performance. That makes it rather hard for me to tout his nomination that strongly today, especially when there are so many other offensive guard candidates with much better credentials than Kuechenberg's.

Bottom line: I hate to say this, but if I had a Hall of Fame vote, I just couldn't bring myself to give it to Kuechenberg at this time.

4. L. C. Greenwood: Defensive end, 1969–1981 Pittsburgh Steelers; finalist six times

Greenwood faces a high candidacy mountain because he played on a dynasty team. Over the years the Hall's voters have placed a ceiling of sorts on the number of Hall of Fame players that they will induct off of dynasty teams. Take a look at each of the dynasties from the 1940s to the 1970s and their Hall representation:

- 1930s–1940s Bears: Dan Fortmann, Bill Hewitt, Sid Luckman, George McAfee, George Musso, Bronko Nagurski, Joe Stydahar, Clyde "Bulldog" Turner (8)

- 1940s–1950 Browns: Len Ford, Frank Gatski, Otto Graham, Lou Groza, Dante Lavelli, Mike McCormack, Marion Motley, Bill Willis (8)

- 1960s Packers: Herb Adderley, Willie Davis, Forrest Gregg, Paul Hornung, Henry Jordan, Ray Nitschke, Jim Ringo, Bart Starr, Jim Taylor, Willie Wood (9)

- 1970s Steelers: Mel Blount, Terry Bradshaw, Joe Greene, Jack Ham, Franco Harris, Jack Lambert, John Stallworth, Lynn Swann, Mike Webster (9)

I don't think the voters intentionally decided on the total of eight or nine players per team, but once the number of inductees gets that high, it simply becomes very hard to justify another induction. A team with ten or eleven Hall of Famers out of its starting twenty-two means that around half of the starters were among the best players ever. That almost strains credulity at some level.

I feel a bit bad for Greenwood because a case could be made that he was the best of the non-no-brainer Hall of Famers on the Steelers. He wasn't as good of a player as Blount, Greene, Ham, Lambert, or Webster, as those five are all considered among the very best ever at their positions. Greenwood also didn't have the case of Bradshaw or Harris, as the four titles and the number two ranking in rushing yards those two had were immediate passes into Canton.

That left Greenwood as a candidate along with Swann, Stallworth, and Donnie Shell. So how did he match up against those three? Let's take a look.

Swann's credentials were rather slim, with only three total All-Pros and two consensus picks. His career reception totals also weren't that impressive, as he caught only 336 passes. On the plus side, Swann did have superb postseason performances and a place on the 1970s All-Decade team, so he looked to be the strongest in-team competition for the eighth Hall of Fame spot on the Steelers' dynasty roster.

Stallworth did post 537 receptions in his career, which was a fairly impressive number given the era that he spent most of his career in. He had a couple of memorable Super Bowl showings, including a performance in Super Bowl XIV that likely should have earned him a Super Bowl MVP award. The downside for him is that he had only three All-Pro nominations, two of which were consensus picks. Stallworth was not a member of any All-Decade team.

The player with possibly the weakest candidacy on that roster was Donnie Shell. Shell had five total All-Pros and three consensus nominations. He was not nominated to either the 1970s or 1980s All-Decade team. There really isn't that much noteworthy about his postseason credentials, at least as compared to the other three players being reviewed.

Now compare each of those career accomplishments against Greenwood's. Greenwood had six total All-Pro picks, with two of those being consensus. He was also a member of the 1970s All-Decade team. In addition, he had a dominant performance in Super Bowl IX and would likely have been the MVP were it not for Franco Harris's 158-yard rushing total that day.

Looking at each of these players' accomplishments, I would rank them in this order:

1. Greenwood
2. Swann
3. Shell
4. Stallworth

A case could be made to put Swann at the top if postseason performances are given extra weight, but I can't see any case where Greenwood would rank any lower than second in this group. He had more total All-Pro nominations than any of the other three, and he tied for the highest number of consensus picks. His All-Decade pick should have put him ahead of the pack of two of the others, and his Super Bowl play was probably equal to or better than all but Swann.

I wouldn't go so far as to say that Stallworth was a mistake pick, but by my estimation he wasn't the best of the available dynasty Steelers. Greenwood was.

Bottom line: I don't want to say that Greenwood should go in because Swann and Stallworth were weak candidates because it implies that he couldn't get in on his own merits. Having said that, Greenwood's candidacy is not as strong as Richard Dent's, another deserving defensive end (number 7 on this list), so Greenwood should not be considered until Dent is in the Hall. After Dent, Greenwood would still be a borderline candidate.

5. Lester Hayes: Cornerback, 1977–1986 Oakland/Los Angeles Raiders; finalist four times

One way to measure whether Hayes belongs in Canton is to see how he matches up against his onetime cornerback battery mate Mike Haynes. Haynes retired in 1989 and was inducted in 1997, so the Hall's voters viewed him as a very strong candidate.

Haynes had eight All-Pro nominations, three of which were consensus. Hayes had six All-Pro nominations, three of which were consensus. Haynes is slightly ahead in that category but Hayes is still in the neighborhood. Haynes was also voted onto the 1980s All-Decade team and Hayes wasn't, so Haynes's edge over Hayes grows a bit bigger.

What did surprise me about Hayes is that I expected him to have a lead over Haynes in the interception category. Hayes had thirteen picks in 1980 and I figured that season would help vault him to a very good career interception total.

It turns out that Haynes actually had more interceptions, forty-six to thirty-nine. Hayes had twenty interceptions in 1979 and 1980 but only racked up nineteen pickoffs in his other eight seasons combined. Haynes played three more seasons than Hayes, but this shows that even with the extra seasons taken into consideration, Haynes over the course of his career was just as consistent a ballhawk as Hayes.

I have to give the Hall's voters credit on this one. Hayes was viewed as being just a step behind Haynes during their careers, and he is still seen that way today. Hayes is probably Canton-worthy, but his wait was also justifiable.

Bottom line: His wait will still be justifiable as long as Dave Grayson is not in Canton. Grayson is the best cornerback candidate and possibly the best Raiders candidate as well (other than Flores). Unless and until Grayson goes in, Hayes should be held out.

6. Gary Zimmerman: Offensive tackle, 1986–1992 Minnesota Vikings, 1993–1997 Denver Broncos; finalist four times

Zimmerman is one of those players who wasn't quite dominant enough to be a first-ballot Hall of Famer. He had nine All-Pro nominations, three of which were consensus, and he did make both the 1980s and the 1990s All-Decade teams, so he has plenty of accolades to make him a viable candidate.

Bottom line: Zimmerman is another player who will likely make it when the voting circumstances are right and the voters don't have two or three slam-dunk candidates to vote in.

7. Richard Dent: Defensive end, 1983–1993 Chicago Bears, 1994 San Francisco 49ers, 1995 Chicago Bears, 1996 Indianapolis Colts, 1997 Philadelphia Eagles; finalist three times

As hard as I am on the 1985 Bears defense in the "Greatest Defense of All Time" chapter, I do believe that they are underrepresented in the Hall. Only two defensive players on that team, Dan Hampton and Mike Singletary, are currently inducted.

Dent's Super Bowl MVP, his having been a leader of one of the great defenses of all time, and his four consensus All-Pros are compelling Hall of Fame–level accomplishments. If his candidacy had one negative, it would be that he was not nominated to the 1980s All-Decade team.

That negative may not be as bad as it might seem at first. The four defensive ends off of that team were Reggie White, Howie Long, Lee Roy Selmon, and Bruce Smith. All of those players are in the Hall. You could also make an argument for either White or Smith to be the greatest defensive end in NFL history. Finishing out of the top four of that group isn't that big of a red mark against Dent.

Bottom line: Had Dent's career happened a few years earlier or later than it did, he likely would have been seen as possibly the best defensive end of his era. As it was, he more than held his own against some of the greats of all time. If that doesn't justify someone for Canton, I don't know what does. Dent should be inducted.

8. Russ Grimm: Offensive guard, center, 1981–1991 Washington Redskins; finalist three times

At some level, Grimm's candidacy would seem to be even stronger than Dent's. Grimm not only had five overall All-Pro nominations and four consensus All-Pro picks, but he was also named to the 1980s All-Decade team.

The reason I say "would seem to be" is that Grimm's competition for the 1980s All-Decade guard spot was not as strong as Dent's competition for the All-Decade defensive end spot. John Hannah and Mike Munchak both made that All-Decade list, but so did Bill Fralic. I don't believe anyone is suggesting that Bill Fralic should be inducted into the Hall, so Grimm didn't have quite as big of a mountain to climb to get on the All-Decade team.

In addition, with the candidacy logjam at offensive guard that I spoke of earlier in this section, Grimm could not be said to be the best available candidate at his position. If he does become a head coach in the NFL someday and can post any type of achievement in that position, I would say that would be the clincher for his induction. Until then he is a very viable candidate but not the best available one.

Bottom line: Grimm is a borderline candidate at best. I would say no for now.

9. Claude Humphrey: Defensive end, 1968–1978 Atlanta Falcons, 1979–1981 Philadelphia Eagles; finalist three times

Humphrey comes into the Hall nomination process with some fairly impressive credentials, including eight total All-Pro nominations and three consensus picks. The voters' history on defensive ends shows that the credential standards at that position are quite high, however. Here is how the current Hall of Fame defensive ends rank by total number of All-Pro nominations:

RANK	DEFENSIVE END	ALL-PRO
1	Reggie White	13
2	Andy Robustelli	11
T3	Doug Atkins	10
T3	Gino Marchetti	10
T5	Carl Eller	9
T5	Jack Youngblood	9
T7	Elvin Bethea	8
T7	Deacon Jones	8
T9	Len Ford	7
T9	Lee Roy Selmon	7
T11	Willie Davis	6
T11	Howie Long	6
13	Fred Dean	4

And here is how they rank as consensus All-Pro picks:

RANK	DEFENSIVE END	CONSENSUS
1	Reggie White	9
2	Gino Marchetti	7
T3	Carl Eller	5

(continued)

(continued)

RANK	DEFENSIVE END	CONSENSUS
T3	Deacon Jones	5
T3	Len Ford	5
T6	Andy Robustelli	4
T6	Jack Youngblood	4
T6	Willie Davis	4
T9	Lee Roy Selmon	3
T9	Howie Long	3
11	Doug Atkins	2
12	Fred Dean	1
13	Elvin Bethea	0

(Dan Hampton is another defensive end in the Hall, but he spent much of his career at defensive tackle, so I didn't include his numbers here.)

Humphrey wouldn't rate very well in either of these lists. His eight total All-Pro nominations would tie him for seventh in that category. His three consensus picks would rank him tied for ninth. He didn't make the 1970s All-Decade team, either, so his candidacy gets no help there. He would slightly lower the standards of the Hall at his position. That makes him a definite borderline case.

Bottom line: Humphrey is like L. C. Greenwood in that he ranks behind Richard Dent as far as defensive end candidates go. Until Dent goes in, Humphrey should be held out. And as was the case with Greenwood, after Dent, it's still a borderline case for Humphrey, and the leaning is toward no. Having said that, the Hall of Fame voters did induct Fred Dean in 2008 and Humphrey's accomplishments are much better than Dean's, so that makes his case stronger.

10. Ken Stabler: Quarterback, 1970–1979 Oakland Raiders, 1980–1981 Houston Oilers, 1982–1984 New Orleans Saints; finalist three times

With hindsight, we can say that in the 1970s there were really only five great quarterbacks. They were, in alphabetical order, Terry Bradshaw, Bob Griese, Ken Stabler, Roger Staubach, and Fran Tarkenton. Stabler is the only one of these five who isn't in the Hall of Fame.

A quick comparison of career accomplishments shows that Stabler keeps up with the other four:

QUARTERBACK	ALL-PRO	CONSENSUS	SUPER BOWL APPEARANCES	SUPER BOWL TITLES
Bradshaw	3	1	4	4
Griese	5	2	3	2
Stabler	3	2	1	1
Staubach	5	0	4	2
Tarkenton	6	1	3	0

Stabler is last in All-Pro nominations but tied for first in consensus picks. He appeared in the fewest Super Bowls but did beat Tarkenton head-to-head for his title win.

The clincher for Stabler's candidacy would probably be that he was one of the three quarterbacks on the 1970s All-Decade team. He beat out Tarkenton and Griese for that honor, so his reputation was still intact as the decade closed out. Stabler certainly belongs with the rest of this group, so I would say yes to his induction.

Bottom line: I still find it hard to believe that a top quarterback in one of the most competitive eras in NFL history is not in the Hall. Stabler should be inducted immediately.

11. Cliff Harris: Safety, 1970–1979 Dallas Cowboys; finalist one time

Harris is a favorite candidate of Dr. Z's, but he is not one of my favorite candidates. One of the reasons for this is that although he had a reputation as an intimidator, from the game tapes that I have seen from the 1970s, he only tried to intimidate the weak.

For example, Harris went after Billy Ryckman in one game. Ryckman was a backup wide receiver for the Falcons who was only in the game because of an injury to Alfred Jenkins. Ryckman was listed with a height of 5'11" and a weight of 172 pounds, but he looked even smaller than that. Harris laid Ryckman out on a play and acted like he had accomplished something big.

Harris also had the famous incident in Super Bowl X when he tried to intimidate Roy Gerela. Gerela injured his ribs while making a tackle on the opening kickoff and it affected his kicking accuracy. He missed his first two field goals in what was a very close game. After the second miss, Harris happened to be close to Gerela and he patted him on the head. He was doing a bit of trash talking and seemed to be thanking Gerela for missing another kick. Jack Lambert saw Harris's head pat and reacted immediately by running over to Harris and throwing him to the ground.

It wasn't just that Harris was messing with an injured kicker that bothered me. It was also the way that he reacted when Lambert threw him down. Harris had a reputation as the Cowboys' hit man, the toughest guy on the team, but what did he do when Lambert, the Steelers' heavy hitter, stood up to him? Harris got up and pointed to Lambert while asking the official to throw a penalty flag.

Had Lambert been ejected, it would have been a huge blow to the Steelers' chances of winning the game, so it was a well-calculated ploy on Harris's part. Lambert wasn't ejected, though, probably in large part because the officials realized that they weren't doing their job by getting Harris off of Gerela.

Harris's move actually ended up backfiring badly, as Lambert's stepping up for his kicker ended up being a rallying point for Pittsburgh to retake control of the game. Gerela hit both of his field goal attempts the rest of the game, and was even able to trash talk back to Harris after one of them.

So to summarize this incident, Harris tried to bully an injured kicker and was faced down by an enforcer. Instead of fighting the enforcer, he yelled to the officials to call a penalty. He also fired up his somewhat downtrodden opponent and got smack talked by a kicker to boot. That sounds a whole lot more like an ineffective instigator than an intimidator.

On the plus side for Harris, he did have six All-Pro nominations, three of which were consensus. He also made the 1970s All-Decade team and is the only safety on that team to not make the Hall.

Having said that, it does beg the argument that just because a player makes the All-Decade team, is that enough to warrant induction into the Hall? It's a great honor, mind you, and should carry a lot of weight, but where does the line get drawn? Louis Wright was also on the 1970s All-Decade team as a cornerback and is the only cornerback on that roster to not make the Hall. Wright had eight All-Pro nominations, three of which were consensus, totals that either equal or surpass Harris's. Doesn't that say that Wright belongs in the Hall in front of Harris? The argument could certainly be made that Wright is the better candidate.

Bottom line: Harris may be Canton-worthy, but as I see it, there are many other players who should be considered for induction before him.

Last but not least, I want to review two other players who haven't been finalists very often, but who are certainly viable Hall of Fame candidates.

1. **Duke Slater: Tackle, 1922 Rock Island Independents, 1922 Milwaukee Badgers, 1923–1925 Rock Island Independents, 1926–1931 Chicago Cardinals; finalist two times**

In some ways I think that Slater should be number one on the entire list, even in front of Bruce Smith. Slater was by all accounts a great player. He was an All-Pro on six occasions and was a consensus pick twice.

This is even more impressive when you consider the circumstances under which Slater earned those honors. He played during an era where blacks had an incredibly tough time getting a fair shake. Bob O'Donnell and Dan Daly in *The Pro Football Chronicle* pointed out that newspapers often said how well Slater blocked on plays and how this was doubly surprising given that he was an offensive lineman and black. If Slater did that well against a stacked voting deck, I can only imagine how well he would have fared with a color-blind accounting of his skills.

Bottom line: It was quite a pleasant surprise to see the Seniors Committee put forth Benny Friedman and Fritz Pollard as candidates a couple of years ago. It reflected well on the committee and the voters showed their respect by rightfully putting those two into the Hall. Slater is just as worthy of being in Canton as those two, so hopefully the Seniors Committee will do the right thing again and put Slater on a ballot in the near future.

2. Jim Plunkett: Quarterback, 1971–1975 New England Patriots, 1976–1977 San Francisco 49ers, 1979–1986 Oakland/Los Angeles Raiders; finalist zero times

Those who tout Plunkett for the Hall say that he is one of a select group of quarterbacks in NFL history who have won two championships. The list is certainly hard to get onto, as there are only sixteen quarterbacks in the modern era (1950 and forward) who can make that claim. Here are those quarterbacks:

STARTING QUARTERBACK	NO. OF TITLES
Bart Starr	5
Terry Bradshaw	4
Joe Montana	4
Troy Aikman	3
Tom Brady	3
Otto Graham	3
Johnny Unitas	3
George Blanda	2
Len Dawson	2
Bob Griese	2
John Elway	2
Jack Kemp	2
Bobby Layne	2
Jim Plunkett	2
Tobin Rote	2
Roger Staubach	2

The non–Hall of Famers on this list are Brady, Kemp, Rote, and Plunkett. Brady will certainly make the Hall once his career ends, so that leaves Kemp, Rote, and Plunkett as the only multichampionship quarterbacks not to make the Hall.

If Plunkett wants to be considered as being among the best of this entire group, he would first have to show that he is more deserving than Kemp or Rote. Let's see how these three stack up in All-Pro and consensus All-Pro picks:

QUARTERBACK	ALL-PRO	CONSENSUS
Kemp	5	2
Plunkett	0	0
Rote	3	1

I was quite surprised to see that Plunkett didn't even get one All-Pro vote during his entire career. He didn't just fail to get any first team votes; he didn't get any votes at all. That easily puts him last on this list, so he could be said to be the least deserving of the two championship quarterbacks.

Bottom line: He's an all-time Super Bowl quarterback, but the lack of All-Pro recognition pretty much eliminates Plunkett from Hall consideration.

11

Art Rooney Wasn't a Victim of Circumstance During His Team's Forty-Two-Year Championship Drought

When Art Rooney finally won a championship in 1974, everyone lauded the "old man." After all, Rooney had been an NFL owner since the 1930s and his forty-two-year wait for a championship was over. They said that his patience had finally paid off, that he was no longer a lovable loser.

That being said, the one thing that I wonder is why everyone was feeling sorry for Rooney in the first place. I understand that he was one of the finest people to ever own a NFL team. His players genuinely cared for him and he for them. But there is one simple fact that seems to be overlooked when talking about his tenure as a team owner: he was a terribly ineffective executive.

The main reason Rooney failed in that capacity is that he didn't do most of the things that owners need to do in order to help their teams to win. If you look at the common denominators of almost every winning football organization, you will find three that are most prevalent. These are:

1. Winning teams almost always pay their players well.

2. Winning teams almost always have top-notch facilities (i.e., training sites, front office, etc.).

3. Winning teams almost always have top-notch scouting/player personnel departments.

Item number 1 wasn't a problem for Rooney, as the Steelers would spend money on top-line players. Pittsburgh paid Whizzer White a $15,000 contract in the 1930s, one of the biggest contracts in the pro ranks at that point. Rooney himself was even quoted as saying that he didn't mind paying a good player good money, but he did mind paying a bad player good money. The record shows that fronting the payroll was something that Rooney would do when the circumstances called for it.

Items number 2 and 3 were areas where Rooney would pinch a penny hard. He was very hesitant to spend money to install effective support structures. The Steelers did not have a very big scouting department for years. For a time in the mid-1950s, Pittsburgh's director of scouting was a full-time mortician who scouted players as a part-time sideline and whose main scouting method was collecting newspaper and magazine clippings. The Steelers' team offices were run on a shoestring budget and their practice facilities were second-rate. Add it all up and you get the complete picture of a poorly run football operation.

It wasn't just the front office that suffered from Rooney's lack of attention. Most of the Steelers head coaches were hired, in part, because they were good friends with Rooney. Walt Kiesling fit this description perfectly and Rooney hired him to be the Steelers head coach on three different occasions, this despite Kiesling's own admission that he was better suited to be an assistant coach.

That wasn't Rooney's only coaching hiring mistake—not by a long shot. The first time Rooney hired Joe Bach, he did it on his priest brother's suggestion. That might not seem like a bad thing, but had he done a little more homework, he would have found out that Bach thought he was much better suited to coaching college football.

After Bach went 10–14 in two seasons, you would have thought Rooney would have learned his lesson, but that didn't stop him repeating both mistakes sixteen years later. He not only rehired Bach, but he again didn't do his homework and wasn't aware that Bach had diabetes until after Bach was his team's coach. Bach improved by one game in his second go-round, going 11–13 before leaving Pittsburgh again.

One of Rooney's coaching hires that could have panned out was Buff Donelli. Donelli was supposed to start his job in 1942, but after two games in the 1941 season, Bert Bell quit as the Steelers coach and left Rooney's team without a sideline leader. Rooney asked Donelli if there was any way he could coach the 1941 season as well. Donelli agreed to help out his friend and took the Steelers coaching job.

This may have worked except that Donelli was also coaching a powerhouse college football team at the time, Duquesne in downtown Pittsburgh. Elmer Layden, the NFL's commissioner, nixed the dual-duty idea, but the Steelers and Duquesne came up with a workaround that allowed Donelli to do both jobs, naming Donelli as an advisory coach for Duquesne and the full-time coach of the Steelers.

The reality of the situation was that Donelli did both jobs for five weeks. This worked until he ran into a scheduling conflict in November when both Duquesne and Pittsburgh had games on the same day.

There are two items of note when it came to this conflict. First, it was Layden, not Rooney, who brought the issue to a head by forcing Donelli to choose. The second is that Donelli decided to leave the Steelers and return to Duquesne. That should tell you all you need to know about Donelli's professional priorities and the state of the Steelers organization at the time. Oh, and by the way, Donelli did not come back to coach Pittsburgh in 1942.

If that wasn't crazy enough, consider that Art Rooney even hired Johnny Blood to be head coach. I mean, if you were ever going to hire a coach, a man to lead your team, I would think the last man you would ever want to hire would be Johnny Blood. Blood was a free spirit, to put it mildly, and was aptly nicknamed "the Vagabond Half-back." He traveled light and liked adventure, the ladies, and a libation or two, preferably in combination.

Blood was known for many things, none of which could be said to reflect the kind of positive role model a coach is supposed to be for his team. He had numerous curfew run-ins with Ernie Nevers when he played for the Duluth Eskimos. He once cut his wrist to sign an autograph in blood for a girl he was trying to impress. By his own admission he showed up to a 1933 Packers practice drunk and Curly Lambeau fired him for it.

The worst of Blood's trangressions would have to be the time he actually missed a game when he was the Steelers head coach. He was playing for a barnstorming exhibition team at the time (things were obviously a lot different back then), and after a game in Los Angeles, he decided to stay on the West Coast to recuperate. He ran out of money and couldn't fly back, so he had to use other transportation to get home. The funny part of the story is that he stopped by to see Ernie Nevers at a game in Chicago on his way back and Nevers asked him why he wasn't with the Steelers. Blood said the Steelers weren't playing that day and right at that moment the stadium's announcer reported that the Eagles had just beaten the Steelers 14 to 7.

Blood admitted that he did not have the right temperament for coaching, so I can't imagine what Rooney was thinking when he hired him to run the team. I mean, I can think of many areas where I would want Blood's expertise. If I wanted someone to go raise some hell with, I'd want to find Johnny Blood. If I needed someone to show me how to ride the railcars, I'd look for Johnny Blood. If I wanted someone to show me where to find some female company for the night, I'd call Johnny Blood. The two things I would never want Johnny Blood to do would be to date my daughter (if I had one) and run my football team (if I owned one).

The only possible reason I can contemplate for Rooney's hiring of

Blood comes from something Dan Moldea wrote in his excellent book *Interference*. Moldea tells of an instance when Rooney hired a coach because the coach owed Rooney money from gambling. Moldea never identified who the coach was, but given Blood's nature and the likely reasons Rooney had for hiring the other Steelers head coaches (most of whom at least could have been considered viable coaching candidates), it is entirely plausible that Blood was that coach. If that was the case, Rooney certainly paid a price of his own while getting his loaned money back. Blood's tenure as the Steelers coach lasted only two full seasons and part of another. He lost twelve out of his last fourteen games and ran up a total record of 6–19.

To be fair, Rooney did make a couple of good coaching hires that didn't pan out largely due to extremely bad luck. Jock Sutherland was able to vault the Steelers into a divisional playoff game in 1947. The team looked poised for a title run in 1948, but Sutherland died of a brain tumor prior to the season. Buddy Parker did make the team competitive in the early 1960s, so much so that they played and lost against the Giants in a game in 1963 that was for a spot in the NFL Championship Game. When Rooney had executive-style coaches like Sutherland and Parker, his teams were competitive, but his track record of coaching hires outside of Sutherland and Parker was almost legendarily bad.

One of the main reasons for this was Rooney's hands-off approach to running the team. He admitted that he let other people run the organization and said that his full-time job was spending five months a year at the racetrack, during which time the Steelers' offices weren't even open. Rooney also had five sons to raise along with running a horse farm and horse tracks, so the Steelers were never even close to being his top priority.

He also left the personnel side of the teams up to his coaches, and given the mediocre state of that part of his team, it should come as no surprise that the Steelers made some big mistakes in this area. To give you an idea of how harmful this was to the Steelers' on-field performance, consider that they had the rights to Sid Luckman, Bobby Layne,

Johnny Unitas, and Len Dawson at varying times and let each one of them go.

All in all, the Steelers were one of the most mismanaged teams in the league during this time, yet the impression given by a lot of the NFL history revisionists is of Rooney being a victim of bad circumstances. I don't want to be rude, but circumstance had next to nothing to do with it.

Just imagine for a moment that the Steelers were a regular business, say a printing company. The owner of this business pays the employees a fair wage and seems to care about the success of the company, but he spends almost all of his time attending to his other business interests. For years he doesn't put money into the printing company's infrastructure. The accounting department is run manually, and the HR department is very small and doesn't have a competitive budget to go out and recruit good employees. In addition, many of the managers in the company are the boss's cronies. They mean well, but they really aren't well suited to running a printing business.

The company goes on like this for thirty years and underperforms for most of them. Finally the owner lets his sons take over. His sons decide to make some wholesale changes to bring the company up to speed with its competitors. They bring automation to the accounting office, beef up the HR department so the company can recruit better employees, and hire professional managers to run the business. After these changes are made, the company goes through a renaissance and becomes very competitive. Eventually, they become the best printing company around.

That is exactly what happened with the Steelers. In the mid-1960s, Art Rooney let his sons, Dan and Art Jr., run the team. It took them a few years to get things going in the right direction, but they made progress very quickly once the new tack was established.

The first big step for these two was when they hired Chuck Noll to be the team's head coach. They then coordinated the building of an incredibly effective scouting group that had one of the best drafting runs ever from the late 1960s to the mid-1970s. Rooney's sons also got the team a new stadium to play in and upgraded the organization's administrative offices. Hell, they even changed the Steelers' uniforms from those hideous ones with the shoulders colored black and gold with the white uniform base to the classic look that is still being used today with some slight revisions.

So even though the record is clear that the Steelers were not very competitive because of the way Rooney chose to run the team, when they finally did win, he was painted as a hard-luck guy who finally caught his break. The funny thing about this is that Rooney said he didn't want people to feel sorry for him because of the team's poor performance. He knew the team was losing because he didn't place a lot of emphasis on it. He didn't want to use that as an excuse but rather as a statement of fact and wanted no sympathy.

And that says as much about Art Rooney as anything. He was a special man, and we should celebrate him for being the kind of man that he was. He added a very welcome touch of humanity toward his players, something that is rare among NFL owners, and the football world was a much better place because of it.

Revising the historical record of his poor management is not necessary to celebrate him, though. If you are a believer in seeing the NFL's formative days through as accurate a historical prism as possible, let me give you a suggestion. Whenever you see the old NFL Films pieces about Art Rooney that extol his personal virtues, applaud loud and long. When you see the videos portraying Rooney as a lovable loser, check your compassion at the door. He got the results that were commensurate with the efforts that he put out.

12

Bert Bell's Gold Watch, or Can Someone Tell Me Why This Man Is in the Hall of Fame?

Bert Bell was one of the NFL's founding fathers and a charter member of the Hall of Fame. He was an owner and a coach for many years but traded in those posts for the role of commissioner from 1946 to 1959.

Bell is credited with many achievements during his tenure as the league's point man. He is always recognized as a pioneer in television because of his implementation of the blackout rule. He is often noted for his strong stance against gambling. Other league accomplishments during his tenure include winning a war with a rival league, expanding to field teams on both coasts, and the reintegration of black players into most teams.

The sheer volume of notable happenings under his leadership

would certainly make it seem like Bell had a very distinguished term of office. A closer look at the historical record shows that the amount of credit he should be given for these occurrences is often marginal at best.

Let's take them one at a time.

The NFL-AAFC War

Bell is credited with having piloted the league to a win in this war, but the NFL actually did worse in the AAFC war than in any other war during its history.

Need proof? Try these facts on:

- The AAFC's average attendance was over ten thousand per game higher than the NFL's.

- NFL teams lost $3 million over the four years the battle raged, and three of its best teams, the Giants, Packers, and Rams, nearly had to declare bankruptcy. Those weren't the only casualties, as the NFL's Boston franchise had to relocate in 1949 and the Lions were also having quite a tough time financially.

- The Packers actually would have gone under if not for the local community once again digging into their pockets to pull them out of the grave.

- The AAFC's Los Angeles contingent, the Dons, outdrew the Rams, and that was a main reason the Rams lost approximately $250,000 during the war. Dan Reeves, the Rams owner, had to take on partners in order to prevent the team from going under. The split ownership eventually led to a toxic front-office environment that even the legendary diplomacy of Pete Rozelle was barely able to maneuver through. This dysfunction continued unabated until Reeves was finally able to repurchase majority ownership of the team in 1962, meaning the AAFC had a negative impact on the Rams organization for sixteen years.

- The Browns were a huge success in Cleveland, something that had to be quite an embarrassment for the NFL considering that the Rams had to leave Cleveland the year before the Browns arrived because they could not make a profit, even in a championship season.

- The New York Giants and the New York Yankees fought to a virtual draw, with both teams teetering on the brink of financial ruin. This certainly was something of a surprise given that the Giants had come off of a division title in the first year of the war. The war went so badly for the Giants that they had to borrow a large sum of money in order to survive, and that debt stayed on their books until the early 1960s.

The biggest reason the NFL was able to outlast the AAFC is that most of the upstart league's attendance was concentrated in Los Angeles, Cleveland, and New York. The other teams in the AAFC could not compete with these three teams and it was this weakness more than any other that cost the AAFC the war.

Compare this with the NFL's battle against the early versions of the AFL in the 1920s–1940s. These wars typically went on for only one season and usually cost the league very little, with the possible exception of the 1926 AFL. The AFL of the 1960s certainly raised expenses but the league also saw a rise in revenues and, at least on the NFL side, there were no instances of teams even coming close to bankruptcy status. The WFL in the 1970s temporarily raised expenses but came nowhere close to damaging the NFL. The USFL's owners were just as rich, if not richer, than the AAFC owners were, yet that league was not much more successful than the WFL.

The circumstances in which Bell had to fight the AAFC were different from the other interleague wars in NFL history, so that has to be taken into account. The NFL did win the war, so Bell has to be given credit for that. Even so, the fact remains that were we to measure each commissioner's interleague war performance on a win-loss record basis, Bell's record would be the worst.

Television

Bell is often lauded as a television visionary, and his broadcasting policies are always extolled as being enlightened rules that encouraged
growth in the league. There are many problems I see with giving him
too much credit for this.

The first is that the Bell's approach to television wasn't created
because of his exceptional broadcasting vision, but was rather more of
a reaction to a problem. The league's blackout rules grew out of the
Rams TV fiasco in 1950, in which a sponsor agreed to reimburse the
Rams a portion of the difference in gate revenue that was lost from having home games televised. The sponsor ended up having to pay the
Rams $307,000 because of a precipitous drop in attendance and, of
course, backed out of the deal after that season.

The loss of fans at the gate was quite frightening, and the following
year Reeves made a deal with a local TV station to broadcast road
games. Home games would not be televised, even in the event of a sellout. The Rams made ample money off of their road games from the television revenue, and once the home games were not shown on
television, the home gate rebounded to its previous level. Bell liked the
results of Reeves's idea so much that he had the rules implemented for
the entire league.

As much as the blackout rule served the league's interests in the short
term, it started alienating fans in the longer term because Bell failed to
realize that television would increase demand for his product. Attendance in the league took a large-scale upturn in the mid- to late 1950s,
which corresponded with the advent of televised games.

But even once the attendance increased, Bell still made no conces-
sions for broadcasting home games that were sold out. Home fans who
wanted to see the games had to resort to traveling to bars that were outside of the seventy-five-mile blackout area. In some cities, bars within
the seventy-five-mile radius did a booming business telecasting games.
Instead of seeing this as an opportunity to build a larger fan base, the
league prosecuted the bars and put an end to the illegal broadcasting.

A visionary is someone who sees opportunities that others cannot. That definition certainly doesn't describe Bell's approach to television. His primary goal with the blackout restrictions was to preserve the home gate, not to set up the league so that it could ride the wave of unprecedented popularity that this new invention gave it. That makes him a gate protectionist, not a television visionary.

Gambling

This is one area where Bell deserves some credit, but not nearly as much as he ends up getting. Let's start by giving him the credit he deserves.

Less than one year after he accepted the commissionership, Bell was faced with an attempted fix of the 1946 NFL Championship Game. Merle Hapes and Frank Filchock, players on the New York Giants, were investigated after being offered a bribe to throw the title stint against the Bears. Bell suspended Hapes for the game, but allowed Filchock to play. After the investigation of the fix was completed a few months later, Bell suspended both players indefinitely.

This leads me to one area where I will come to Bell's defense. He has been criticized quite often for not suspending Filchock, especially considering that Filchock threw six interceptions in that game, which is still a championship game record. The second-guessing revolves around the question of why Filchock was allowed to play while Hapes wasn't. If Filchock was as guilty of not reporting the attempted bribe as Hapes was, shouldn't he have been prohibited from competing in the game as well?

I was of that mind-set until I looked at the issue from Bell's point of view. The one thing that would have cleared the league and Filchock was if the gamblers' goal of having the Bears win by more than 10 points was not reached (the spread was Chicago −10).

The best way to help the Giants reach that goal was to have their starting quarterback in the game and not banned from the stadium. Had Filchock not played, New York would have had to rely on Emery Nix as their passer. Nix was in his second and last NFL season and had thrown a total of twenty-seven passes in his career. There was no way Nix was going to stop the Bears, so Bell took a chance on Filchock being able to pull things out. It worked in a way, as the Bears won 24–14, thus making the bet a push.

In the aftermath of the fix attempt, the league voted to expand the commissioner's gambling police powers significantly, allowing him to bar players for life in the event of any type of action that could possibly affect the outcome of a game. Bell used these new powers to implement a rule prohibiting all players, owners, and other team personnel from entering casinos. He also set up a predecessor to NFL Security by hiring former law enforcement officials to serve as monitors for this type of behavior.

As good of a start as Bell got with the Hapes/Filchock incident, there are a number of other incidents that make the claim that he kept the sport clean seem at least somewhat dubious. Some of the biggest names in the sport were party to these incidents, including Carroll Rosenbloom and Bobby Layne.

Rosenbloom was brought into the league by Bell to stabilize the Colts ownership situation and save that franchise from going under. Rosenbloom certainly accomplished this, but he brought along some baggage while doing so. According to Dan Moldea's book *Interference*, Rosenbloom had very close ties to many organized crime figures, was a known gambler, and was reported to have placed heavy bets both for and against his team while owning the Colts. Legend also has it that he bet a large sum of money on the 1958 NFL Championship Game. Pete Rozelle investigated him for just this sort of thing fairly early on in his commissionership, so it is highly unlikely Bell didn't have an idea of what was going on. The fact remains that, despite a significant volume of evidence, Bell never publicly investigated his good friend.

The one recurring theme in just about all of the government investigations into gambling and the NFL in the 1950s included or centered on the Detroit Lions and their leader, Layne. Don Dawson, a convicted sports gambler best known for being linked to Len Dawson by an NBC report the week before Super Bowl IV, said that Layne fixed games and shaved points on a regular basis, both when he was with the Lions and when he moved on to Pittsburgh later in his career.

Paul Hornung corroborated this contention in his autobiography when he told of an incident where Layne made a decision that caused Detroit to tie a game instead of going for a possible win. Hornung said that the Lions were deep in the opponent's territory but Layne eschewed attempting a game-winning field goal because a three-point win wouldn't have covered the spread. He tried throwing a touchdown pass on fourth down and missed and the Lions tied the game.

Layne reportedly also helped spread the gambling mind-set throughout the Lions locker room. This is part of the reason Detroit had multiple players punished when Rozelle investigated the league's gambling subculture early in his commissionership. (On a side note, Dawson also said that Layne was only one of many players with whom he did business, which is another black mark for Bell.)

Even Bell himself was rumored to bet on NFL games on a regular basis, if Bill Radovich's story in *The Pro Football Chronicle* is to be believed. Radovich claimed that during a break between depositions in the *Radovich v. NFL* case his lawyer, Maxwell Keith, told him that he was going to confront Bell with the name of a gambler with whom Bell supposedly placed bets on NFL games on a regular basis. The confrontation never happened because Bell didn't make it to the rest of the deposition. Radovich implied that Bell was kept from returning in part because he feared this very line of questioning. In *Interference*, Moldea confirms that Bell did have a significant number of underworld contacts around the country and used them to gather information with which to keep the game clean. Radovich's claims are unsubstantiated but not impossible to believe given Moldea's information, and they still somewhat dull the luster of Bell's commissionership.

Curtailing On-Field Violence in the NFL

Another area where Bell gets a lot of credit for helping to improve the NFL's image was in stemming the tide of on-field violence that overtook the league in the 1950s. By that time the league had a bad reputation for being something akin to the modern-day NHL. This negative image cost the league a lot of bad PR, including a scathing *Life* magazine article in 1955.

The press coverage wasn't yellow journalism, either, as the NFL had a very real problem with the game being far too violent. Late hits, cheap shots, "bootie plays," and vendettas were commonplace at that time. The players knew full well that the league wasn't going to crack down on the violence, so they effectively had to police themselves.

It would be inaccurate to say that Bell failed miserably in attempting to change this culture because he barely even tried to do so. He did very little to enforce clean play and even denied that there were enforcers on every NFL team, something that was common knowledge around the league.

Bell also did nothing to punish George Halas after the Ed Meadows/ Bobby Layne incident in the 1956 Western Conference Championship Game. Meadows nailed Layne from behind after Layne handed the ball off on a running play, even though Layne was at least six yards away from the play when Meadows got to him. The hit gave Layne a concussion and knocked him out of the game. It was a major reason why the Bears won 38–21.

This was the highest-profile occurrence of dirty play and came at a time when the league was hip deep in negative press coverage about this very type of thing. Bell could have suspended or fined Meadows and/or the Bears organization, an action that would have shown the world that the league was not going to put up with those kinds of shenanigans.

Bell did nothing of the sort. His response to the incident was to try to whitewash it. He proclaimed that the Bears and Meadows were not guilty of trying to knock Layne out of the game. His lack of action in this case simply fortified the idea that the commissioner's office was not interested in doing anything to clean up the game's violent tendencies.

To be fair, there is one way that Bell addressed the violence issue. He was very concerned that fights and injuries not be shown on television.

He thought it would be a bad influence on kids watching the game to see late hits, punches being thrown, or cheap shots knocking players out of games. His belief in this was so great that the NFL actually had language in its CBS contract that required the network to do all it could not to show fights or injuries. If Bell was either unwilling or unable to control the league's Wild West mentality, he does have to be given credit for trying to cover up the problem.

The *Radovich v. NFL* Case

The most far-reaching of the issues that Bell and the league faced during his tenure was the *Radovich v. NFL* lawsuit. Bill Radovich played for the Lions in 1945 and then jumped to the AAFC's Los Angeles Dons so that he could be closer to his cancer-stricken father. He tried to take a minor-league football job in California after he left the Dons, but the team had a blacklisting agreement with the NFL and denied him employment on that basis. Radovich sued the NFL under the Sherman Antitrust Act and the case went all the way to the Supreme Court, which ruled for Radovich in 1957.

The issue this created for the NFL was that the ruling essentially made the league subject to antitrust laws. Prior to this case, the issue of how the antitrust laws applied to the NFL was undetermined. Major League Baseball had been exempted from the antitrust laws in 1922, but the legal waters for extending this exemption to any other professional sport were uncertain at best.

And that is the reason why this ends up as a black mark on Bell's tenure. The league didn't have to allow the issue to get to the Supreme Court. Radovich's first attorney, Joseph Alioto, actually dropped the case because he didn't think it could be won. The NFL had won two lower-court rulings in the case and by that time had already proven its point regarding how it would treat players who jumped leagues. Since Radovich eventually settled out of court, it is likely that the league could have avoided taking this case to the limit and exposing its antitrust flank had it just been willing to fork over a relatively small amount of cash to Radovich. The league owners were probably as responsible for pursuing this case as Bell was, but the fact is that it happened under his tenure, so he has to bear some level of responsibility for the harm this court loss caused the NFL.

West Coast Expansion

Bell is only occasionally credited with pioneering the NFL's West Coast expansion, but it was Dan Reeves and Dan Reeves alone who expanded the league to the left coast. The Rams lost $50,000 during their 1945 championship season in Cleveland, and Reeves could not afford to absorb the losses any longer. At the 1946 league meeting, he requested permission from the league to move the team to Los Angeles. The rest of the owners voted him down when he first proposed the idea, and he had to threaten to pull out of the league in order to force them to agree to the move. I have yet to read one description of this that details any influence-peddling on Bell's part to get the move approved, so Reeves gets full credit for ensuring the NFL's Manifest Destiny.

Integration

Bell is also only occasionally credited with this, but again the record shows that if anyone deserves recognition for it, it is once again Reeves. The league had been segregated for fourteen years when Reeves signed Kenny Washington and Woody Strode in 1946. Reeves wasn't necessarily being altruistic in the matter, as some local civil rights activists were clamoring to possibly sue due to the city offering a stadium for a white team but not offering a "separate but equal" facility for blacks. Nevertheless, there is no evidence that the league officers had any say in the matter at all, so Bell cannot be given any credit for this.

If anything, Bell should actually be held accountable for not integrating the entire league during his tenure. The Washington Redskins were an embarrassment with their racist policies and never integrated when Bell was leading the league. The Redskins only integrated after their owner, George Preston Marshall, was threatened by the federal government to either integrate or face legal action. Even after the majority of the league was integrated, most teams had unwritten quotas that only allowed a certain number of black players to make the roster each season, which is another cloud over the league's racial policies under Bell's leadership.

Far be it from me to say that Bert Bell did not do anything to help the league. He did implement the NFL draft, which has been touted as the most effective enforcer of parity the league has ever seen. For the record, though, let's take a closer look at why Bell might have seen the draft as a good idea.

The most likely reason he wanted the lower-rung teams to get some form of competitive benefit is that he had one of the worst records of any owner in the league. Take a look at his teams' records over his thirteen-year ownership run:

YEAR	WINS	LOSSES	TIES
1933	3	5	1
1934	4	7	0
1935	2	9	0
1936	1	11	0
1937	2	8	1
1938	5	6	0
1939	1	9	1
1940	1	10	0
1941	1	9	1
1942	7	4	0
1943	5	4	1
1944	0	10	0
1945	2	8	0
Total	34	100	5

What a terrible record this is. His teams notched only two winning seasons and both of them came during the war-depleted roster years. Bell's teams put up two or fewer wins in eight of the thirteen years and finished either last or next to last in their division in all but one season.

A big part of the reason his teams' records were that bad is that Bell was a terrible coach. He was the head coach of the Eagles from 1936 through 1940 and coached the Steelers for two games in 1941. He ran up a 10-46-2 record during that time, or a winning percentage of 19 percent. According to Michael MacCambridge's book *America's Game*, that is the worst record of any coach in NFL history who coached five or more years. Since Bell seemed incapable of building a good team and was having a lot of problems signing players, it isn't surprising that he would come up with the idea of a draft.

It is often stated that the reason he did this was to give weaker teams the highest draft picks, thus allowing them to get the cream of the crop. While it is true that the draft gives the weakest teams dibs on the best players, the overall benefit that a club receives from having a higher drafting position is limited to one draft pick, as a moment of thought will show. In Bell's day, the club that drafted first theoretically got the number 1 pick and the best team got the number 10 pick. The worst team then had the number 11 pick, which is actually one pick worse than the best team got at the end of the first round. Another way to put it is that after the number 1 pick, the championship team drafts one pick better than the worst team in the league for the balance of the draft.

The value of the number 1 pick in the draft is significant, but the real value to the Eagles, and to every other team in the league since then, is that the draft guaranteed them exclusive negotiating rights with a certain number of talented players. This eliminated player signing competition between teams, and if anyone was going to benefit from, or be an understandable proponent of, a reduction of league Darwinism, it would be Bell.

The funny part is that Bell's teams didn't benefit from the draft. His teams' pre-draft record was 9-21-1, or a winning percentage of 30.7 percent if ties are counted as half-wins/half-losses. His post-draft record was 25-79-4, or a winning percentage of 25 percent.

I'll try to end this on a positive note by pointing out Bell's shining accomplishment. The NFLPA was formed in 1956 and over the course of the next year worked to get the league to recognize it as the negoti-ating arm for the players.

Bell worked very hard to get the association league recognition and was nearly successful at getting this done during the 1957 owners' meeting. He had the votes beforehand, but once the proposal was on the table, he was double-crossed by Redskins owner George Preston Marshall and the proposal failed because of Marshall's opposition.

Bell realized that from both a legal and an ethical standpoint the league needed to recognize the union, Marshall notwithstanding, so at a congressional hearing in August that year, he announced that he was unilaterally recognizing the union. His justification for doing so was the section in the league's constitution that allowed him to act "in the best interests of pro football."

That move took some moxie and benefited the league, its players, and its fans. It also made up a bit for the complete screwing the play-ers received from Bell's draft idea and the elimination of free-market conditions that came along with it.

I just wish Bell had shown that kind of moxie and foresight in the other areas of concern the league faced under his leadership. If he had done that, I would better understand his place in the pantheon of NFL greats. As it stands now, his induction strikes me as a reward for long-term loyalty rather than for an uncommon level of accomplishment.

13

The Greatest Defense of All Time. Period.

I have to admit to being something of a sucker for a "best ever" discussion. I enjoy bantering back and forth with readers about whether Dwight Stephenson or Mike Webster was the greatest center of all time (Stephenson gets my vote) or if Jerry Rice is the best player in NFL history (and I happen to think he is). I may not agree with the other person's contention, but most of the time I can at least understand the basis of his stance.

As much as I enjoy these arguments, I'm always a bit perplexed when I hear someone say that any defense other than the 1970s Pittsburgh Steelers is the best of all time. There are many people today who say that the 1985 Chicago Bears or the 2000 Baltimore Ravens defenses have eclipsed the Steel Curtain as the greatest. Those defenses had never eclipsed Pittsburgh's in my mind, but, in the interest of full disclosure, I have to acknowledge a bit of subjective prejudice in this matter, as some of my earliest football memories revolve around rooting for the 1978–1979 Steel Curtain championship teams.

Even with this leaning on my part, I like to think of myself as a responsible and open-minded football historian who wants to give credit where credit is due. I decided to apply Jamesian Theory to the greatest defense argument to see where it would weigh in on this matter.

Over the years, Bill James espoused three different ways of measuring team greatness: dominance in the team's best season, dominance over a period of time, and a player-by-player analysis of the teams in question. If either the Bears or the Ravens want to be labeled as the greatest defensive unit of all time, they should be able to top Pittsburgh in at least two of these categories, or win one and tie another at the very least.

Single-Season Dominance

Single-season dominance is the weapon of choice whenever the Bears/Ravens backers are stating their team's claim. There is no doubt that each of those teams had dominant runs, so let's compare them against the Steelers' most dominant single-season runs.

The Steelers had a couple of overpowering defensive runs, but their most impressive one occurred in 1976. Over the last nine games of that season, Pittsburgh allowed a total of 28 points, or only 3.1 points per game. They pitched five shutouts in those games and allowed less than 6 points in all but one contest. At one point Pittsburgh's defense went twenty-three straight quarters without allowing a touchdown, and they only allowed two touchdowns during that entire stretch.

Another feather in this defense's cap is that the Steelers' playoff chances were riding on their performance. The team had started off 1–4 in part because the defense gave up 110 points in those five games. If that wasn't sufficient motivation for the Steelers D to tighten things up, Terry Bradshaw was injured in week 5 and missed four of the next six games, making Mike Kruczek Pittsburgh's signal caller. The defensive run was the main reason Pittsburgh ran off nine straight wins to end that season and make the playoffs.

The only downside for the 1976 Steelers is that they didn't win the

Super Bowl, but that wasn't the only dominant Steel Curtain run. The 1972 Steelers ran off a 9–1 season-ending run largely due to the defense allowing only single-digit points in six of those ten games. The 1975 Steelers also allowed single-digit points in six of nine games. Even when this group was getting long in the tooth in 1978 and 1979, they could still be counted on to carry their fair share. The 1978 defense allowed 14 or fewer points in eleven of their sixteen games. The 1979 defense wasn't quite that good, but they still gave up only single-digit points in six games that year.

Contrast those runs to the 1985 Bears. Between weeks 6 and 12 of the 1985 season, Chicago held their opponents to a mere 39 points, or an average of 5.6 points per game. The Bears pitched two shutouts during that time, held five of their opponents to single-digit scoring, and never allowed more than 10 points in a single game. In the last three games of that stretch the Bears allowed only 3 points, and one of those games was a 44–0 thrashing of Dallas that sent notice to the rest of the league that this was a truly great defense.

As awe-inspiring as the Bears' run was, it was bookended by two stretches that weren't anywhere near as great. During the first five games of the 1985 season, Chicago allowed 88 points. Fifty-two of those points came in two games, including 28 points given up in week 1 to a Tampa Bay offense that would end the season with the Bears being ranked twenty-first in scoring offense.

The last four games of the season weren't that much better. Miami scored 38 points against this defense in their memorable *Monday Night Football* win over Chicago, and the Bears' next three opponents put up 33 points. Taken as a whole, the Bears gave up 159 points in the nine other games outside of their dominant stretch, or an average of 17.7 points per game. This isn't an extremely high total, mind you, but it is over three times as high as their midseason run.

The Ravens also had a very dominant stretch. Baltimore posted four shutouts in 2000 and held eleven of their sixteen opponents to 10 points or less. Only three teams were able to post more than 14 points against them. In one seven-game stretch near the end of the season, the

Ravens allowed a mere 56 points in seven games. Twenty-three of those were in one game, so in the other six games Baltimore allowed only 33 points. Their playoff run was just as impressive, as they gave up only 20 points in their three playoff wins.

After reviewing each team's accomplishments, I just can't give any of them a distinct edge. Keep in mind that I'm not knocking either the Bears' or the Ravens' performances. What I am pointing out is that the Steelers were just as dominant by this measurement and that they have just as much of a claim to single-season dominance as Chicago or Baltimore.

Dominance over a Period of Time

We can start this part of the analysis by excluding Baltimore from it. As great as the Ravens defense was, it was still only a one-year unit. As such, they simply cannot compete in the dominance over a length of time discussion. The Bears can, so let's take a look at their record in this area.

The Bears' defensive regular-season dominance from 1984 to 1988 matches up very well with the 1970s Steelers runs. The Steelers were dominant for a longer period of time, but let's just say for the sake of argument that the Bears' five-year regular-season performance was impressive enough to allow Chicago to claim some form of equality with Pittsburgh in this area.

Where they can't claim any form of equality is in postseason performance. To illustrate this point, consider that Chicago played in nine playoff games between 1984 and 1988 when the Bears defense was still at the top of its game. Here are the scores from those games:

GAME	CHICAGO	OPPONENT	RECORD
1984 NFC Divisional at Washington	23	19	1–0
1984 NFC Championship at San Francisco	0	23	1–1
1985 NFC Divisional vs. New York Giants	21	0	2–1
1985 NFC Championship vs. Los Angeles Rams	24	0	3–1

(continued)

(continued)

GAME	CHICAGO	OPPONENT	RECORD
Super Bowl XX vs. New England Patriots	46	10	4–1
1986 NFC Divisional vs. Washington	13	27	4–2
1987 NFC Divisional vs. Washington	17	21	4–3
1988 NFC Divisional vs. Philadelphia	20	12	5–3
1988 NFC Championship vs. San Francisco	3	28	5–4
Total	167	140	

The Bears gave up 140 points in those nine playoff games while barely finishing over .500. If the 1985 playoff games are taken out, Chicago was 2–4 and allowed 130 points in those six games, or nearly 22 points per game. The Bears' post-1985 playoff performances are the reason why when people refer to the dominant Bears defenses of the 1980s, they simply refer to the 1985 season and nothing else.

This phenomenon is what I call the dumbing down of the meaning of defensive greatness. Before the 1985 Bears, whenever people talked about great defenses, they always spoke of units that had multiple-year runs of greatness such as the 1960s Packers, the Cowboys' Doomsday I and Doomsday II groups, Miami's No-Name defense, and Minnesota's Purple People Eaters. All of those teams had their share of single-season greatness, and each of them won Super Bowls with the exception of the Vikings, but they all also had long stretches of dominance. No one who touted the abilities and accomplishments of these teams needed to limit the discussion to only one year's worth of play.

The 1980s Bears' regular-season showings were more than sufficient to keep them in the discussion with their defensive predecessors. After they suffered through the multiple playoff debacles, however, a lot of the mystique of Chicago's defense wore off. Many members of the media (along with all of the Bears fans) still wanted to remember this unit as one of the best of all time, but they knew they couldn't do so if they used the previous measurements of defensive greatness. The solution to this was to revise the definition of what constituted legendary defensive status from multiple years down to only one year.

In my eyes, that isn't a revision of the definition of greatness. It's a dilution of required accomplishment and doesn't reflect well on the Bears' claim to being number one. It is also the main reason why the Ravens were allowed to join this discussion in the first place. There was no reason why the previous standards of defensive excellence needed to be thrown aside and it was due as much to the Bears' popularity as it was to their level of greatness.

Charisma is not an acceptable substitute for achievement, however, and the facts clearly show that Pittsburgh trumps both Chicago and Baltimore in this area by a wide margin.

Head-to-Head Positional Comparison

In grading the head-to-head comparisons, I had to choose whether to measure a player based on his best single season or if he should be measured on the strength of his career. I ended up going with the career performance method because an individual defensive player's single-season performance can be very hard, if not impossible, to put into historical context. His overall historical career context is much easier to gauge. In the end, it came down to making a choice between using a small or large measurement of performance. In that case, I'll go with the large measurement every time, and that's what I did here.

The big downside to the career measurement method is that Baltimore can't effectively be included in the comparison. Eight of Baltimore's eleven starters in 2000 were either not with the team or not starting anymore in 2002. That lack of longevity basically eliminates the Ravens' ability to compete in this arena. Plus, as I mentioned earlier, if Baltimore has any claim, it would be as the best one-year defense, not as the best defense of all time. That leaves this matchup as one between the Bears and the Steelers.

The first criterion I used to grade the matchups is the number of All-Pro and consensus All-Pro nominations a player had. Just as was done in the Hall of Fame section, the consensus All-Pro picks were culled from *The ESPN Pro Football Encyclopedia*. The consensus picks also carry just as much weight here as they did in the Hall of Fame comparisons, as I wanted to give a large reward for players who achieved the highest positional honor the league has to offer.

Another resource I used in this analysis was the historical positional rankings from Rick Korch's 1993 book *The Truly Great*. Korch is a respected football historian, and in his words he "interviewed several hundred experts—players, former players, coaches, assistant coaches, historians and sportswriters" to help him determine who the greatest players were at each position. Korch ranked over two hundred total players and typically would rank at least ten players at every major position.

Korch's book is a very good reference for this comparison not only because of the depth of the rankings and the large amount of research that went into them, but also because of the timing of its release. All of the Steelers players had retired by 1993 and only a couple of the Bears players were still active starters, so Korch's study basically encompassed the entirety of each team's run of greatness.

In each positional ranking, I will list both players' accomplishments and then judge which team has an advantage at that position. The advantage rankings will range from push (if the players are equal), to slight edge, to edge, to big edge, to huge edge. There will be one point awarded for each step up the edge ladder, which means there will be a maximum of four possible points at each position.

The players at each position will be the primary starters during the bulk of each team's run. Again, *The ESPN Pro Football Encyclopedia* was quite helpful with this, as it lists the primary starters for every team since 1950. Players who are enshrined in the Pro Football Hall of Fame have their names in bold italics.

Left Defensive End—L. C. Greenwood vs. *Dan Hampton*

Greenwood was one of the dominant pass rushers of his era and would likely be in the Hall of Fame were there not a good level of resistance to Steelers players from that era due to there already being nine players from that team in the Hall. Hampton was not as dominant a pass rusher as Greenwood but was just as dominant a player, as his Hall of Fame induction proves.

They both had six All-Pro selections in their careers, but Hampton has a slight advantage in that area because three of his selections were consensus, whereas only two of Greenwood's selections were consensus. Greenwood was ranked as the twelfth best defensive end of all time in the Korch list and Hampton didn't make the list at all, so that would be in Greenwood's favor. Greenwood was also a member of the 1970s All-Decade team, while Hampton was not a member of the 1980s All-Decade team.

Even so, the Hall of Fame nomination probably carries more weight than the All-Decade team and Korch's list. Although it could be argued that Greenwood belongs in the Hall, Hampton is already there. The positional advantage here has to go to Chicago. **Slight edge to Bears. Bears lead 1–0.**

Left Defensive Tackle—*Joe Greene* vs. Steve McMichael

McMichael was certainly one of the better defensive tackles of his day, but Greene changed the way the defensive tackle position is played with his tilt tackle stance, and he was nearly unblockable during his prime. Greene was listed as the third best defensive tackle of all time on the Korch list and McMichael was not listed at all. McMichael was an All-Pro on five occasions, a record that is nothing to sneeze at, but it pales in comparison to Greene's eleven All-Pro nominations. Greene was also a consensus All-Pro four times to McMichael's one. In addition, Greene is in the Hall of Fame and McMichael is not, and McMichael likely will not be voted in. **Big edge to Steelers. Steelers lead 3–1.**

Right Defensive Tackle—Ernie Holmes vs. William "The Refrigerator" Perry

Perry is certainly the more celebrated player due to his antics while lining up in the Chicago offensive backfield, but let's not also forget that he was a fairly good tackle. That notwithstanding, I give this to Holmes for one simple reason. Holmes's play early in his career was so good that historians often say he would have had a Hall of Fame career were it not for some off-field issues. Perry was never thought of as having Hall of Fame potential and was held back by his own off-field conditioning issues. Holmes also had two All-Pro seasons to Perry's zero. **Edge to Steelers. Steelers lead 5–1.**

Right Defensive End—Dwight White vs. Richard Dent

Both were very good pass rushers who didn't get the credit they deserved because they weren't the best defensive linemen on their teams. Dent had five All-Pro nominations, none of which were consensus. White had four All-Pro berths, but none of his were consensus either. Neither appeared on the Korch list. Dent has generated more Hall of Fame support than White, though the anti-Steelers backlash has to be accounted for. Even with that caveat, Dent wins this one. **Edge to Bears. Steelers lead 5–3.**

Left Linebacker—*Jack Ham* vs. Otis Wilson

Wilson was fast, strong, athletic, and an All-Pro on two occasions. That's a pretty good record, but Ham was an All-Pro for seven consecutive seasons and six of those were consensus picks. Ham also ranked as the second best linebacker of all time on the Korch list and is usually thought of as the consensus choice for the best 4–3 outside linebacker of all time. That makes this one fairly easy. **Huge edge to Steelers. Steelers lead 9–3.**

Middle Linebacker—*Jack Lambert* vs. *Mike Singletary*

How can either one of these all-time greats be given an edge here? Both were All-Pros nine times, with Singletary having six consensus picks and Lambert seven, so that could be a reason to give Lambert a slight edge. Lambert ranked second in the Korch rankings and Singletary fifth, so that could constitute another reason for giving Lambert a slight edge. Even so, they both were so dominant and their records so nearly identical that I simply can't choose a winner between them. **Push. Steelers lead 9–3.**

Right Linebacker—Andy Russell vs. Wilbur Marshall

Marshall is the better-known player in large part because of the attention he received when the Redskins acquired him as a free agent in 1988. He helped lead the Redskins to a Super Bowl, so that also gave him more of the spotlight.

Marshall may have garnered more attention because of those things, but Russell was probably just as good a linebacker over the course of his career. Russell had seven All-Pros with zero consensus All-Pros compared to Marshall's four All-Pros and two consensus. Neither made the Korch list. To be fair, three of Russell's All-Pro rankings came before the foundation of the Steel Curtain was in place, so it could be said that the All-Pro rankings are a push. That's how I would see this positional ranking as well. **Push. Steelers maintain 9–3 lead.**

Left Cornerback—J. T. Thomas vs. Mike Richardson

This is one of the harder rankings because neither player was that good. Richardson did have one All-Pro to Thomas's zero. Richardson also started six seasons to Thomas's four, another number that indicates he was probably a slightly better player than Thomas. **Slight edge to Bears. Steelers lead 9–4.**

Right Cornerback—*Mel Blount* vs. Leslie Frazier

Frazier was a four-year starter for Chicago with zero All-Pros to his credit. Blount was a six-time All-Pro, consensus All-Pro on one occasion, and was voted onto the 1980s All-Decade team. Blount was also listed as the third best cornerback of all time on the Korch list. Another feather in his cap was that he changed the way the game is played by forcing the implementation of the Blount rule in 1978 that limited the amount of physical contact a cornerback could have on receivers running downfield. This one is no contest. **Huge edge to Steelers. Steelers lead 13–4.**

Strong Safety—Mike Wagner/Donnie Shell vs. Dave Duerson

Wagner was the Steelers starter at strong safety from 1971 to 1976 and fared quite well for himself, as evidenced by his four total All-Pro nominations (zero consensus). Duerson was just about as good as Wagner in the All-Pro voting, tallying three total All-Pros and one consensus, so that would seem to make this category a push.

The big issue here is how much credit Pittsburgh should be given for Donnie Shell's performance in the later years of the Steel Curtain. Shell was an All-Pro for five straight years (1978–1982) and consensus three times. He has also been a finalist for the Hall of Fame, so if his contributions were fully accounted for, it would give the Steelers a large edge. As it is, some of Shell's performance came as a backup in the Steel Curtain's prime years and some as a starter in the waning years of that unit. The Bears have no equivalent player in their secondary so Pittsburgh's edge at this position is significant. **Edge to Steelers. Steelers extend their lead to 15–4.**

Free Safety—Glen Edwards vs. Gary Fencik

Edwards is one of the least known of the Steelers defenders because he was traded to San Diego in 1978 after Shell established himself as the starting strong safety and Wagner moved to free safety. Even so, Edwards's contributions to the Steelers defense can't be overlooked. He was voted All-Pro three times, although none of them were consensus rankings.

Fencik's record is appreciably better than Edwards's, as he was named All-Pro in six seasons, with one of those rankings being consensus. The only issue with Fencik is that he was similar to Andy Russell in that four of his All-Pro rankings came before the Bears defense really established itself as a dominant unit. Had Edwards done a bit more, I would probably give this a push, but Fencik's overall achievements are so much better that I think Fencik deserves the nod here. **Edge to Bears. Bears add two late points to make the final score 15–6.**

Here are the rankings by edge type:

EDGE TYPE	BEARS	STEELERS
Push	2	2
Slight edge	2	0
Edge	2	2
Big edge	0	1
Huge edge	0	2

I know there are some people who will think this ranking system is unfairly weighted toward the Steelers, but the fact remains that Pittsburgh's Steel Curtain had the greatest collection of defensive players of all time. There is no other defense in the history of the NFL that can say it had three players who could make a strong argument for being the best player of all time at their position. Joe Greene, Jack Ham, and Mel Blount could all definitely make that argument. Jack Lambert can't quite make the argument of being the best middle linebacker of all time, as Dick Butkus or possibly Ray Lewis have that claim locked up, but beyond those two, Lambert has just as great of a claim as the best as any other middle linebacker. That's four all-time greats along with three other Hall of Fame candidates (Greenwood, Russell, and Shell).

As great as the Bears were, they had only one player who could make a valid claim for the best of all time at his position, that being Mike Singletary. Lambert was just as good as Singletary but he was probably the fourth best player on his own defense. That should illustrate as much as anything why the Steelers win the head-to-head personnel matchup hands down.

In the end, I know this is a subjective issue on many levels, and there are many Bears and Ravens backers who will say those defenses are the best no matter how many comparisons I go through. No matter how I look at it, however, I simply cannot see how either of those defenses could be considered better than the 1970s Steelers. Pittsburgh won more Super Bowls, was great for a longer period of time, was just as dominant in their single-season runs, and had a huge personnel advantage. The Bears may have been the flashier defense and certainly possessed a unique level of charisma, and the Ravens carried a bad quarterback to a championship, but the Steelers were the better defense by nearly every criterion imaginable.

14

The Greatest Wide Receiver of All Time. Period.

There are more than a few elite wide receivers in the NFL today. For some of these players, such as Marvin Harrison, Torry Holt, Randy Moss, and Terrell Owens, there have been some discussions over the past couple of years about the possibility that they might eclipse Jerry Rice in at least one of the major wide receiver statistical categories. As these four start getting closer to Rice's marks over the next few seasons, there will also be the inevitable discussions about if any of them should be considered the greatest wide receiver of all time.

I can already give you the answer to that question: No. Not just no. Hell no.

The reason I am so adamant about this is that the gap between Rice and these four is extremely large, much larger than many seem to understand. As I mentioned in the previous chapter, I prefer making an objective argument to a subjective one, so let me show you three objective reasons Rice is, and almost certainly will remain, better than these four.

1. None of these four is likely to pass Rice's overall statistics by the end of their careers

Rice's lead is so big that it isn't even a cinch that any of these four will top any of his regular-season career totals.

To illustrate this, take a look at how Rice's career statistics measure up to the other four as of the end of the 2007 season.

CATEGORY	RICE	HARRISON	+/-	HOLT	+/-	MOSS	+/-	OWENS	+/-
Receptions	1,549	1,042	-507	805	-744	774	-775	882	-667
Receiving yards	22,895	13,944	-8,951	11,864	-11,031	12,193	-10,702	13,070	-9,825
Receiving TDs	197	123	-74	71	-126	124	-73	129	-68

Now let's compare each active receiver's current pace in these categories and see how many seasons it will take them to break Rice's records if they keep that pace up. The table below shows each receiver's current production level, the amount they are behind in each category, and the approximate number of seasons it would take them to equal Rice's records.

CAREER TOTALS THROUGH 2007

CATEGORY	CAREER TOTALS	PER SEASON PACE	+/-	NO. OF SEASONS
		HARRISON		
Receptions	1,042	87	-507	6
Receiving yards	13,944	1,162	-8,951	8
Receiving TDs	123	10	-74	7
		HOLT		
Receptions	805	89	-744	8
Receiving yards	11,864	1,318	-11,031	8
Receiving TDs	71	8	-126	16
		MOSS		
Receptions	774	77	-775	10
Receiving yards	12,193	1,219	-10,702	9
Receiving TDs	124	12	-73	6
		OWENS		
Receptions	882	74	-667	9
Receiving yards	13,070	1,089	-9,825	9
Receiving TDs	129	11	-68	6

Now let's put this into an age context. It would take Marvin Harrison six more seasons of catching eight-seven passes per year to top Rice's career reception total. Harrison will be thirty-six years old coming into the 2008 season, so he will have to continue producing at this level until he is forty-one. That seems to be highly unlikely to happen, and even if it does, it will only put Harrison in front of Rice in one category. Harrison would have to tally 1,162 yards a season until the age of forty-four to pass Rice's career yardage total. Add the age factor to Harrison's serious knee injury last year, and the chances of him breaking even one of these marks seem slim.

The odds are not much better for any of the other receivers. Holt would have play past his fortieth birthday and maintain a higher pace in his late thirties than Harrison would. Moss's seventy-seven receptions per season pace is a mark he has equaled or bettered only six times in his ten seasons in the NFL, so it seems unlikely that he could keep up that mark until the age of forty-one. Owens has the worst chance of any of the four, as he will be thirty-five years old coming into the 2008 season and has to play at least six more seasons to have any kind of chance of beating even one of Rice's marks.

Regardless of some of the hype that is bound to come up in the next few years, unless and until any of these players starts putting up these kinds of numbers when they are in their very late thirties, it cannot be assumed that they will take Rice's place on the statistical throne.

Even if some of Rice's regular-season career totals do fall, that would only give someone a claim at possibly being the best regular-season pass catcher in NFL history. There is more to being the best wide receiver of all time than catching regular-season passes, however.

2. No one can match Rice's playoff statistics

If there is one part of Rice's career that sometimes seems underestimated, it is his postseason level of dominance. In twenty-eight career playoff appearances, Rice caught 151 passes for 2,245 yards and 22 touchdowns.

To give you an idea of just how dominant those figures are, compare them to Harrison's career playoff numbers through the 2007 season:

fifteen games, 62 receptions, 862 yards, and 2 touchdowns. The spread is even bigger for the other three in receptions and yards, as Harrison's numbers are easily the second best of this group in those totals.

To put it another way, Harrison could add one of his regular-season average totals to his playoff totals and he still would not top Rice in any postseason category. In fact, any of the other receivers could add their regular-season averages to their postseason marks and none of them would top Rice in any measurement (although Moss would tie him in touchdowns).

As impressive as Rice's overall lead is, it probably doesn't quite do justice to the amount of distance he has over everyone in this group. Just consider these facts:

- At this point, Rice had more postseason receiving touchdowns than Harrison, Holt, Moss, and Owens combined.

- Rice alone had fourteen games with at least one touchdown reception; the group has only sixteen among them.

- Rice's eight 100-yard receiving games are only one less than the combined group total.

- His fifty-six receptions in the three 49ers' Super Bowl playoff runs would place second among the group's overall playoff totals.

Harrison, Moss, and Owens all currently start for playoff-caliber teams, so they will almost certainly close the postseason statistical gap between now and the end of their careers. Having said that, I should point out that in the five playoff games they played in during the 2007 postseason, this trio posted a combined thirteen receptions for 170 yards and two touchdowns. That is barely any better than Rice's Super Bowl XXIX stat line of ten receptions for 149 yards and three touchdowns. It also shows why Rice is without a doubt the king of the postseason world and why he will hold that title for a very long time.

3. Rice was the greatest blocking wide receiver of all time

Even if some insanely high late-career statistical burst puts one of these four into Rice's regular and postseason statistical stratosphere, he would still be far behind Rice in another category: blocking. Blocking is a subjective criterion to be certain, but the general consensus of coaches, scouts, and football historians is that Rice was the greatest blocking wide receiver of all time.

It can't even be said that any of these four was the best blocker of his era. Moss's lack of blocking effort was one of the reasons Merrill Hoge called him out a few years ago. Harrison prides himself on being the type of receiver who catches the ball and tries to find a soft spot to avoid getting hit, so getting physical with defenders isn't his game.

Owens and Holt score okay in this category, but they certainly don't have a highlight reel block to match up with Rice's fantastic blocking night against the Rams in 1989. Anyone who saw that game will never forget Rice's incredible persistence in throwing multiple downfield blocks to help John Taylor turn two short passes into a 92-yard touchdown and a 96-yard touchdown. I won't weigh in on how much this category should count when grading the best-ever wide receiver, but it does have to count for something, and none of these four is anywhere near Rice's blocking neighborhood.

I know in the end that this type of analysis is subjective. I happen to think that Jerry Rice could be the greatest player in NFL history, not just the greatest wide receiver. If anyone is going to beat him out for the greatest wide receiver honor, however, that player is going to have to beat him in all three categories listed above, not just in one or two. I simply can't see any way that Harrison, Holt, Moss, or Owens will be able to do that. That's why I say that Rice will still be the best wide receiver of all time for at least another generation.

PART FIVE

AN NFL
BUSINESS
REVIEW

15

NFL Socialism versus NFL Meritocracy: A Cautionary Tale

The NFL likes to think of itself as meritocracy, a place where on-field success translates into overall success for players and teams. Vince Lombardi's quotes have been the mantra of more than one successful CEO, and the NFL's meritocratic environment is often touted by businesses as a bastion of inspiration for capitalism.

It's actually kind of funny to me that the NFL is touted as the most American of sports due to these meritocratic ideals. There are some things about the league that do represent the best parts of American life, or at least what we think of as the best parts, but the business structure of the NFL is anything but meritocratic, or even capitalistic. In fact, the NFL's business structure is something that any socialist party would be proud of.

For those who might not believe this, let me enumerate the most prevalent of the league's socialist policies:

- Each team generates different levels of revenues, but almost all of the revenues are given to the league for equitable redistribution.

- The heads of state (the owners) are discouraged and in some cases prohibited from competing with one another in the realm of non-shared funds. Some of the NFL's owners are among the best capitalists the world has ever seen, but their capitalistic urges are largely suppressed by this part of the NFL's financial structure.

- The workers have a party that is supposed to represent them, but it does so sparingly. The NFLPA over the years has twice won back the free agency that the owners took away from the players in the 1920s–1930s, but in both cases the union gave it back to the owners in exchange for relative peanuts. The NFLPA also has a very spotty track record of supporting its older players.

- The league has a history of exhibiting a large amount of control over the media. This control makes the NFL extremely effective at reducing or eliminating negative stories about it. The league and its best players are also largely immune from critical analysis because the media must stay on their good side to keep the information flow going. All of these don't add up to quite the level of media suppression that former Communist states once enjoyed, but it is has equaled a controlling environment nonetheless.

- As much as I enjoy NFL Films, in this instance I can't help but make the connection between it and the propaganda arm of an effective socialist regime. The NFL Films marketing and PR power cannot be overstated, especially when it is partnered up with other messaging arms of the league. For example, if the NFL, in conjunction with NFL Films and a large number of willing media members, bangs the drum of the value of the NFL draft to maintain competitive balance, any competing message of the value of an open player market will almost certainly not be heard by the public.

- The power of the commissioner as judge and jury, with no real due process or independent arbitration board in many cases, smacks very much of Big Brother knowing best.

No Socialist Overthrow

The NFL's socialism reaches very far into the on-field competition as well. It wasn't always this way and it didn't happen overnight. It was done on a piecemeal basis over the course of many years, as detailed by the following time line:

- **1920**—The initial action item of the very first meeting of the APFA (the predecessor organization to the NFL) after establishing the league's organizational structure wasn't to set up common scheduling. It wasn't to set up balanced officiating or to arrange a divisional league structure to allow for a true championship game. No, the initial action item was assigning one of the league members to collect player names from each team for the purpose of assigning exclusive negotiating rights for those players to those teams. That move alone helped destroy half of the professional players' free agent market.

- **1930s**—The next step in the process was the implementation of the reserve clause. The reserve clause gave teams the right to extend a player's contract for one more year past the initial term of the contract. Its earliest forms also allowed for a revision of the salary to any term the owner desired, though later versions of the clause allowed the owner to reduce the value of the contract by a maximum of 10 percent. The league ended up following baseball's lead and made the reserve clause a perpetual contract extension for the life of the player's career.

- **1936**—This was the year the owners finally finished off player free agency. From 1920 to 1935 the league still allowed for competition for college players coming into the league. Bert Bell provided the impetus to eliminate this type of competition by suggesting that owners assign exclusive negotiating rights to the college players as well, a process known today as the NFL draft.

- **1960s**—The Rozelle Rule was adopted in the early 1960s and took the reserve clause restrictions to another level. Teams were allowed to bid on players whose option year was up, but this rule gave the commissioner the power to award compensation from the raiding team to the raided team in the event of a signing and effectively killed off any player movement in this area.

Even with the advent of today's free agency, the competition between teams for players operates more like a regulated business than a free market. There is limited competition for workers when they first join the workforce and almost all of that competition is for the lower-end players who are not drafted. There is competition for workers after they are in the workforce for four years (which also happens to be the average length of a player's career), but that competition is largely blunted by a hard-line stance on expenses. The best workers often never have a chance to test their free market value due to having franchise tag restrictions placed on them.

The common denominator of all of these moves is that they were made to keep costs down by eliminating competition between teams. The end result of them was the building of the quasi-socialist player distribution structure that rules the NFL today.

The Real Reasons Football Is Popular

Once the NFL achieved great success using these methods, an assumption was made by the league and many in the media that the organizational setup of the NFL was a large contributor to its popularity. I for one don't think the NFL's popularity growth had much to with its business and player distribution structures being inherently superior. There are many other reasons that better explain football's rise to predominance. These include:

- The field layout and timing structure of football make it the best fit for television.

- Baseball, basketball, and hockey all have very long seasons and their playoffs have always been best-of-five- or best-of-seven-game series. The NFL has a very short schedule and a one-shot playoff structure, both of which heighten fan anticipation.

- Football's scoring system makes it the most enjoyable sport to bet on.

- Compared to the daily grind that fantasy baseball can be, the once-a-week nature of fantasy football makes it the most enjoyable fantasy sport to play.

- Football is the most violent of the major sports.

All of these items pass along huge benefits to the popularity of football and have absolutely nothing to do with the organizational structure of the league.

Even with its inherent visual advantages, the NFL still somewhat lucked into capitalizing on the advantage that television gave it. Up until the 1960s, college football was the premier brand of football in the United States. The colleges could and should have been the leader in the television world, but they feared television just about as much as the NFL did. Both entities viewed TV as a necessary evil that could siphon away gate revenues instead of seeing it as a way to help build a much larger fan base. The colleges were so scared of TV that they implemented policies placing severe limitations on how often a team could appear on television. That allowed the NFL to take the early lead in the televised football world.

The second phase of the NFL's television dominance was also due to circumstance. When the AFL came along and found an effective way to use TV (they actually pioneered the revenue sharing system and Pete Rozelle copied it for the NFL), the NFL was forced to respond and had to join up with the television networks in order to keep up with their competitor. College football had no such existential occurrence and therefore was trumped as America's football leader when TV turned out to be the golden goose.

Warning Signs

The NFL's position as the leading sport on television has been unchallenged for the past thirty-plus years, and over that time the league seems to have forgotten about the serendipity that helped vault them to the top position in the first place. Being in the top position for that long has also dulled some of their senses when it comes to how they approach their customers and media partners. There are many different instances of this that I'll cover shortly, but first I would like to share an experience I had while working in the hotel industry that I think relates strongly to the NFL's current circumstances.

Back in the early 1990s, I worked in the front office/reservation department of a name-brand hotel in Central Florida. This hotel's parent organization had recently implemented a new pricing philosophy called revenue management. In a nutshell, the revenue management philosophy says that if you have three hundred rooms to sell on a night and there are four hundred customers who want rooms, you should set your pricing structure up so that you can sell your rooms to the three hundred customers who are willing to pay the highest prices.

The philosophy is very straightforward, but it was made more difficult for us because of the nature of our hotel's customer base. Our property had three major customer segments: corporate, groups, and transient. The corporate bookings came from companies that we gave discounted rates to in return for their committing a certain number of annual room nights to us. The group segment typically consisted of organizations that would book convention meeting space with the hotel and receive in return a number of rooms at a discounted rate. The transient segment consisted mostly of business travelers who weren't associated with any of our corporate partners.

After we installed the revenue management software, we gave it a few weeks to collect information on our customer base. It then gave us recommendations as to how we should price our rooms. We happened to install the program during a time of record transient demand at the hotel, so, of course, the system told us to allocate as many rooms as possible to that segment.

The transient segment tends to pay the highest prices because they typically consist of last-minute bookings. Because these rooms were booked at the last minute, these customers were not price sensitive and would book the room no matter how high the price was. All they knew was that they had last-minute business in our area and had to get a room come hell or high water.

In the first few weeks after implementing the software's pricing strategy, it looked like we had hit a gold mine, as the hotel was generating record daily and monthly revenues. We were even able to raise our standard rates by as much as $20 per night and found no shortage of takers for that higher price, as the transient demand was that high.

All seemed well until the transient demand dropped after our peak season. Those next few months gave us an object lesson on the problems that come with focusing too much on one part of the customer base.

The first problem we found was that by committing too many rooms to the transient segment, we hadn't allocated enough rooms for the other segments of our customer base. Our staff and management had become so focused on doing all we could to generate transient business that we reduced our focus on our corporate guests and groups. The corporate and group customers started to feel alienated, and it became more difficult to get their business back once the transient demand dropped. In some cases we lost future corporate bookings because we didn't hold aside some rooms for last-minute bookings from those customers during the transient demand explosion. We were under no obligation to do so, as corporate and transient bookings are done on a first-come, first-served basis, but the corporate customer base didn't care about that. They had been loyal guests for many years and were not very understanding when we had no rooms available for them.

We learned our lesson and in future years made an effort to balance our approach so that we could maximize the high transient demand while not damaging our relationship with the other facets of our customer base. We may have left some money on the table during the peak months, but we ended up more than making up for it the rest of the year.

Customer Service Isn't a Priority
in a Socialist State

The problems we had at the hotel are just the kinds of issues that could be on the NFL's horizon. For proof, consider some of the following warning signs.

1. **Fan dissatisfaction with the limited availability of the NFL Sunday Ticket package and the NFL Network**

The NFL Sunday Ticket package allows viewers to see any NFL contest with the exception of blacked-out local games. This package would interest millions of fans across the country, but it is only available to DirecTV customers. Since DirecTV currently commands approximately 15 percent of the television market, that means that about 85 percent of the U.S. television viewing audience has no access to this package. The main reason the league went with DirecTV was up-front money. DirecTV now pays $700 million per year for exclusive access to the Sunday Ticket package.

The issue for the league in this area is that chasing this up-front money could cost them with some of their most loyal customers. Consider that there are approximately thirteen to fifteen million fantasy football coaches in the United States. If the large number of gamblers and hard-core fans (i.e., ones who would order Sunday Ticket to follow their team) is added to the fantasy coaches, the number of viewers who would be the target market for the Sunday Ticket package could total anywhere from fifteen to twenty million.

DirecTV says there are approximately two million Sunday Ticket subscribers. Even assuming that some potential subscribers will still see Sunday Ticket at a sports bar or at a friend's house, these numbers clearly show that the market penetration of Sunday Ticket among its target audience is not nearly as high as it could and should be.

Instead of trying to get the Sunday Ticket package to the populace, the NFL has spent most of its efforts trying to get NFL Network (NFLN) included in every cable/satellite provider's basic package. One of the main tactics they used to try to accomplish this was by placing late-season games on NFLN.

Their hope was that fans would overwhelm their local providers with complaints about not being able to see the NFLN games, but the groundswell of support didn't pan out like the NFL wanted. Fans wanted to see the NFLN games but weren't going to spend much, if any, time pestering their local providers to put NFLN on the air. That illustrates a somewhat alarming level of ambivalence for a league with possibly the hardest-core fan base of any sport in the United States.

In addition to the U.S. market, the NFL needs to consider the impact of its Sunday Ticket policies on building an overseas fan base. I say this because of an e-mail I received from an NFL fan in Brazil. This Brazilian American football backer bought the Sunday Ticket package in 1998 and became a Broncos fan during their second Super Bowl–winning run.

After that year, the fan tells me that DirecTV stopped broadcasting all of the games live as they did in the United States. The new policy was to send four games to Brazil live and show the rest on tape delay. At that time, the cost of the Sunday Ticket package was still cheap, somewhere around $40 U.S.

Once Rupert Murdoch bought DirecTV, the Brazilian fan continued, he merged it with another South American satellite service and canceled all sports packages except soccer. The NFL was now only available on two channels, ESPN and a local Brazilian station.

After this happened, the only way this fan could watch the Broncos was to buy the NFL Game Pass. This package would allow him to view Denver's games on the Internet, but it cost $240. This fan says that is too much money for him to pay and is too high for that market. He also suggests that the NFL could see international growth if it were to emphasize the Internet market, but says the league needs to offer content flexibility packages that let fans pick their options à la carte for a lower price.

As impressive as this fan's dedication was to seeing his team play, it was just the tip of the iceberg. He was initially writing me to inquire about the cost for one of my books to be sent to Brazil. He wanted to read about the NFL so much that he was willing to incur the high price of international shipping to do so. He also joined a Brazilian association for football fans and met Tony Gonzalez when Gonzalez made his way down to Rio de Janeiro. In addition, this fan says that two of his friends got to see the NFL draft live and in person, and proclaimed that it was a once-in-a-lifetime experience for them.

Think about this for a moment. The NFL is looking to expand internationally and here is a South American fan who is part of a grassroots movement to spread the word about the league. In addition, he is willing to spend money to see his team play on television, and that would likely make him more effective in popularizing the league among his friends. This should be a dream come true for the NFL in its international fan quest, but instead of making it easy for him to proselytize about pro football, the league makes it quite hard due to rigid pricing and limited access to its games.

The DirecTV and NFLN deals may provide the league with larger margins and more control over their premium programming packages, but their limitations are significant. They shut out a very large percentage of the potential customer base, much like our hotel shut out the corporate and group segments while chasing the transient customers. Some of our customers eventually found other lodging options when we made it harder for them to stay at our hotel. The NFL needs to be concerned that these fans will do the same thing and find something else to do when they can't watch an NFL game.

2. The NFL as media outlet

The NFL and the media have always had a symbiotic relationship. The league gave newspapers, magazines, and television networks an unparalleled rating and readership juggernaut. In return, those outlets gave the NFL not only a wide amount of coverage, but also what was basically a friendly style of coverage.

Even though the NFL had a positive relationship with the media, it still always tried to exert a certain amount of influence over the media's coverage of its sport. That often led to an uneasy peace at times, but for the most part, the press and the league mutually benefited from pro football, so it all worked out well.

That approach seems to be changing of late, due largely to the NFL's mutation from a pure sports entity to a combined sports/media outlet over the past few years. NFL.com has changed from being largely a promotional Web site to more of a standard sports media site, and the NFL Network is now competing with the major television networks for game broadcast coverage.

Both of these changes are turning the symbiotic relationship into more of a survival-of-the-fittest contest. That is leading to what could become a major battle between the NFL and the fourth estate. The first skirmishes of that conflict are already happening on four fronts.

The first is the league's new policies on media outlets' use of video content. The NFL recently implemented a policy prohibiting newspapers or other organizations from using more than forty-five seconds of video from postgame news conferences or interviews from the locker room. This policy also extends to preseason games, training camps, and practices. These organizations also cannot store the forty-five-second pieces on their Web sites for more than twenty-four hours. They must also post hyperlinks to NFL.com and to individual team Web sites.

The NFL is doing this because it knows the value of video content on a Web site. It doesn't want any media outlet, large or small, to be able to compete with it in this arena. The NFL is perfectly within its rights to do this, mind you, as it is only enforcing this rule for occurrences on its facilities. The downside is that it does put the NFL at loggerheads with a lot of competing media sites, ranging from large outlets such as ESPN.com down to local newspaper sites.

The second is the league's attempt to place limitations on sideline cameras from local television affiliates. In 2006, the NFL barred all but one local "pool" crew from the sidelines on game day in what it said was an effort to reduce on-field traffic congestion. The media saw this move for what it was, an effort to eliminate video competition. Two Missouri state senators evidently came to the same conclusion, as they filed legislation challenging the league's policies. This forced the NFL's hand and the league changed the rule to allow up to five local camera crews field-level access.

The third instance of this competition is the league's new pattern of funneling the bulk of the breaking injury/contract stories through

NFL.com and the NFL Network instead of through standard media outlets.

The fourth is floor space. The more the NFL becomes a media outlet, the more floor space it requires at the big media events. Because of this, the league has partitioned the best spaces at media functions for itself and caused many media outlets to have to do their jobs with much less space than they had in previous years.

It is one thing when the league tries to manipulate the media to get the type of coverage that it wants. It is entirely another when the league starts competing with the media and potentially costs reporters their jobs. As this competition heats up, it will cause a lot of negative feelings as newspaper and magazine circulations continue to decline over the next few years.

As harmful as those negative feelings might be, the NFL at some level probably doesn't feel it has to care about that. If the *Washington Post* or the *New York Times* gets peeved at the NFL and decides to give the league less or even zero coverage, the NFL knows that its fans will just start reading other newspapers or Web sites. In other words, those sites know they cannot afford not to cover the NFL, so they will be forced to find ways other than video content to attract readers and viewers.

This may not be good news for the NFL. I say this because I believe there are five reasons why fans go to sports Web sites. They are (in no particular order):

1. To get the news of the day

2. To read columnists with strong opinions

3. To read investigative stories

4. To watch video clips

5. To do fantasy league research

Of these five, the NFL can easily do three. They can offer the news of the day, do video clips, and give out fantasy league research. The league can do these without any chance of negatively impacting itself from a public relations standpoint.

The other two are nowhere near as easy. The NFL will certainly not want to do investigative stories on itself. No NFL reporter is going to scope out the Michael Vick dogfighting angle because of the extreme harm the story would cause the league. I don't necessarily knock the league too much in that case, as that type of reporting is necessarily confrontational and would be quite difficult to manage in a league-owned vehicle.

It is the strong columnist reason that is really the gray area for the league. The NFL would certainly like to draw as much on this area as it can, and it has been successful on this at some levels. Cris Collinsworth is one of the most opinionated announcers around, and yet the NFL had no hesitation in hiring him to be the color commentator on its live game broadcasts. I have also heard strong commentary from NFLN personalities such as Jamie Dukes, Tom Waddle, and Mike Mayock, so the league is showing that it will accept a difference in opinion.

Having said that, the NFL's general approach to media coverage has always been to target the fan who isn't interested in hearing anything negative about players, coaches, or teams. The league often follows the player's credo that says "always credit, never blame" when it comes to analysis or commentary. I'm all for positivity, but they take that idea and go to ridiculous lengths with it. In some cases the league's coverage of itself feels like a Norman Vincent Peale cult gone wrong. This tendency will keep the league from effectively competing with other outlets on the strong commentary front.

Dominating three of the five fan desires from a Web site sounds great, but it could leave the league in a bad way because all the rest of the media have left to distinguish themselves are the investigative stories and strong commentary. That means that not only will the mainstream media dive into these areas more, but the independent sites will too.

If that doesn't sound bad, consider that the Vick dogfighting story very likely would not have gotten legs had it not been for Mike Florio and his Web site ProFootballTalk.com. Florio prides himself on not being a part of the mainstream media and uses this outsider status to go after stories that other members of the media can't or won't tackle. It was Florio who kept the Vick story going when it seemed all but certain to die, and it isn't a stretch to say that without Florio, Vick may not have been either charged or convicted.

As impressive as Florio's persistence in pursuing this story was, it could be only the tip of the iceberg of negative coverage for the NFL. For every Florio there are blogs like Deadspin.com or TheBigLead.com that also like to break controversial stories. To use an analogy, these blog sites are like the hard-edged newspaper columnists and reporters from years ago, but on steroids. Just like Florio, they see themselves as pseudo–media outlets at best and are therefore less apt to follow the decorum that newspaper or magazine columnists had to abide by years ago.

Fans are relying more and more on these independent blogs for out-of-the-mainstream controversial stories and very hard-hitting commentary. As these independents gain in popularity, the mainstream sports media sites may eventually feel compelled to go after more of the fringe/rumor type stories to keep from being scooped.

All of this makes me think back to the approach that Pete Rozelle took toward the media. Rozelle was the consummate public relations man and he possessed a certain genius for getting the right type of press coverage for the NFL. For the league to do anything that would have given it negative coverage among the media would have been foreign to Rozelle's way of thinking, and competing with the media would have been anathema. Rozelle also knew that one of the benefits of making friends with the media is that when times got tough, the media would feel more compelled to help the league out.

When the mainstream outlets do start targeting the independents by going after those fringe stories—and I feel very strongly that this will happen sooner rather than later—the NFL will be faced with more potential negative media coverage than at any time in its history. If that had happened when Rozelle was in office, any number of friendly media types could have offset it. That won't likely be the case today, and that can't be good for the NFL.

3. Too many NFL teams are not the number one sports team in their market

For those who might doubt whether the NFL could ever fall off its perch as the number one sport in the United States, I suggest taking a look at some of the local markets where the NFL team is not the preeminent sports franchise.

There are numerous instances of this. I grew up in Michigan and left there about twenty years ago, and I can say without a doubt that the Lions were not the number one sports team when I left and they still are not now. Michiganders feel much more of a connection with the University of Michigan or Michigan State University in a football sense, but it goes even deeper than that. I believe that sports fans in that state have a much closer bond with the Tigers and Red Wings than they do with the Lions.

The counterargument to this is that the Lions have done so badly over the past fifty-plus years that, of course, the area's other, more successful sports franchises are going to be more popular.

My first retort to this is that consistent success doesn't always equal support. The Browns still have one of the most loyal fan bases in the league despite experiencing many stretches of mediocrity and leaving town for three seasons. It is also worth noting that the Tigers and Red Wings both went through significant parts of their history where they were less than competitive and yet they still eclipse the Lions in popularity by a mile. There's a reason they call Detroit Hockeytown.

Another retort to that argument would be that it isn't just bad teams that are having issues winning the local-market battle. I live in Florida now and we have three largely successful pro teams in the Dolphins, Jaguars, and Buccaneers. These teams have not lacked in on-field success, yet Jacksonville and Miami have both had a history of trouble selling their stadiums out. The Jaguars even had to go so far as to black out some of the seats in their stadium to ensure sellouts, and things are still touch and go on that front.

I can also illustrate the relative inability of these teams to connect with Sunshine State fans with the litmus test that is an integral part of living in Florida. Just about every person in this state is identified in part by the college football team they root for. In fact, one of the first questions on meeting someone new in Florida is, "Are you a Seminole, Gator, or Hurricane?" This often leads to friendly rivalries between neighbors and coworkers and is so prevalent that it is a clear indicator that college football is king in Florida, not pro football.

These aren't the only two areas where the NFL is not the lead sport. In Atlanta the Braves certainly seem to be the lead team over the Falcons. The Patriots are coming off of a dynastic run yet they are not the number one team in the New England area, as their dynasty still hasn't led them to overtake the Red Sox. No NFL team was ever able to establish dominance over the Los Angeles market and beat out the Dodgers. The Titans certainly aren't going to overtake the Volunteers for the lead spot in Tennessee football fans' allegiance any time soon. I would also question whether the Colts or the Panthers are more popular in Indiana and the Carolinas than basketball is.

All of these examples show that while the NFL has national predominance, it has a ways to go to achieve this predominance in all of its local markets. This also provides proof as to why the NFL needs to ensure that it has a strong media presence across platforms and providers.

4. You call it a game, I call it a business

The common denominator in these examples is that the league seems to think it doesn't have to care about all of its customers in order to make a good profit. This lack of interest in keeping the overall customer base happy has led to the creation of an unhealthy competitive environment. Do you think that the Lions, Cardinals, Saints, or any of the other NFL teams that have gone through twenty-plus-year periods with limited or zero on-field success would have been as willing to do so had they been losing money? Of course not, but with the protections that the league's structure has built in to spread the wealth and limit the financial benefit of on-field competition, these teams don't have any compelling incentive to do better.

Another way to put this is that there is a constant tug-of-war between the business side and the game side of pro football. The business side always wants to make the most money, but fans watch the NFL for the game side of things. In too many cases, the business side is winning this war because the socialism of the league makes it too damn easy for them. Organizations can pay most of their attention to their team's financial areas and grant only cursory attention to the game side of their team with little or no effect on their bottom line. In many cases, teams seem to have made the conscious decision that there is no real need to take care of the game side of things because there is little money to be made on that side (as reflected in the St. Louis Rams executive's comment in *Sports Illustrated* that the ownership wanted the team to get to the playoffs but not to win the Super Bowl, because winning the Super Bowl costs the team money).

Winning Isn't Everything: The Financial Disincentive of the NFL

To further illustrate my point, consider the following. Starting with the 2007 season, the difference between the NFL's salary cap and salary floor (which is the minimum amount of money a team must pay to its players) will be approximately $29 million. From a purely financial standpoint, the only reason a team would want to spend up to the salary cap is if that $29 million investment was going to bring in more than $29 million in nontelevision revenue such as gate receipts.

Given the current state of gate receipts in the NFL, this move would rarely be a winning situation for the team. According to a 2005 estimate in *Forbes*, twenty-five NFL teams had gate receipts totals between $30 and $45 million during the 2004 season. Only six teams topped the $45 million mark and only two topped the $55 million mark. In other words, there is only a $25 million gate difference between the top and bottom game revenue teams, or $4 million less than the difference between the salary cap and salary floor.

The lack of potential upside in gate receipts means that teams don't have much incentive to spend money on players. NFL teams might also have a tough time financially justifying spending more money in the coaching area. This is part of the reason why after the 2006 season, despite there being a strong pool of veteran coaches and high-profile college coaches available, most teams pursued the low-cost option by hiring either relative unknowns or ex–head coaches with mediocre NFL head coaching win-loss records.

The Most Important Word in the NFL's Lexicon: Integrity

I don't want to sound like an alarmist, but there is a real danger if there is no tie-in between on-field performance and financial success. The danger is that it could affect the integrity of the game. We hear comments all the time about how player integrity could affect the game. For example, any player who has issues with drugs, gambling, women, or shaky personal finances could possibly put himself into a situation where he is asked to do something that could have an undesirable impact on the outcome of games.

As harmful as the above situations could be, a situation where a team has little financial incentive to win can be just as damaging. If NFL fans ever start believing their team cares solely about money, those fans will stop giving their hearts to the teams. This would be catastrophic to the league and now is the time to prevent it from happening. If the NFL really wants to turn itself into a meritocracy, if it really wants to reward teams and players, and by proxy those teams' fans, for excelling on the field, it is in the league's best interest to tie more of a team's financial success to its on-field success.

This doesn't require an elimination of the current socialist structure, but rather a reduction in the totality of that structure. I believe the best way to do this is by embracing the philosophy that there are ways of enhancing on-field competitive balance while still allowing the league to receive the benefits of the "league-think" environment.

Here are two suggestions I have for doing this:

1. Eliminate the draft
The current player distribution structure ensures that every team will

always have a certain number of talented players committed to their organization for a guaranteed period of time regardless of the team's level of play. What the NFL is trying to do with this brand of socialism is prevent the instabilities inherent in a capitalist structure. I understand that having teams fail is not good for business, but there should be no fear of a quasi-capitalist structure as long as certain fail-safes are implemented.

Keeping this in mind, I propose that the NFL draft be replaced by a collegelike signing day. This process would end up being a lot like the recruiting battles that colleges wage for high school players each year. The biggest benefit to this system is that the worst teams would no longer be able to simply plug along at the status quo and receive a guaranteed number of top-notch players. For example, if the Lions have a 2–14 season under the current system and are given exclusive rights to deal with the best quarterback in the draft because of this, it is a way of rewarding them for having a lousy season.

Rather than give the Lions that pick, make them fight for it. Let them come to the hot rookie prospect and show him that they are the best team for him. Yeah, I know, the last thing we need is to pump college players' heads with more delusions of grandeur, but don't forget the benefit here. The bad teams can no longer coast by with a half effort. They would have to try even harder to get that big quarterback, and if they didn't, their fan base would be quite upset with them and possibly make them pay financially.

One of the arguments against this is that it would ruin the competitive balance of the league. That's where the fail-safes come in.

The first fail-safe is the fifty-three-man roster limitation. Roster limits and the limited number of yearly openings per team would prevent teams from being able to overstock on players.

The second is the limited number of starting roster spots and the high pay that goes along with them. That fail-safe would ensure that teams with bad records would have weapons with which to battle for the best players. A starting spot on a bad team is worth a whole lot more than a backup spot on a good team, and players would be drawn accordingly.

The third is the rookie salary cap. This cap would ensure that an NFL team would have to approach this system the way that a fantasy football coach in an auction league does. Teams would want to target certain players and determine the highest amount they would be willing to pay that player. If the player were paid more by another team, the team would need to have a backup plan for targeting another player.

2. Divide some of the television monies based on the television ratings that each team draws

The idea of equitable distribution of television monies is so ingrained as a fail-safe for the small-market teams to be able to compete with the large-market teams that any mention of change is often seen as heresy. I don't agree with that mind-set, but there is certainly some validity to it. Having said that, isn't there a way to at least partially reward teams for their overall contributions to the television package?

Let me show you what I mean by comparing the television rating contributions made by Dallas and Atlanta. According to the *2007 NFL Record & Fact Book*, the Dallas television market was the sixth largest in the NFL, with over 2.3 million TV households to its credit. Atlanta had the ninth largest market with just over 2.2 million TV households.

The household presence is nearly equal, but does anyone believe the Falcons' television impact is equal to the Cowboys'? The Cowboys are one of the prime-time players in the NFL's television package because they have a long track record of success and they try very hard to appeal to a large base of fans. If they don't get a benefit for being the sixth largest market, shouldn't they get a benefit for doing the extra work to build themselves up into a dominant national TV player?

One idea to reward them would be for the NFL to implement a more limited form of television revenue sharing. What if it put 75 percent of the television revenues into an equal share pool and placed the other 25 percent into a pool that rewarded teams for their television contributions? This type of system would give a financial incentive to teams for landing nationally televised games and generating Nielsen ratings. This would create competition among teams for the nationally televised spots, and since the nationally televised spots generally go to the best teams, it would force teams to do more to win.

As odd as this might sound, this change could be a boon for small-market teams. Just imagine for a moment how the Buffalo Bills of the late 1980s–early 1990s might have fared under this system. Buffalo is currently the third smallest market in the NFL, but if they were able to put together another team like that Bills group, which was certainly one of the most popular teams in the NFL, it would give them an advantage over their larger-market brethren.

Don't get me wrong. I am a firm believer in the right of every owner to run his team as he sees fit. If he wants to run one of the most profitable teams by pinching a penny hard like Mike Brown, more power to him. If he wants to throw lots of cash around like Jerry Jones and Daniel Snyder do, that's good, too. I simply don't think that any business or sporting interest is served by having too many protections for lousy organizations. Survival of the fittest may be too harsh of a mantra for any sports league to embrace, but it sure beats the mantra of preserving the weak at the cost of the strong.

16

Why the NFL's Blackout Rules Make No Financial Sense

I am one of those people who likes to think green. I wouldn't go so far as to call myself an environmentalist or anything like that, but I am all for trying to cut my household's energy usage.

One of the ways I do this is by installing compact fluorescent light bulbs (CFLs) that are rated as Energy Star by the Environmental Protection Agency. CFL bulbs, according the Energy Star Web site, "use about 75% less energy than standard lighting, produce 75% less heat and last up to 10 times longer." It is estimated that the average U.S. household would save $50 per year on its electric bill by changing to CFLs.

Despite this, there are reports of people who don't want to switch to CFLs. In some cases the reason given is the mercury content in CFLs. The mercury issue is rather specious, as CFLs are no more dangerous than many other potentially hazardous household products like paint, gasoline, or batteries. In addition, even though CFLs do contain mercury, the amount of energy they save reduces overall mercury pollution that is emitted by coal-burning power plants.

In other cases, people don't want to switch to CFLs because, frankly, they simply don't want to have to change. They have used incandescent bulbs for years and, darn it, no one is going to make them change if they don't want to.

The resistance these people have to CFLs reminds me a lot of the resistance the NFL has to revising or eliminating the blackout rules. To illustrate my point, let's take a team with a history of on-field success, say, the Miami Dolphins.

The *2007 NFL Record & Fact Book* says that the Miami–Fort Lauderdale market has 1,538,620 TV households. If we estimate three people per household, that equates to 4,615,860 potential television viewers. If we assume that the people living in the Miami–Fort Lauderdale market are the only people who would attend a live game, that means that the Dolphins have to sell 75,192 seats at Dolphin Stadium to these 4.6 million people. That equates to the Fins having to post a 1.6 percent market penetration to achieve a stadium sellout.

That percentage doesn't take into account fans living outside of the Miami–Fort Lauderdale viewing area. Having lived just outside of Orlando for twenty years, I can guarantee you that a significant percentage of the Dolphins' seats are sold to people in central Florida or in markets north of the Miami–Fort Lauderdale area. The Orlando–Daytona Beach–Melbourne area alone is estimated to have nearly 1.4 million TV households. If that market were to be included in the potential stadium audience, it would nearly double the number of possible ticketholders, thus significantly reducing the South Florida market penetration the Dolphins would have to reach to sell out their stadium.

Now here is the crazy part about blackouts. Let's assume for a moment that all of the Dolphins' stadium ticket sales came from the South Florida market. If the team ended up selling tickets to 1.5 percent of the Miami–Fort Lauderdale populace, they would sell only

69,238 seats. This would result in the Miami–Fort Lauderdale area being blacked out for the game that Sunday.

Think about that for a minute. By the team missing its market penetration goal by one-tenth of 1 percent, there would be roughly 4.5 million people unable to see the Dolphins play on television. What is especially odd about this is that the NFL doesn't even take an interim step and allow its local fans to pay for the privilege of seeing a blacked-out game from home.

Does any of this make sense to you? Aren't these tactics going to alienate the South Florida populace? Are the Dolphins more likely or less likely to garner more fans by keeping them from watching the team's games?

Let me put this another way. If you were running the Dolphins, wouldn't you want as many people as possible to see your team play? If there were thousands or tens of thousands of fans in the metro area who wanted to see your team play, and if they were willing to pay for that privilege even if they didn't come out to your stadium, wouldn't you let them? Would you want to make it harder or even impossible for them to become customers? Or would it be your goal to make it as easy as possible to be an NFL fan?

One might think that dropping the blackouts would actually help generate the valuable television ratings that make the huge network contracts possible. It might if the Dolphins or the NFL actually ended up being financially punished for the lack of a sellout, but that isn't the case. If the Dolphins can't sell out their stadium, the local populace and the local television affiliate are the ones who are punished. This is why you see so many TV stations purchasing blocks of tickets on the eve of the blackout. It is in their best interest to have the game televised, especially if it is only going to cost them a few thousand dollars to do so.

What do the Dolphins lose for not selling out the stadium? Nothing except the lost revenue for the unsold seats. The Dolphins don't have to pay back the local CBS or Fox affiliate for ad revenues lost due to the difference between the Dolphins game and the replacement show. And when the television contracts are renegotiated, you can be sure the NFL will tout Miami–Fort Lauderdale and its 1.5 million-plus television households as a potential audience. I don't mean to pick on the Dolphins, as their organization does care about winning and they do make a tremendous effort to sell tickets and be a part of the community, but there isn't any logical reason why the local television affiliates and fans should have to pay like this.

And for the life of me I can't figure out why the local affiliate can't broadcast another game in the Dolphins game's place. Does the NFL think that local fans are going to say, "I was going to stay home and watch the Patriots-Jets game on Sunday but it's being blacked out because Miami couldn't sell out their stadium. I think I'll go to the stadium and see the Dolphins game instead!"

I can't see any logical reason for the league's line of thinking on this. Why wouldn't it want as many fans as possible to see as many of its games as possible, blackout or no?

The reason is that the league is treating blackouts like those behind-the-times people treat CFL bulbs. They have done it this way for so long that they are set in their ways and aren't going to change. The blackout rules actually made sense when they first came into play during television's infancy in the 1950s. Television was a novelty back then and people would stay home and watch TV simply because a show was on. Well, TV's novelty wore off a long time ago, but the league has never willingly adjusted its rules to keep up with the changing times.

So what can be done to change this? The biggest catalyst could be if the networks and their local affiliates get fed up with losing the local markets and insist that the NFL do something about this issue. Why should CBS or Fox lose their ability to broadcast games in, say, the Phoenix market if the Cardinals don't care about sellouts? They shouldn't. If the NFL won't eliminate the blackout rule, the networks should try to negotiate a penalty that has to be paid by the local team to the local affiliate to offset their loss of that market.

Prescription for Change

A Call for a Historical Statistical Revolution

The NFL is not noted for its willingness to embrace new statistics. There are many instances of this, but the best example of this hesitance can be told via the story of the sack.

The sack started to become a viable potential statistic in the 1950s with the advent of the pass pocket and multiple wide receiver offenses of the Browns and the Rams. The ability to collapse the pocket became a necessary strategic goal, and the idea of a pass rush started to gain popularity among football fans. The idea started to become even more prevalent when Larry Wilson of the Cardinals helped popularize the safety blitz in the early 1960s.

Even with the impetus of those two occurrences, what really started the ball in motion to get sacks official recognition was when Deacon Jones coined the term "sack" in the late 1960s. After that happened, it gave the concept semantic legs, and the word started to get used more and more often. By the late 1970s, "sack" was an all but ubiquitous phrase on NFL broadcasts and in print. It became so ingrained in the football vocabulary that Topps football cards started listing unofficial sack leaders on their team checklist cards.

Despite all of the progress in the general acceptance of this play as an extremely important one, the league still did not track sacks as an official individual statistic. They tracked these plays from a team stand-point under the heading of "Tackled, Attempting Passes," but the NFL still would not credit individual players for sacks.

So why wouldn't the league do this? According to an article in *Pro Football Weekly*, the reason is that Seymour Siwoff (the head of the Elias Sports Bureau, the official statistical arm of the NFL) did not think the sack was worthy of being tracked. Siwoff was quoted as saying that a sack was due more to the effort of the defense as a whole rather than to the effort of an individual.

That comment is so specious on so many levels that it almost strains credulity to think that Siwoff actually believed it himself. The "team effort" comment could be made about any type of statistic. And to imply that Deacon Jones or Harvey Martin only got sacks because of the rest of the defense, and not because they were phenomenal pass rushers, is simply bunk.

That same *Pro Football Weekly* article also quoted Siwoff as saying that the only reason sacks became official statistics is that the league put pressure on Elias to do so. He also claimed that player agents wanted to use sack totals as contractual incentive clauses and were pressuring the league to officially track sacks because of this.

What was most disturbing to me about Siwoff's comments is that he seemed to show no interest in tracking the sack statistic on his own. This obstinacy is also reflected in the league's/Elias's lack of interest in verifying John Turney's unofficial sack statistics.

For those of you who are not familiar with Turney's work, he is a researcher who spent years tracking down individual sack totals for the seasons prior to 1982 (the first year that Elias listed sacks as official indi-vidual statistics). Turney reviewed play-by-play sheets and game films going back to around 1960. When he was done compiling his totals, he asked the league and Elias to verify them. They declined.

Since then, Turney has been on a crusade of sorts to get the sack totals reviewed. Sportswriters across the country have also joined to help publicize his labors, but all of the effort has been to no avail up to this point.

I am frankly at a loss as to why this would be, but noted football historian Bob Carroll has put forth one line of thinking as to why the league shouldn't verify Turney's sack totals. Carroll believes that starting the sack totals in 1982 is perfectly acceptable. He suggests that other historical football researchers have found discrepancies before and that the league doesn't go back and change its totals because of their work, so why should do they do so for Turney?

As much as I respect Carroll's opinion on a number of football subjects, I can't disagree with him more on this particular point. To state that the league should not try to go back and make their statistical records as accurate as possible is frankly ludicrous.

To use an analogy, think about how using this approach to new information would affect the scientific community. Would anyone think of telling the Egyptology field that it should not verify the findings of the group that claimed they unearthed the tomb of Nefertiti because we already knew enough about that era of Egyptian history? Or would it be right to tell astronomers to not bother verifying the findings of scientists trying to locate planets in other solar systems because we already have plenty to review with the eight planets in our solar system?

Or to use another tack on this, what would Carroll himself say if a similar suggestion were made about his specialized field of research? If anyone suggested to him that if he were to find anything else out about the football world of the 1920s, the football research community should shun his work because they already know more than enough about that era, would he be okay with that?

There is also a big difference between Turney's work and that of most other researchers: Turney's is verifiable. According to Peter King, a complete collection of game footage exists going back to around 1965, so there are at least eighteen seasons' worth of individual sack totals that could be verified. I would argue quite strenuously that as long as a full collection of tape from a particular season exists, there is no rational reason why the league should not commission someone from the Elias Sports Bureau to work with, or even independently of, Mr. Turney to proof his numbers. I could understand stopping the tracking as soon as the league got back to a year where the full season of film no longer exists, but otherwise it seems to be a no-brainer decision.

That doesn't mean that it will get done, and the most likely reason it won't is that the Elias group isn't on board with statistical changes. That isn't entirely surprising, as Bill James railed against Siwoff and company for years for their attempting to hold a monopoly on information.

He did this in many ways. James made it one of his goals to try to get more raw information into the public's hands. He also raised the average fan's level of understanding of baseball by pioneering, publishing, and popularizing new statistics. Today's baseball fan is used to the idea of having such relatively basic statistics as batting averages versus left- and right-handed pitchers as a standard part of a player's statistical line. Twenty-five years ago that wasn't the case, and James is really the reason for that change.

In the same way that James argued for a baseball informational free flow, I would argue for the same type of free flow in football. Monopolizing the information is only hurting the interest in football statistics. If analytical football research is going to find its way to the same level of acceptance as sabermetrics, information will have to be shared widely and openly with the public.

I want that to happen, so I say it is time to start a statistical revolution in the analytical football world. There are a number of ways to get this revolution started. They are:

1. Verify Turney's numbers
This is the most logical starting point. Turney's works have already been heavily publicized, so the public has already been primed for them. His work has the additional benefit of being limited to a single statistic. That statistic is well known, uniformly accepted, and under-

stood as being an important performance measurement. Turney's works are also quite heavily researched, so the lead time to get the statistics verified would likely be short.

Verifying Turney's numbers would not only be a great way to start the analytical football revolution. It would also be a terrific way to generate additional interest in this field and give the league a huge PR boost at the same time.

Just imagine the possibilities. The league could make an announcement that it was going to confirm the historical accuracy of Mr. Turney's sack research and announce its findings at a future date. The most preferable announcement date would probably be around the time of the Hall of Fame voting during Super Bowl week. Sportswriters are always starving for fresh material then, and this would more than fill their need. It would also be a great way for the league to better celebrate its history.

The league could even spread the announcements out over a period of time by releasing the revised statistics in five-year increments. The first year could have the sack totals from 1977 to 1981, the second year the totals from 1976 to 1972, and so on.

The Seniors Committee could also use these announcements to help get one of their candidates enshrined. Say for a moment that Harvey Martin came up for nomination during the release of the 1977–1981 sack totals. Martin's best seasons came during this time, so that would likely do a lot to better illustrate how well he did during those years.

Since the league has a ton to gain and nothing to lose by making this move, I say it should put the same kind of pressure on Elias to do this as it did back in 1982 to get Elias to start tracking this statistic in the first place. Elias has been a loyal partner of the league for a long time, but Siwoff's group needs to serve the best interests of the league first in this matter. If Elias doesn't want to do this, the league should consider finding another statistical arm for this, maybe STATS Inc., or even commission its own people to work on it. If the NFL was corporate enough to drop CBS in the mid-1990s after getting hundreds of millions of dollars from that network over the years, one would think it could be corporate enough to do the same to a stat company if that company wasn't working in the league's best interest.

2. Embrace a new set of statistics/metrics

There are probably some readers who are asking the question, "What type of statistics do we need that we don't already have?" That is just the type of question I asked myself when I started researching the *Scientific Football* series.

The answer to the question is that there are dozens of useful statistics that should be added to the official set. The reason for this is that the amount of information tracked on a standard football play-by-play sheet is really limited and consists primarily of eleven items:

1. Down and distance

2. The starting and ending yard line on the play

3. The time remaining in the quarter on that particular play (a stat that is often incorrect)

4. The names of the players who carried the ball at some point on the play, be it as a runner, passer, or receiver

5. The result of the play

6. The tackler on the play

7. The score of the game if it changed on the play

8. A running tally of the number of first downs gained

9. Which team won the coin toss (or tosses if the game goes to overtime)

10. Which goal line each team was defending

11. A running tally of the overall third- and fourth-down efficiency and number of first downs gained at the end of each quarter

And that is about it. This type of situational information certainly has value, but it still only tells the "who/what/where" that happened on a play. The "why and how" parts of a play are missing, and they contain the most valuable information.

Since those items are not available on a play-by-play sheet, that is where the statistical revolution has been headed up to this point and where it is going in the future. I will cover the new statistics more in a bit, but for now I'll say that the mantra of the stat revolution should be to make the how and why information available to the public.

3. Give the public access to game footage

The best way to make the how and why information public is for the NFL to open its kimono and allow both fans and the media access to its film library.

This is probably the most important item in getting the football statistical revolution rolling. I say this because it was the key to Bill James getting fans involved in sabermetrics. James was a great writer and made statistics more interesting, but he also made his methods accessible. Fans were able to apply his methods to their own research, and that is what started the groundswell of sabermetrics to become what it is today.

Football won't be able to do that until its fans are able to apply their own research methods to the game. Fans want to feel like scouts or coaches, and the only way to tap into that feeling is by allowing them to look over game footage.

This should not be limited to today's footage, either. The NFL should also allow open access to its historical game footage. I feel just as strongly about this because there is hardly a week or two during a football season that I don't get an e-mail from some fan wanting to know how to get a hold of historic game footage. Most of the time they want coaches' film so they can do some kind of breakdown of their favorite team.

That would be a radical departure from the NFL's current policy for archival tape access for the public, which is zero. I even asked NFL Films for press-level access to old footage one time and was told that the archives are not available for anyone to see, press member or not. The staff at NFL Films must get the "access to game footage" question even more often than I do, as their Web site has a note stating that game footage is not available.

The obvious question is, why isn't this footage available? With the level of demand out there, it would seem like a no-brainer move on the league's part. I'm not even asking that the league give the information away for free, far from it. This could be an incidental revenue proposition for the NFL in a significant way. It would also likely prove to be very profitable, as the costs for upkeep and distribution of digital files are dropping due to the commoditization of digital technologies.

The league could build this up in stages. In the first stage they could make the raw coaches' footage available. If that worked and was profitable, the league could then add play-types tabs to each play and charge an additional fee for access to this type of material. The league could also just offer raw footage and then offer tabs to certain organizations, such as colleges or think tanks or media companies, for a fee.

Colleges might actually end up being a big moneymaker for the league in this area. For those of you who might think I'm off base on this one, consider this. College students make up a significant percentage of sports fans and a huge percentage of analytical sports nuts. These students want access to this information. For proof, consider that the University of Georgia is actually already offering a scientific football class.

A great number of colleges offer sports management classes, and a game tape/statistical review for football would fit right into that curriculum. The NFL could partner up with the collegiate community and turn this into both a moneymaker and a fantastic marketing opportunity to the young demographic they are always looking to target.

What's odd about the NFL's resistance to this is that the league made a big deal a few years about how it was working with IBM to digitize every play of every game it had on tape. There was one IBM commercial in particular that showed one fan telling another fan about the NFL's tape digitization project, and it gave the impression that the footage was going to be available to the general public. I understand the benefit that IBM would get for running commercials of this sort, but why would the league do it? It made fans think that games would be available to them when they weren't, and that isn't good PR.

Even if the league is hesitant to make its film library available, the least it could do is work with DirecTV to implement the option of having any network-broadcast camera angle available to a DirecTV viewer. This had been announced as a possible DirecTV upgrade a few years ago, but it still hasn't happened. If this option were implemented, it would at least let fans and researchers record games from an all-22 angle and do research based on that.

But that would be only a short-term fix. The long-term fix is for the NFL to join the iTunes/iPhone/YouTube generation and give fans access to as much digital information as they are willing to pay for.

4. Found the establishment of a football scientific community

I know that may sound crazy on the face of it, but I can easily envision a scenario where football research could be treated like a true scientific exchange. What gave me the inspiration for this thought was when I watched a show on astronomical planet hunters.

These scientists spend years looking throughout the galaxy for stars with planets. After one researcher believes she has found a planet, she then sends her research out to the world and lets other scientists review her work. The other scientists will then point their telescopes at the star and run the measurements to see if their research concurs with the theory that a planet is orbiting the star. If and when the community as a whole concurs with the original findings, the planet is then considered confirmed.

This type of thing could easily translate to football research. In today's world, if a dedicated Raiders fan/researcher says that Cliff Branch belongs in the Hall of Fame, he has very little other than the basic statistical record to back him up.

What if that researcher were able to go back and review Al Davis's claim that the one thing that Mel Blount feared was Branch going deep on him? As it stands now, Davis's remarks are strong anecdotal evidence at best, but there is no statistical evidence to back him up.

If the footage were made available and that researcher wanted to back his claim up, he could spend hours watching the footage and then post his findings on a football science blog or message board. A Steelers fan in turn might watch the tapes and point out something that showed Branch didn't dominate to the extent that the Raiders researcher said he did. Or he might do a completely separate tape review and point out how Branch did against, say, Louis Wright as a negative for Branch's candidacy.

Maybe another way to put this is that many fans want to feel like scouts. They want to know the game on a different level than they do today. The only way they are going to be able to do this is by breaking down game tapes. Some fans will look for things such as line splits. Others will look at coverages. Still others will want to review pass blocking. It all adds up to an increase in the interest of some of the most passionate fans in the base.

In any event, the idea is that this type of thing would start an intellectual exchange and would drive a significant amount of interest in pro football. And that is something we all want to see.

One other point I would like to make is that there was a line in one of the NFL Films *Lost Treasures* series where Ed Sabol said someone asked him why they keep all of the old footage. Sabol said the footage was like the skeleton of the NFL's history and that you don't throw away the bones.

As noble as that statement is, and as much as I am certain that the Sabols revere NFL history as much as anyone on this planet, the most effective way to ensure the footage is kept is to make it valuable. Having the footage stashed under lock and key makes it rare, but it does not make it valuable. Giving the public access to it, on the other hand, makes it very valuable.

Examples of Statistics/Metrics That Could Drive the Revolution

There are literally dozens, if not hundreds, of possible statistics that could drive the revolution. Over the years many different sets of unofficial statistics have been compiled by various sources. The most common unofficial statistics include the following:

- Yards after catch
- Areas on the line of scrimmage where running plays are directed (i.e., run up the middle, run to left tackle, run to left end, etc.)
- Number of pass attempts for wide receivers, tight ends, and running backs
- Yards per attempt for wide receivers, tight ends, and running backs
- Segmentation of receiving statistics into short/medium/deep/bomb depth levels. This is already being done to some extent, but it isn't anywhere near ubiquitous. Even when a receiver's performance is segmented into depth levels, it almost never includes pass attempts.
- Dropped interceptions
- Interceptions by type (i.e., tipped at line, due to drop by receiver, due to quarterback being hit, etc.)
- Success percentage for pass attempts to receivers
- Inclusion of penalty passing yards into total yards gained by anyone in the passing game

There are many other possibilities of occurrences on the playing field that could be tracked as official statistics, but these nine would definitely be the low-hanging statistical fruit.

As strong of candidates as these nine are, there is a downside to any football statistical tracking method. This is something that I covered in *Scientific Football 2006* in an essay titled "Objectivity vs. Subjectivity— The Quandary of Football Statistical Tracking."

If there is only one message that I get across in *Scientific Football 2006*, it is that there will never be a set of football statistics that are completely objective. The simple reason for this is that the game of football isn't set up for it.

Baseball is set up for purely objective analysis. The reason for this is that baseball has a subjective arbiter: the umpire. On every pitch, the umpire has to make a subjective call of ball or strike. It doesn't really matter if the pitch was a ball or a strike. The only thing that matters is what the subjective opinion of the umpire was regarding the pitch. Once he makes his determination of ball/strike, from a statistical standpoint the subjectivity is removed. That pitch is now and forever a ball or a strike.

The game of football does have some of its subjective portions clarified into objective measurements by the officials. Almost all of these involve contact with the ball. An official will rule whether a pass was caught, or whether a ball carrier broke the plane of the goal line, or if the ball was tucked or not.

Once you get away from players who made contact with the ball, the refs almost never make judgment calls other than the occasional penalty. This limits the number of purely objective plays that a scorer can track. It is this lack of objective material that has slowed the field of football research down."

There are two examples from the list of nine that illustrate the subjectivity point quite well. These are:

1. **Yards after catch.** This statistic is subjective because there is no definitive way to state where a catch began. Most researchers track these yards from where the receiver first touched the ball. I don't agree with that methodology because at that point the pass has yet to be caught. Even if that part of the methodology works, it can often be subjective as to what yard line the receiver caught the pass at. If the ball was first touched right on the yard marker, one spotter might track the pass from that yard line while the other could have a slightly different angle and track it from the next yard line. I know it's only one yard, but these two items show that yards after catch have two significant subjective elements.

2. **Hole areas where running plays are directed.** I did a full season's worth of running game breakdowns during my research for *Scientific Football 2006* and I found that there are huge variances in the hole areas that are credited by different scorers. Some would

call an off-tackle play a run to the outside, while others would call that same play a run over the tackle. The tracking methodology varied so dramatically from one scorer to another that I don't even pay any attention to the run area statistics anymore.

This type of subjectivity may mean that some statistics will never pass the litmus test for being "official," but that doesn't mean they lack value to both fans and researchers.

The good news is that none of the other seven statistics listed above are that hard to track. Most of them are also very objective in nature. Even the ones that do have something of a subjective angle to them (i.e., number of pass attempts and interceptions) should be fairly easy to work around if the scorers were given a clear set of guidelines.

Performance Metric History

Below is a list of all of the metrics that have been covered in the *Scientific Football* series from 2005 to 2007. The year number next to the metric indicates the year the metric was initially introduced.

Bad decision (2005): A quarterback is charged with a bad decision when he does something with the ball that either leads to, or nearly leads to, a turnover. The most common bad decisions are forcing passes into coverage or staring at receivers.

Catchable pass (2006): A pass that a receiver has a reasonable chance of catching. The rule of thumb is whether the pass is within the receiver's catching frame.

Coverage sack (2005): A sack that occurs in the pocket more than three seconds after the snap.

Deep assist coverage (2006): Coverage where a safety is responsible for helping another defender cover a pass downfield. Compare to direct coverage.

Depth level (2005): A measurement of how far downfield a receiver was on a pass attempt. It is measured from the point at which the receiver touched the ball. Short passes are 1–10 yards downfield, medium 11–19, deep 20–29, and bombs are 30-plus yards downfield.

Direct coverage (2006): Coverage where a defensive player is directly and actively responsible for covering his man. Direct coverage can occur in either man or zone coverage. In zone coverage the defender has to be actively trying to cover the receiver for it to count as a direct coverage pass.

Forced incompletions (2007): Any incomplete pass that a defensive back is physically responsible for causing. It is a combination of passes defended, stripped/dropped passes, and plays where a hit by a defensive back causes an incompletion.

Garbage sack (2005): When one defensive player gets a sack due to the pass-rushing efforts of another defender. One typical example of this is when a defensive end crashes the pocket from the outside and forces the quarterback to step up into a well-blocked defensive tackle. The tackle was only able to get the sack because of the defensive end's pass rush, so he is credited with a garbage sack.

Good recognition sack (2005): This type of sack is given when a defensive player makes a sack because he didn't bite on a fake by the offense that was supposed to take him out of position. A good example of this is when a defensive end reads a bootleg pass correctly.

Individual effort sack (one-on-one) (2005): A sack where a defensive player beats an offensive player one-on-one for a sack.

Missed passes (2005): Inaccurate or dropped passes that cause an incompletion. Missed passes are used to measure how successful a quarterback/wide receiver/tight end could have been if not for the mistakes. They also help measure how lucky a cornerback was in coverage.

Near interception (2006): Near interceptions are either dropped interceptions or interceptions that landed close enough to a defender that he could have had a chance to catch the ball had luck been on his side.

Not at fault interceptions (2006): Interceptions that occur for reasons other than bad decisions or inaccurate passes.

"Other" sacks (2005): The type of sack that is credited when a sack doesn't fit into any of the other categories. The most common "other" sack is the gimme sack. Gimme sacks most often occur when a quarterback trips over a lineman's foot on his drop and is downed by a defensive player.

Passing tree (2005): A schematic that teams use to describe the types of routes a receiver can run. The schematic is expressed in a format that resembles a tree, hence the name.

Point of attack success percentage (2006): The percentage of time that a defensive lineman or linebacker defeats a block on a running play directed at his gap.

Pursuit plays (2006): Plays where a defensive lineman either chases a play down from the backside of the play or goes five-plus yards downfield to make a tackle.

Pursuit sack (2005): A type of sack that occurs when the quarterback is scrambling out of the pocket but is still looking to throw the ball downfield when he is sacked. Compare to run sack.

Run sack (2005): This type of sack is credited when a quarterback starts to run after dropping back to pass the ball. The quarterback must be out of the pocket and pull the ball down, tuck it away, and be running toward the line of scrimmage for a play to be noted as a run sack.

Scheme sack (2005): A sack where a defensive player gets it due to running a stunt or a blitz.

Snotbubble (2007): A play where a defensive back breaks up a pass with a big hit. I named the metric snotbubble in honor of the term Lawrence Taylor used to describe when he would nail a ball carrier. LT said a little snotbubble would come out of the player's nose, hence the term.

Stripped/dropped pass (2006): A pass that a receiver starts to catch but then has the ball stripped away by the defender.

Success percentage (2006): The percentage of plays in which a player does something successful. Successful plays include completions (for offensive players), incompletions (for defensive players), and penalty plays that go in the player's favor.

SYPA (Success Percentage × Yards Per Attempt) (2006): A metric that combines both success percentage and YPA in an effort to measure a player's overall effectiveness.

TYPCA (Total Yards Per Catchable Attempt) (2006): A metric that measures the number of yards a receiver gains when a catchable pass is thrown his way.

Weighted bad decision percentage (2005): Bad decisions are given point totals based on the amount of damage they cause. Weighted bad decisions are those point totals expressed as a percentage of total pass attempts.

YPA (Yards Per Attempt) (2005): A quick barometer of a player's efficiency.

These certainly aren't the only metrics that can be tracked. It also doesn't hurt to have multiple groups tracking the same metrics. Aaron Schatz and his group of researchers at FootballOutsiders.com (authors of the annual *Pro Football Prospectus* series) have been doing an excellent job pioneering new play-by-play statistical methods for a few years now. A number of the metrics they track are similar to and/or based on metrics initially found in the *Scientific Football* series, but in many cases they have added interesting twists to the metrics that help them analyze the numbers in different ways. And that is what football science is all about—different researchers doing research and comparing/contrasting it to the work done by other researchers.

Where Do We Go from Here?

In his brilliant book *The Lexus and the Olive Tree*, Thomas Friedman explained how the democratizations of technology, finance, and information were fueling the globalization engine. The availability of resources that these democratizations gave to the masses empowered people in a multitude of ways. They lowered the entry-level price of starting many types of businesses and thus made it possible for the average person to become an international investor, run a retail outlet, or become a publisher.

There are thousands of fans who want to become scouts and/or football statistical analysts, but they cannot because the resources aren't available to them. In much the same way as the aforementioned democratizations empowered the general public, the availability of football videos and an expanded statistical database would empower these fans to chase their football dreams.

The only ones who should have anything to fear from expanding the availability of these resources are those who are currently benefiting from the monopolization of this type of information. I happen to be one of those people, but I realize that the future of analytical football is dependent on the participation of the public. I am more than willing to give up my place in the monopoly to see this field expand to the next level.

The expansion won't happen if the public doesn't demand the information, though. That's why I encourage anyone and everyone who reads this book to do something to get this information out there. Send an e-mail to the NFL. Write a letter to ESPN. Post a blog on your local newspaper's Web site, or better yet make a Web site of your own and get it linked to as many other blog sites as possible. Call in to your local radio station and make it a topic of discussion for that day. Once the groundswell of support reaches a critical mass, the information doors are certain to open. So if you want to see more analytical football in the future, join the revolution and make your voice heard!

Index